Transition to A New World Order

What We Leave Behind for the Next Generation

B. Bahramian

Transition to a New World Order

What We Leave Behind for the Next Generation

B. Bahramian, Ph.D., MBA
Director & Professor
University of Maryland

authorHOUSE®

AuthorHouse™
1663 Liberty Drive
Bloomington, IN 47403
www.authorhouse.com
Phone: 1-800-839-8640

Published by AuthorHouse   04/14/2016

ISBN: 978-1-4772-2902-6 (sc)
ISBN: 978-1-4772-2901-9 (hc)
ISBN: 978-1-4772-2900-2 (e)

Library of Congress Control Number: 2012911186

Print information available on the last page.

The Dedication Page

This book is dedicated to my love, Afsar for her passionate support and guidance in developing the ideas presented here, as a partner and genuine advocate of humanity in all aspects of social and political developments for mankind through her short lived life. It is also acknowledged to all freedom loving people around the world, seeking non-violent changes in political structure of their societies, honoring democratic values to improve the standard of living and struggling against tyrannical regimes.

Disclaimer

This book is designed to provide information and ideas only. This information is provided and sold with the knowledge that the publisher and author do not offer any legal or other professional advice. In the case of a need for any such expertise consult with the appropriate professional. This book does not contain all information available on the subject. This book has not been created to be specific to any individual's or organizations' situation or needs. Every effort has been made to make this book as accurate as possible. However, there may be typographical and or content errors. Therefore, this book should serve only as a general guide and not as the ultimate source of subject information. This book contains information that might be dated and is intended only to educate and entertain. The author and publisher shall have no liability or responsibility to any person or entity regarding any loss or damage incurred, or alleged to have incurred, directly or indirectly, by the information contained in this book.

Table of Contents

Introduction

Based on the evidence that has surfaced since 2008, it is apparent the governing bodies of a large number of nations have failed to deliver on the social contract between these governments and their citizens. In addition, the implicit contract between nations participating in the globalization of the world economy has been breached. This breaching suggests a critical need to analyze these international relationships in order to assess the viability of the globalization process as it affects the current economic and political world order. Here it seems evident that both the so-called capitalist and the communist systems have major internal defects and cannot deliver or serve the best interests of their citizens in the 21st century. As is obvious then, a systemic analysis of both national and international shortcomings must be accomplished in order to identify underlying problems and to pose some solutions to the most egregious of these shortcomings.

To do so, a number of critical issues are investigated and analyzed in the various chapters of this book. Potential solutions to a number of these problems will be discussed for their viability.

Key to these analyses will be a focus on the failure of developed, developing and under-developed nations to promote political, economic and social systems that recognizes, and attempts to correct, the great disparities in the economic and social condition of significant number of their citizens. The reason for this failure, that is to say, is an over-riding failure to define and enforce "human rights". The recent populous uprisings in the Middle East are good manifestation of this phenomenon that has upset or discard the tyrannical rules.

Even in the United States, the richest of all nations, some 13,000,000 American children do not get enough food daily to sustain their physical and mental well-being. In addition, there are an estimated 3,500,000 homeless Americans. This reflects, to a great degree, the egregious income disparities in the United States (and elsewhere) where a small portion of the citizenry live in luxury, while a substantial portion of the population live in poverty. Without proper dynamic governmental measures to correct problems such as these, we can never achieve the form of equitable economic prosperity that fosters a greater care for the rights of the individual. To accomplish this, a greater emphasis on an integrated system to make use of education and technology in delivering sustainable economic growth for the future is paramount.

Leaving this issue aside, it is also obvious that the over-riding problem of unequal social, political and economic outcomes results, to a great extent, from the failure of many governments to restrain the political activism of significant elements of the business community. More so than is readily evident, significant elements of the business community act as "sovereign powers" ignoring or otherwise minimizing their contribution to the public interest of their respective home nation. Thus, a new government-business relationship may need to be realized in order to realign the responsibilities of the business community to the public at large.

Evidence of this can be found in the decline of the services provided both by government and the private sector. This failure is causing many industries, especially high-tech ones, to fail in achieving their objectives. In many cases, outsourcing has become a nightmare for both the company and its customers.

The starting point for all of these changes suggests strongly that renewed priorities must be given to the need for (a) adequately feeding the people of all nations, (b) providing these people with access to basic infrastructural resources, including health care and educational systems that adequately provide for their physical and emotional well-being, and (c) most important of all, putting in place educational systems that meet the spiritual and vocational needs both of the individual and the nation as a whole.

Given the international nature of many of these problems, the goals and effective role of the United Nations must be revised and made more consistent with the world as it exists. Its focus must be on actively promoting the rights of the individual, matching the deeds with words. For example, a United Nations assembly should be capable militarily and politically of protecting the citizenry of any nation both from aggression by other nations and especially from any abuse of the indigenous citizenry by its own government. Only in this manner will "human rights" be given the priority that should be accorded them.

To insure that these and similar needs discussed above are no more than utopian dreams, the role of technology and its potential power for stimulating progress to more democratically committed governments will be set out and amplified. The projected results of these analyses can then be used in the policy formulation process and the resulting plans of action that will serve the needs of the individual.

Due to the fact that the process of nation building involves well-orchestrated, interwoven, and multi-disciplinary planning, the major issues and disciplines are addressed in different chapters of this book.

Chapter I. Transition to a New World Order

If we are to survive, we must have ideas, vision, and courage. These things are rarely produced by committees. Everything that matters in our intellectual and moral life begins with an individual confronting his or her own mind and conscience in a room alone.

Arthur M. Schlesinger, Jr.

Global Vision on Global Economy

In spite of the advancement of technology at a speed not experienced before comparative to all of history, and an unprecedented access to information around the globe, the overall quality of life for a majority of the world's population is declining drastically. Technology designed to improve the quality of life is now woven within the very fabric of human existence for many people and the lifeblood of the commerce of nations and the world. Yet the overall quality of human life for many has not improved, and for some has drastically declined at a pace in step with the advancements of the technology.

One of the underlying problems in the rich versus poor nation dichotomy is that many of the more advanced nations are dominated by the interests of the business community with, in many instances, the elected (or appointed) government taking a more passive role in the governance system than is otherwise acceptable.

Considering the poverty level of almost two-thirds of the world's population, a new world order is needed to insure that human needs are met, and the potential for world-wide terrorism is minimized. The richer one-third of the world's population must find solutions to this over-riding issue if their own well-being is not

1

to be destroyed. The current poverty level of the world's population alone needs the direct attention of an effective governing system, beyond the systems of elected officials representing parties or empowered appointments. Some believe that at this point in damage control, only a new world order can improve the overall quality of living. Some philosophies seem that they can also benefit homeland security; an imperative aspect during a time of terrorism threats. Although there are several underlying problems in the rich versus poor nation dichotomy—politics, commerce and financial stability, are aspects of this decline in living standards, which need to be carefully modified.

United States President Calvin Coolidge was justly right when he said, "The business of America is business." He could not have sent the message any clearer. This is an aspect of life that the society—has learned to embrace and at the least accept in support of capitalism.

This attitude is still portrayed confidently today by more governments than ever before. The theory that only a new world order could reverse the damage of today's level of poverty does make sense. This passive attitude has compelled political figures to act in the best financial interest of their governing areas and political contributors rather than the quality of living of the citizens. An aggressive government would not just realize and accept the vital role that business plays on the economy. An aggressive government would also create effective ways to balance between the economic social classes, not just the corporations. Though there is an undeniable accuracy in President Coolidge's statement, the fact still lies that what is good for the United States may not necessarily mean the same benefits for the world as a whole. As a matter of fact, it is becoming apparent that even in the U.S. this relation needs a major overhaul—the growing Occupy Movement across the globe is good evidence of this transition. In most cases, a problem needs to get worse before attention is given for repair. The current state of the world and the quality of life is no different. As President Coolidge indirectly portrayed many years ago, American business and balancing the economy has been and remains a priority for the US. Today, a prime example of how out of control the imbalance has become would be through government assistance programs within the United States. While the information is public knowledge that the American government has made welfare more readily available for citizens than small business loans, most people are shocked when they learn the current statistics.

Even back in [1]2003 in The Complete Idiot's Guide to Economics, Tom Gorman explained the different roles the government plays in maintaining the balance between wealth and poverty. The overall job of the government, in this aspect, is to manage the economy—in a nutshell. "The federal government implements economic policies aimed at generating full employment as well as low inflation." This includes job creation tax benefits for corporations that benefit wealthy Americans. While creating jobs is a worthwhile cause, the overall figures have to balance out in the end. [2]"When small businesses that generate community jobs and revenue get pushed out by franchises and wholesalers; a gap is created between the classes."

Though the government creates assistance programs to aid in the fight against poverty, these programs come hand in hand with specifically outlined eligibility requirements. And although welfare statistics are currently high in richest nation on earth, a good percentage of the people who need assistance; are unable to qualify. Doesn't this violate human rights? If a government who cannot afford, so to speak, to fulfill their elected obligations of providing the bare essentials to survive, wouldn't a new world order be the solution? The same can be said about the economic development programs that government has been initiating. The government has taken the initiative to create these programs but yet passively managed their effectiveness. For example, as recently as of this writing, news reports are that the state of Massachusetts

3

allowed welfare recipients to spend $200,000 of Federal taxpayer money on alcohol, tobacco and lottery tickets! This is a direct effect of the government's lack of attention to spending reports and case management.

A new world order that regulates the standards of government can encourage more women and minority owned businesses, and aggressively support them with the resources needed to survive. By opening up a business, one is generating revenue for the community, creating jobs for residents as well as making a potential profit for themselves. With the current economy on such a deteriorating path these last few years, small businesses have suffered significantly. From a political standpoint, governments as a whole have often caused more damage to the economy in their attempts to make adjustments. The strategies and focus areas change as each leader takes the reins. This constant change in power, and in turn, change in focus, and weakens economic flow and social structure of any society.

Based on international statistics and information published in almanacs, the world population has surpassed 6.5 billion inhabitants as of early twenty first century. About one third are living in more advanced industrial countries, and the other two third are surviving in advancing areas, with well over one billion living in poverty. All nations are seeking higher standards of living and more prosperity through further economic developments, one way or another. However, the requirements of the two camps vary substantially. In the first camp, societies are generally looking for more economic development in terms of wealth expansion, or more "securities", primarily lead, portrayed, and promoted by business enterprises. Whereas in the second camp, people are struggling for basic necessities of life, such as commodities and infrastructure services for more productivity at home to yield more job opportunities and prosperity. Both camps need global economy to expand, however, their visions and objectives are quite different.

In more industrious and advanced countries, it is the business enterprises that need the economic expansion, which are generally coupled with more greed, and of course more prosperity. In advancing countries, requirements for advancement are geared to fundamental elements of life, which are led by their respective governments. Therefore, the vision for global economy has different perspective for different nations at need with global economy in mind. If all statesmen would have considered the planet Earth alike as a whole—like a true family of nations— then the solutions for globalization would have been much easier to diagnose or cope with. Free trade versus protectionism (restrictive trade practices), technology transfer issues, including patent protection rights, financial mechanisms, planned economy and many more factors affect the process for formulating an acceptable, and more reciprocally-based business relation between the respective countries.

In many advancing countries, enforcement of patent laws of the West are compromised, since local industries are not bound by any regulations or discipline to abide by, especially through the use of Internet to acquire a technology to use. International corporations are naturally hesitant to transfer their developed technologies and know-how to a foreign entity without a reasonable compensation. This, in effect hampers trade as well as joint venture businesses across the globe. Consequently, the development plans or industrialization venues in the receiving countries get affected. For example, during the past decade, China established joint venture enterprises with German, French and the U.S. industries to help curb poverty in China, and create productive employment in the country using the technologies of the respective host countries. However, after a while, once enough technical workforce was trained and they learned the know-how of the business, contracts were cancelled and the adopted technologies found their way by the Chinese enterprises into other parts of the globe, starting to compete with the original owners/developers of technologies at a much lower price and quality. It happened in oil industry, delivering exploration tools and technologies, refineries, railway system, electronics, etc. On one side of the equation, the receiving partners or countries are thirsty for new technologies to adopt for their economic growth, on the other side, the burden of all that research and development costs by the contributing country would be ignored without any due compensation. This is a great dilemma for both parties to be resolved, if the guest countries need the technology of the host partners, otherwise the speed of progress or development would be seriously affected. In any case, the competitive environment dictates the most efficient and lean operation, delivering high quality goods and services in much disciplined manner for a successful business endeavor. Most businesses in advanced countries enjoy the availability of skilled and knowledgeable workforce in their project implementation. For any advancing country to engage in development or industrialization program, necessary skilled workforce need to be trained to support such objectives. No industry can survive with un-skilled labor force. To produce high quality products efficiently and be competitive in the market, the necessary workforce parallel with other development programs must be assembled and trained in the society. This training program, or production of workforce, need to be regarded as infra-structure tasks of the country to be integrated in harmony with other activities for implementation of development programs. Solutions in today's broken services are not in patch-up operation or temporary remedies, rather a radical and fundamental design and program for applications. Well trained and devoted workforce can guarantee the most efficient and acceptable deliverables. Problems in today's delivery systems are lack of job responsibilities of workforce as directed from top management or strategists to bottom; i.e., contacts with end-users—watered down quality of work. Job conscience need to be addressed and made a requirement at all levels, from management to supervisors to labor.

The best design, or product, or service which is well thought of, or produced at the top by competent experts or designers, on the way to the end-users' hand passes through a number of stages—managers, bureaucrats, supervisors, and finally a clerk or even a low earning labor to transmit the goods or services to the end-users. If in this process, individuals at every level are not well trained and competent in delivery system, the product, or for that matter, service will fail. In other words, the quality of the deliverables will be watered-down step-by-step and the end-user will suffer from a bad quality product or service. This can be witnessed in our everyday life in insurance services, banking, security services and many other public and private services. Under such circumstances, global economy and even development programs will greatly suffer. All levels of delivery systems need to be manned with competent, trained professionals and monitored for quality of goods or services being rendered.

The Need for Criteria on Economic Advancements

With a new world order and implementation of the respective philosophies, which focus more on economic stability and decreasing the gap between the wealthy and the working class; it will securely strengthen the global economy. This is vital to the overall quality of life for all people. Most businesses today require the implantation of current technology and successful global trading. The use of modern technology can contribute to the economy by solidifying the demand for the mass manufacturing industry; ensuring jobs. Technology can also advance the production of a company by saving labor costs, time and other expenses. Although these advancements also progress business opportunities and in turn, careers—the dependency has created additional expenses for citizens to maintain, and to ensure job security. Global involvement is becoming pervasive in industry and business. Most businesses large and small are involved in some way in global trading, whether directly with vendors and customers or with the trade or use of products or goods manufactured outside their country. In the Unites States, the stimulus plan that President Obama implemented presented a strong start in solving the issues the country faced in 2008. This stimulus offered aggressive stages for a long-term plan of attack by focusing on both economic growth, freedom of technology to improve the quality of life, as well as the importance of global trading. Even still, this is just one country. Although the US has a long reputation of global involvement with good and bad results, no one country has the power to save the world from the possibilities ahead.

In a time of on-going war and terrorism, a new world order is a logical choice. Global relations are designated and defined in treaty and trading laws. Yet, we can see through the tragic events in recent years that terrorist threats have drastically advanced life altering realities. The United States has been viewed as the "safety-net" for the world, so to speak. The Land of Opportunity and Freedom. Yet, over the last few decades, the United States has been involved in conflicts with global issues, some unrelated to the United States in no other way but indirect financial gain, though maybe guised under other intentions. During this same time, world poverty has grown to the discouraging 1.4 billion people affected today. (Bureau of Labor Statistics, 2012) A great deal of human suffering and environmental damage is caused by the growth of population. The world population is presently estimated by the United Nations to be over seven billion people. The total population has grown steadily for the last several hundred years. There are seven times as many people on earth as there were just two hundred years ago. The earth's resources are finite and while more even distribution could raise the standard of living for most, there are not enough resources for more people in the future. Most authorities and experts believe we will reach a global population of ten billion by the year 2050. Most increases are happening in poverty stricken areas, where this is least affordable. Education and health care resources are needed in these areas to slow the population growth. Education, as a backbone and infrastructure of any society, will assist in not only increasing the prosperity level of countries, it will curb the population growth, which is getting out of hand in many under-developed nations. It is also very instrumental in people's moral of participating in their own affairs in developing democratic values, as well as innovative measures leading to a more stable and sustainable society, fertile to attract investments and in turn increasing job opportunities.

Education can shape the prosperity and standard of living of any society—on population control, industrial development, creation of job opportunities and productivity. Therefore, planned educational programs with strategic objectives that a society needs—at large—to meet the nation's objectives, cannot be left to private enterprises to deliver this vital role. A harmonious participation and cooperation between industries, financial institutes and government as a catalyst to set policies would be needed for any country in order to shape the programs, rather than putting financial hardships on the students. After all, it would be the industries that benefit from this educational undertaking! Job opportunities need to be tailored and created to the need of the country, and the support systems need to be in-placed for interested students to be able to pursue their careers in different levels—practical technical training, professional levels, and research alike.

Social responsibility of individuals can be regarded as the prime social structure of any society in forming the political and progressive development of the nation. Their participation or lack of, in every aspect of development will affect their standard of living and the values a nation is pursuing for itself. The culture of participation and disciplined responsibility of citizens in any society safeguards the democratic values and advancements— in economic, education, culture and arts, provided adequate educational training are available to all to enjoy this privilege. Divestment in major corporations, led by the U.S. universities, under protests and pressure from students in 80's brought the South African Apartheids to their knees. The same might happen anywhere in the world, not paying attention to the causes of uprisings and protests. Faith in humanity is at stake.

There are many who say that the poverty level across the world is a direct effect of passive government action. Governments have taken little initiative to ensure the improvement of the overall quality of life and an end to poverty altogether on a global stage. The poverty statistics can and will affect the quality of life for all individuals and their communities. People cannot spend what they have not earned. Unemployment does not just affect the financial advancement of the individual. This leads to a lack of spending back into commerce or property foreclosures which decrease neighborhood property values.

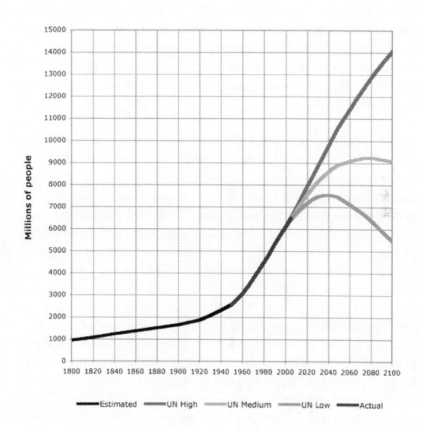

World Population History and Forecasts According to the United Nations

The US and other Western countries teetered with financial collapse beginning in 2007. A great deal of this was caused by the US financial system, leading to mortgage crisis. The power of the dollar and the lack of government monitoring, or entanglement of government and corporate interests combined, allowed many financial institutions and mortgage companies to get away with predatory lending tactics for so long that many industries, including the real estate and credit industries suffered critical damage. "Due to the subprime mortgage crisis, creditors are not willing to lend money to the people. Since subprime lending

11

has almost ceased, it is affecting the subprime buyers the most." (Mortgage Cases, 2007) The picture of the overall quality of life is now painted differently. If the government can allow the greed of businesses to run roughshod over ethics and the security of so many citizens, one can only wince when surmising what the future might hold.

The destructive role of businesses in influencing any government policy will affect the democratic process, and undermines the political faith of people in their government. Government processes and elected officials that are serving their people must be above the partisan influences of political parties or businesses alike in order to be able to deliver the most efficient and productive solution for the ills of their society. In most advanced societies, lobbying is strictly forbidden. Governments and political institutes are designed to serve the people in their social fabric, rather than ruling over them! Furthermore, advertising and commercial promotion of any political agenda or candidate for an elected office is demeaning the intelligence of society and need to be eliminated in any democratic election process. This principle by itself can reduce the influence of money in political campaigns, which is very destructive, manipulative, and devastative in any society. Influence of commercial entities or interest groups in political processes of society would lead to favoritism, corruption, and eventual totalitarian state. Public debates and equal access to public media between different candidates would be stimulating and promotes political though process and democratic values.

In their annual meetings, the more industrious advanced countries advocate for the global economic development programs in different countries to curb hunger, revolts, and provide security at home. The blueprint they all present are based on "Free Trade" to advance prosperity levels in all areas. NAFTA did not achieve that after nearly 20 years. Even the sale or import of bananas in certain countries upsets WTO relations amongst certain members at political level. Protectionism is still the dominant factor in all trade relations or business endeavors across the globe. At different stages of development in any society, the policies need to be adjusted with respect to values and long-term aspirations of that society. In order to introduce and develop industrialization, probably some protection would be beneficial for their economy to grow. Later on, to monitor the quality of goods and services within the country, foreign competition can help to establish good standard for their goods, attracting foreign investment and getting into international market, which would expand the productivity level and economic prosperity of the nation. Examples are numerous—ranging from Japan after WWII, to Thailand, South Korea, and India alike. Policy makers need to weigh the low-rate labor costs versus quality goods they will be providing to the market place. Globalization has created an arena for the most quality product at the least cost to be delivered at the most efficient manner to the end-users' hand. Only the most efficient systems are going to succeed. Considering the diverse interests of different business entities, in the most competitive world economy, the advancing countries are faced with aggressive business practices and new political environment to cope with. Considering the fact that global economy has created a fierce competitive environment for companies from the industrial nations to do business in advancing nations, policies and government strategies in receiving countries are influenced beyond the capability of those nations to resist temptations. It affects their planning on products they need, or services they desire for their respective economic growth. In support of their respective constituents, and protecting their own interests, the advanced countries from the first camp will, naturally, support their own business enterprises, and they need to influence the receiving partner(s) for their home products or services—marriage of politics & business. That's the beginning of "conflicts" that one can witness at all levels of governance—in trade, joint ventures, and even between the industrial countries at international competitive market. Subsequently, it will serve as the springboard for corruption, butchering democracy to ensure

13

their continued rule to benefit from privileges, and beginning of autocracy—gradual death of democracy.

Economic hardships, lack of job opportunities, bleak horizon on prosperity level and advancement in any society will result in people's lack of interest or participation in the affairs of their own society, and this dissatisfaction gradually leads to unrests, protests, and sometimes violence. However, unless the masses get organized and structure a solid political formation to voice their desire or demand, their movement does not get anywhere. And that's where tyrannical regimes do best in preventing such a mass movement to form, and filling the vacuum!

Human Rights & International Business Developments

To deprive a man of his natural liberty and to deny him the ordinary amenities of life is worse than starving the body; it is starvation of the soul, the dweller in the body.—Mahatma Gandhi

Humanity has valued Human Rights as early as 2500 years ago, as described in the documents surfaced at different libraries, museums, and public places such as the United Nations. Although many civilizations and cultures recognized the value and importance of human rights in their societies, implementation of appropriate measures to reflect the rule of land has been marred in the history of mankind. It is ironic to note that the political developments have always been paralleled with the growth or the degree that society has valued for human rights of its citizens. Interpretation of the values, or to the degree human rights would confer with respective societies all depend on the ruling body of that society—it has always throughout the history been treated in that manner. Roman Empire, Persian Empire, Greeks, or even Egyptians, they all had recognized the necessity and value of respecting human rights in their governance. To what extent they practiced is questionable. Throughout the history, one could observe the abuses on human rights, contrary to their

14

declared intent in practically every society—political opponents in Roman Empire were thrown in front of lions, beheaded in Spain of medieval era, or executed by Adolf Hitler, and tortured and brutally get murdered in today's Iran under another medieval ruling clan. Can we call this development of rule of law in defense of human rights? Formation of the International organization, United Nations, was supposed to legitimize and observe a universal law for defense of human rights in all country members.

In early 21st century, one could witness the atrocities conducted by Serbs in the old Yugoslav peninsula, with the UN playing little attention to enforce its mandates! Iraq's aggression, and consequent violations of human rights by its dictator in 80s, or the abuses of power exercised in Zimbabwe after a fraudulent election by the ruling group in 2008, or the Iranian ruler's violation of human rights, imprisonment and torture of protesters after the so called "election" of 2009, were all ignored by the paralyzed United Nations and the industrial nations. Although we are still living in 21st century, and humanity has not reached its full maturity to recognize and value the human rights, different societies gradually are reaching or nearing the perfection in observing these values, experiencing democracy in their respective societies. The past century has been good evidence to the fact that observance of human rights in any society is coupled with the growth of democratic values, and hence further development of economic infrastructure, leading to prosperity for the nations involved. Full implementation of human rights in a democratic society creates multiple dimensions in economic development, with potentials for benefiting from a global economy at large.

Populous uprisings in the Middle East early in 2011 were good manifestation of the desire of the people—Jobs, Productivity, Economic Prosperity, and curbing corruptions. All political doctrines and ideological discussions were replaced with basic pragmatic issues in support of their economic and human values. They might not fully understand, or even practice democracy;

however, they do understand the value of "participation" in every step of the way towards democracy—planning, decision making process, and implementation phase of projects or programs to benefit them all. A transition to democracy is powered by people's participation in all major affairs of any society, leading to economic development and prosperity for all. Sitting on the side-line, waiting for others to change or modifying the governing bodies will result in a ruling body fueled by lack of participation of its constituents and eventual totalitarian system. Selecting the most appropriate industry, technology, service or even products to promote in a given society to a large extent depends on the form of governance of the receiving nation. South Africa was a good example of this phenomenon. The end of apartheid and election of Nelson Mandela to form a democratic government in the country was the beginning of economic expansion at global level, bringing more prosperity to the nation. Unfortunately, the industrious countries, in search of more economic development at home, cannot afford to observe all the necessary values of human rights in their dealings with advancing nations, causing many nations to suffer from this double standard. It has a double edge effect: it lowers efficiency in conduct of business and planning, and leads to the abuse or waste of funds that often end up in farm lands and personal accounts! Corruption at government level can be contributed mainly to lack of people's participation in the political process and welfare of state and society. In other words, open system will benefit the masses, whereas the closed system will flourish dictatorship and corruption, which at the end will result in the collapse of the governing regime.

The desired economic development in any advancing nation will not be achieved unless the right environment is created for that nation to prosper. Of course, one of the primary factors in the lack of such an environment is the fierce global competition amongst the multinational or international companies in seek of lucrative business deals to secure a steady growth for their shareholders at home and produce higher stock values! Otherwise, without steady growth in the value of their stocks, the CEOs do not last very long, and are replaced with an individual who can deliver! The question is whether the international companies can prosper in their dealings with democratic form of governments? During nineteenth and twentieth century, mankind has witnessed the growth of colonialism and later support of totalitarian regimes by international enterprises, through their own governments— militarily or otherwise—to secure lucrative business deals. Naturally, such arrangements could not materialize under a democratically elected and operated government. Therefore, support for dictatorship and puppet regimes expanded from East to West and other continents for the gain of a few business enterprises at any cost. With the rise of democracy across the globe and awakening of masses, or their desire to secure a higher standard of living, the process for such companies are changing too. The role of supporting governments is changing alongside to reflect the realities of world today, performing business transaction in a new environment. In other words, the international business development for a global economy to grow, presently in early 21st century, has obstacles and hurdles to overcome. The solution is multiplex, and not simple to resolve, unless the issues are treated in a visionary manner by statesmen, and not politicians. The objective needs to deliver a "Win-Win" solution for all parties concerned.

If a new world order becomes reality rather than just a conspiracy theory, how would this benefit the world as a whole and within the United States? As mentioned earlier, the United States has become more and more lenient with immigration tolerance and assistance. The United States has put the quality of life of American citizens at risk by providing free operating hand to financial sector of society to dictate the faith of humanity. Freedom to illegal immigrants; will also throw off the balance of American economy. According to statistics gathered by the Center for Immigration Studies, "there is no way to know if the current trend will continue, but these very high unemployment rates for immigrants and natives raise the question of whether it makes sense to continue admitting so many new immigrants. In FY 2008, some 1.45 million new immigrants (temporary and permanent) were given work authorization." (2009)

These statistics alone are alarming. With a new world order implementing more just/fair governments across the world—all people would have the same rights and freedoms. There would not be a few countries more advantageous than the others, drastically decreasing the "urge" to migrate to another country or start a war.

As with all countries, US citizens have their own expectations of their government. They exercise political freedoms by electing the officials to represent them; make decisions for them. They put our faith in elected representatives expecting them to make the right decisions for the working class as well as the wealthy. Citizens expect the protection of their human rights by the law enforcement and the judicial systems. The path of the future does not just rely on the security and fulfillment of the basic human rights of American citizens. From a global aspect—there are various parts of the world where violation of human rights has become part of everyday life; never to be questioned. [3]In 2010, 15.1 percent of all US citizens lived in poverty. The US poverty rate in 2010 was the highest poverty rate since 1993. Between 1993 and 2000, the poverty rate fell each year, to a low of 11.3 percent in 2000. Children represent a disproportionate share of the poor in the United States; they are 24 percent of the total population, but 36 percent of the poor population. In 2010, 16.4 million children, or 22.0 percent, were living in poverty. From a resource standpoint alone, global trade and open seas are vital to business and the quality of life in most nations. Today, there is no country in the world that could successfully operate unaccompanied. Many people are of the opinion that the United States involvement in the war in Afghanistan demonstrates their dependency for global trading. A new world order can re-establish these open lines of balanced trading, secure importing, and cost effective exporting, without harming the economic balance.

Truly unifying the world as one entity would require the entire population to readjust their lifestyle, their way of life, and their mindsets. The definition of human rights would be redefined in a sense. Homelessness would be eradicated. People would not fall victim of identity theft, Internet scams, predatory lending, or be able to get away with white collar crimes against each other. Although the concept of a new world order would without a fraction of a doubt takes away some of the freedoms that American citizens have grown accustomed to—they are in essence, just a single piece to the bigger puzzle. A new world order will balance the quality of life globally; as a whole. The decision of which government is more beneficial all boils down to the individual person. Yes—the wealthier people will be affected more gravely when it comes down to having their "freedoms" stripped from them. But in turn, thousands of people who are living in poverty or homeless will be able to benefit from a better quality of life. As a whole, we need balance in society to achieve equality. We can choose between poverty levels increasing across the globe or limiting the excess living of a few. By laws of the trickle effect, the key to economic survival is ensuring the constant flow of money through the cycle from wholesale to retail to consumer which creates and maintains all phases of employment. In the current economy, given both the unemployment and poverty rate, the bulk of the cash flow is cycling through only certain areas. The wealthy spend their money in high-end stores rather than franchises like Wal-Mart that produce thousands of jobs. They spend their funds on high-end luxuries which rarely trickle down to the working class end of the chain unless serviced or maintained. This essentially adds to the gap between the wealthy and the working class. How does the current government attempt to decrease this gap? By implementing progressive income tax. Allowing the rich to maintain their tyranny, so to speak, in return for adhering to pay their higher tax brackets.

The world is changing. Societies have either depleted or replaced the more traditional resources for advancement with modern technology. How does this affect us as a whole? In more ways than we are capable of creating an effective defense. First and foremost, this concept has created a certain leniency for society. Goals have become about cutting corners for the sake of saving time and money. In some cases, we have sacrificed the quality for the quantity that could be mass produced. We can see this from the decline of homemade goods on the market and the influx of As-Seen on TV products or infomercials. US President Woodrow Wilson was prophetic with his statement about business—the business of America has become, in laments terms, enabling society to become lazy.

All of these realizations of today's society might not have been directly caused by the passiveness of the government. However, the passiveness of the government combined with the array of government types across the globe has definitely played a heavy role in the overall quality of living for many societies. Since society, as a whole, has grown almost dependent on modern technology, securing open trade lines and structures under a new world order are imperative for survival. The Technology-Democracy-Development paradigm proves this. There is no denying how the use of technology has advanced us as a society. Technology has advanced tremendously from 1990s through today. Yet even then, the impact of modern technology on the advancement of society was widely known. Looking passed the obvious ways technology could advance the business aspect of society, we can see advancements for the quality of life itself.

"Good scientific communication via the mass media [technology] is especially important in those areas directly and strongly affecting people's lives—for example, before, during and after natural disasters such as storms, volcanic eruptions and earthquakes, as well as in the general area of global change or depletion of natural resources" (World Conference on Science,

1999) We witnessed this during and immediately after the September 11th tragedy. Although the terrorist attacks were carried out in a few places, it directly affected the entire world.

Due to technology—media, Internet and business—the world was able to come together, rescue people, and create relief strategies. At the same time however, the passiveness of the United States government was evident as well. This passiveness or overload of responsibility, allowed businesses to take advantage of these same tragedies as a way to generate profit. Companies were selling memorabilia with promises to donate proceeds to families in need or the cleanup efforts at Ground Zero. This deceit could only be possible because of the lack of social and government responsibility.

Taking this one step further, we can see the same affects in the still increasing casualties of 9/11. Volunteers who assisted in the rescue and cleanup of Ground Zero are to this day, suffering or dying from respiratory issues. The government that was expected to provide adequate health care facilities to aid these type of disease and tragedies, are unable to even accurately identify the underlying issues—nonetheless cure them. The balance not only for and between different social classes, but also the balance between nature and human nature is needed. We have utilized technology to advance society at the expense of destroying the earth itself. The ozone layer, global warming, globalization. All these current world issues are an indirect result of the abuse of the privilege of technology. Today, almost every business advertisement encountered bears a mention of their social networking website as an additional way to contact or keep updated on that specific company. Yet how many times do you encounter a hairspray commercial that includes the damage aerosol can have on the ozone layer?

The governments are abusing their power for the further advancement of businesses rather than increasing the overall quality of life. How is this priority even defined? Through the years of influence by monetary gains. Maybe the time has come for a new world order to ensure the protection of human rights in the future. With the world in the condition that it is in between poverty, war, global warming, globalization, government corruption—do we really have a choice for survival?

Just as a man would not cherish living in a body other than his own, so do nations not like to live under other nations, however noble and great the latter may be.

Chapter II. Democracy and People's Governance

"All compromise is based on give and take, but there can be no give and take on fundamentals. Any compromise on mere fundamentals is a surrender. For it is all give and no take".—Mahatma Gandhi

Political Institutions:

Mankind, throughout the long history of civilization has developed a system of governance to serve him best. Coming either from a rural, agrarian society or urban grouping—people have structured a system to serve their needs. Initially, due to lack of political institutes, religions had played this role to manage the societies. As civilizations grew, local rulers, kings and emperors were devised to protect and govern their societies. Influence of religions in the affairs of societies, through kingdoms or otherwise, were exercised and lessons learned during the past number of centuries, lead to development of political institutes to replace the autocratic rules of religions. Renaissance in Europe was a turning point for the separation of religious rule from politics and governance. Consequently, development of republic—government of the people for the people—was devised, leading to formation of political institutes and rule of law to protect people and their societies against tyrannical form of ruling elite.

In this process, maturity of political systems, especially industrial revolutions helped the managing groups—governments—to respect people's private opinion, beliefs and faith without the need for any religion to set any civil rules or regulations in conduct of everyday affairs of society. This led to freedom of all religions in those societies without any clash, and the religions were protected from the harms of political tantalization—separation of religion from operation of governments. This is the general trend and evolution of political systems separate from different religious orders for different nations to manage their civil affairs on economic growth, political and social affairs, education, job creation, well-being and trade, etc.

Political development of societies will mature when people in a given geographical region, for their common interests create and establish a serving entity, to be called government. Contrary to medieval eras, in the twenty first century, fully developed societies are governed by people themselves through a self-elected institute, called government to serve them, rather than rule them. If the true meaning of a government is based on such notion that the institute is to represent people, by people, and for the people, then any influence of power or interest groups in any form, financial or otherwise, on operation of such institute will divert the society towards a totalitarian system of governance.

Governments, which are normally elected by its citizens, need to be small and efficient in providing the common infra-structure services for its constituents – the people. Individuals or businesses alike can benefit from a common basic platform to prosper and grow from. Of course, lack of functioning political institutes create political vacuum, which leads to autocratic and tyrannical form of government, which might be used by a religion to take advantage and influence a governing system—Spain of early 20th century, Israel, and Iran. Unfortunately, all tyrannical regimes, in order to prolong their grip on power, will not allow any political institutes to form to organize the society, and this will hinder the implementation of any democratic measures in the society. People's participation in any political structure to develop democracy and prevent corruption, which is one of the main essence in any nation building, is mandatory.

Political institutions do not flourish under dictatorship or tyrannical systems. Most dictators govern without the checks and balances of a governing body. All dictatorships have commonalities that have led to their demise. They usually have totalitarian regimes and maintain power through fear and control. They often foster cult like personalities by feeding propaganda to the masses. The modern dictator of North Korea, Kim Il-sung implemented school prayer thanking him and commissioned all art to focus on him. Saddam Hussein had images of himself produced and displayed as statues, murals, and about Iraq. The Roman Senate is the creator of the dictator, originally formed for emergency reasons in the event of uprisings. A dictator was in power over all politicians with no liability for actions, and usually limited to a six-month term. Lucius Cornelius Sulla was later appointed dictator and did not have the term limit and ruled for two years. Julius Caesar succeeded him and served until his assignation. The office of dictator was then abolished.

Many dictators come to power at times of crisis or uprising. Napoleon Bonaparte rose from an army general to rule France, crowning himself emperor for life. He had a highly successful military career and was initially very popular. He controlled all facets of the French government and the press. Upon his invasion of Russia a coalition of European armies surrounded France and his army soon declared mutiny, eventually forcing him into exile.

A great deal of dictators had distinguished careers as military commanders previous to acquiring power. Saddam Hussein served as the general of the Iraqi Army. Manuel Noriega, who came to rule Panama, had a long standing military record. Muammar Qaddafi was a military leader who took power of Libya in a September 1969 military coup. While numerous dictators have been military leaders who gained power during a coup, some have been appointed. For instance, Adolf Hitler, was appointed chancellor by President Paul von Hindenburg. Upon the death of Hindenburg, Hitler became the Führer.

The majority of dictatorships end with the death or ill health of the dictator or as violently as they begun. After decades of rule Fidel Castro's health deteriorated and he handed the reins of

Cuban government to his brother Raul. The United States invaded Panama and captured Manuel Noriega and imprisoned him. Hitler committed suicide when the German Armed Forces were defeated and Josef Stalin and Vladimir Lenin both died after strokes. Benito Mussolini of Italy was killed by Communist partisans and Saddam Hussein was taken from hiding in a mud hole by United States Armed Forces to face justice and was executed. Muammar Qaddafi's last place of refuge was in a drain pipe under a road in Sirte, before he was killed.

Dictators are inclined to violate human rights and frequently are guilty of genocide and remain in power for long periods. Besides death or a citizen overthrow of government, which is usually difficult as dictators control their country's military, change can only occur with the intervention of other governments or the United Nations. Organization for example, Human Rights Watch, investigate and publicize the human rights violations of tyrannies and dictatorships and pressure governments for reform. Because of the technology and accessibility to cell phones and the Internet, some evidence of human rights abuses have made their way into the mainstream. Perhaps the recent removals and resignations of dictators signal a trend toward elected rulers who allow their citizens the basic freedoms that many of us take for granted today.

There are current examples of tyranny throughout the Middle East region. Protests are prevented by the ruling regimes, no matter how peaceful participants behave themselves, and eventually leading to uprising of masses, violence and chaos. Beginning with nineteenth century, and more in 20th century, a new concept of democratic form of governance was introduced to complement the idea of republic. Democracy flourished with the growth of labor force, and industrialization in the West. Trade unions, parliaments, financial institutes and the common rules for all citizens to enjoy were formed and developed over the past couple of centuries. However, it must be emphasized here that democracy can only work in a society that is well educated and informed. Education is not simply reading and writing abilities; knowledge base and good judgments need to be developed in a given society.

It is a changing world, therefore, societies need dynamic set of rules or constitutions or political structures to benefit from and operate within. Role of business enterprises in manipulating the governments and lobbyist activities need to be barred in order to achieve a true form of democratic government. To ensure full development of democracy in any society, people's participation in all aspects of government is essential. This is the process for any advancing nation to realize and engage themselves at all levels, and enjoy the participation of its people into all development programs, industrialization, education, economic planning and investment, defense and political development; to understand, digest and gradually implement the democratic values.

Industrial growth, economic growth, and advancements in any society are geared directly to the degree of democratic values that society can exercise. It is not possible to inject or import the idea of democratic form of governance to a society, unless the people do realize the need and discipline themselves in accepting the limits and advantages of such a system, respecting human rights of all individuals. In other words, ruling by decree or kingdom is over, and advancing nations are realizing that the best approach towards prosperity is the rule of law, respect for human rights, and impartial political institutions to serve and protect them. Awakening of societies in 20th and 21st centuries are the result of this demand by nations, leading to protests, upheavals and revolutions. If societies are denied a progressive evolutionary change, and are severely confronted, historically this leads to violent change—a revolution.

What would happen if the world would unite for the sole purpose of ensuring a strong, stable government and reverted back to the old social and economic order? The days of kings and emperors, ruling with religion to maintain order. When comparing the effectiveness of the different types of governments which have been implemented throughout history, with the issues the world faces today—a monarchy type government seems like a possible solution. If religion, once again, was the string that linked everyone together under this monarch, would this prove that society—as a whole—could benefit more from a government run without the separation of church and state? More importantly, are those benefits worth relinquishing the people' right to religious freedom—amongst other rights?

There are many aspects to consider when weighing out the pros and cons of a monarch government. Looking at historical monarchies of the past, one can clearly see both the benefits and the setbacks of this type of government. In certain ways, however, the advantages and disadvantages showcased in the past somewhat contradict each other. Yet to create such a government in the current time would be extremely difficult without rebellion. This type of government would also be a bit hard to utilize in today's society since the amount of religions present today, override the concept behind the once practiced divine right of kings. There are very seldom civilizations present today who possess the structure and belief needed to adhere to a government ruled by the divine right of kings, such as the Middle East and parts of Europe.

Today, there are several monarchs still present throughout Europe, Asia, Africa and Oceania. Some ruled with the backing of a religion and some without. However, the most famous and successful monarchy of history is within England. The success of England's power over loyalty from the people can best be witnessed by the recent publicity from the Royal Wedding. Hundreds of thousands of people, both within England and throughout the world, gathered to witness the marriage of the newly wed Duke and Duchess; William and Kate. This marriage managed to unify the entire world with publicity but also opened up the educational realm for what a monarchy truly stands for—peaceful unity.

In today's society, though a monarch may not be implemented, there is similarly in essence, one social class which predominantly overpowers the other. Some may stand to say that the wealthier class has more "political pull" than the working class. Others may say that this pattern of rule by the government is grounds for the conspiracy theory behind a new world order.[4] However, as better explained by The Daily Kos, this type of relationship is more commonly justified as ". . . people of similar minds, shared interests and massive resources intending to do what is best for themselves operating synergistically outside the eroding democratic structures that used to protect us." (Bing, 2011) Although this statement pertains to the discussion of the government in England, the concept of government secrecy and true intention can be implemented throughout the world.

Looking at historical patterns, there is no doubt that religion played a huge role in ancient governments and the success thereof. For many years in various parts of the world, rulers used religion as the grounds to unify and control, so to speak, their people. During these ancient times, civilizations such as the Aztecs and Incas, who played a vital role in evolution, used religion as a sense of leverage over their people—using faith to bind their power. "As Hinduism, Buddhism, and Island in Southeast Asian empires, and both Islam and indigenous beliefs in Mali, provided sanctions for rulers, for both the Aztecs and the Incas, religion played a central role in legitimizing the power of ruling elites and in sanctioning warfare and the exaction of tribute from conquered territories." (Goucher, et al, 1998) Despite the effectiveness of this ideological glue that held both society and empire together, how long did it actually last? In these times, human sacrifice was not only utilized by rulers, but also justified as the same—there is no surprise that rulers struggled until they were conquered by the next reign.

29

Over the last few centuries, there have been many more religions being discovered and freely practiced. Due to this influx in religion, the separation of church and state is almost vital to ensure continued religious freedom. It is this same influx that has caused governments such a monarchy to become less effective and more difficult to implement. People today are not as "scared" so to speak, to go against their government, as they were in ancient times. Implementing a monarchy which rules with religion in today's day and age, would mean taking away the religious freedoms of the people. It would also call for the world to follow the same religion. Who is divine enough to make this call? The majority of society would agree that no one bears this divine right to make such a decision for the entire world.

As the concepts of religion grew stronger and more diverse, world emperors and rulers found themselves with increased competition from religious leaders; making the power over their subjects less effective. It is quite simple to adhere to a certain lifestyle if there is no other lifestyle being presented as an option. This was the goal of ancient rulers; through the use of religion. In order for rulers to remain in power—they felt—was by discrediting those who stood as opposition. More religions meant more people following different beliefs. This theory can be shown in the ancient Romans. Even though the Romans ruled by religion, their religious beliefs were based on the ideologies of several religions combined. "State religion looked after the home of the Roman people, as compared to the home of an individual household." (Roman Empire)

This concept only shows that as nations develop amongst themselves, the power that the emperors or rulers have over the people decreases. This is where the separation of church and state becomes an important and equally supported division. In essence, this separation gives some of this power back to the government—in regard to ruling the politics—while giving equal power to religious leaders for individual faith. In essence, the

30

people themselves have more faith in their government when they feel their government does not take advantage of them. In this specific case, the separation of church and state decreases the fear that the government is using religion to control their subjects. Britain is the best example of how a monarchy can evolve and change over time to accommodate the changing times and nations within the rule.[5] "The English monarchy starts . . . in 1066, with William the Conqueror, and continues to exist to this day. This makes the British monarchy one of the oldest in Europe." (The Royal Universe, 2009) This specific monarchy outlived its own bloodline, continuing their rule. There was even "a dark period in the 17th century when the people suffered from temporary delusions and created a republic." (The Royal Universe, 2009)

By Britain allowing this republic to develop, it directly went against the concept of the divine right of kings. However, in my opinion, it also—as a complete contradiction—strengthened the government in the eyes of the remaining followers because it showed the government's willingness to let the people grow amongst themselves; while still leaving the option of their protection available. This is the ultimate example of the effective "rule of law." By allowing the republic and eventually the democracy to develop while the monarchy of England still stood intact, Britain showcased the strength of the government itself. The government enabled the change, encouraged the change and in some ways supported the change (by not intervening with war or opposition) all while maintaining their own rule with their remaining loyal subjects.

As one can see, the history of the world's governments have long been pressed through their own trials and errors. Some monarchs of earlier times failed by over-implementing, so to speak, their divine rights. Others fell victim of the pressure of up and coming religious leaders. However, England and Britain have proven that a monarchy can successfully outlive generation after generation if utilized leniently; leaving room for change in changing times. In essence, by following the rule of law and placing the growth of a nation before the individual needs and rights of the governing body, a country can benefit greatly from this type of government. This success also shows that religion can play a vital role in this process, remaining in essence, and the string that linked everyone together under this monarch, but does not necessarily need to be strictly implemented and enforced upon all subjects. The power behind the concept of the separation of church and state can be a useful tool to a successful monarchy. However, the fact still lies that in the current state of the world affair, as a whole, implementing a unified monarchy—might pose nearly impossible.

The United States has outlived many Presidents from several political parties, all following their own list of priorities. The democratic system has showcased many benefits for American citizens but has also put American citizens in many jeopardizing situations such as war and poverty. Some may stand to say that the different reigns in presidency may be an ongoing direct effect of the instability of the current economy. Without question, the United States must make some drastic changes to their current government system in order to bring the economy back to a healthy, stable trend for the future. Whether the current government is specifically tweaked to such a point that a comfortable compromise between government and people can be met or a complete revamp of the government itself is done; this change is vital to our existence.

One of the major/outstanding differences between the UK policy making process and the US is on the continuity in many strategies, policies and programs that are adopted or conducted in the UK system of governance, no matter which political party is in power, versus regular change-over of guards, policies and values that are changed every time a new administration is elected in the US. In most industrial countries, professional political elites are leading the governments to a stable political and economic direction/or environment, whereas in the US politicians are generally elected based on the amount of funds pumped into their campaign coffers, without much expertise or attention to the candidate's relevant political, administrative, professionalism or economic experience!

The Change is Needed Now

Lack of structured political institutes with discipline and organizations to lead the people to success or implementation of advanced development measures amongst people will cause totalitarian system to rejuvenate or flourish. Non-organized criticism will fail; and that's exactly what tyrannical regimes want—don't allow the opponents to form a cohesive entity! Therefore, the solution for such a misfortune is for the people to create local, cohesive civil network with activists across the country for a solid network of participants to actively participate in a non-violent resistant – a civil non-obedience movement for change they desire.

As we continue to slowly transition in time, technology continues to transition with us, at a much faster rate. These advancements in technology have left most Americans either dependent on the technology or subject to unemployment due to the technology replacing their position. Business owners are investing in more long term savings in overhead costs due to the speed and accuracy of using technology over manpower. Due to the cost and rate of inflation, most American business owners are outsourcing the remaining work overseas to further decrease the overhead costs, rather than create (or keep rather) jobs in the United States. This has had a tremendous negative impact on the economy and lack of resources within.

At this rate of inflation, crime, unemployment, poverty and declining economy, may be an evolutionary approach to a newly formed government may be needed. With every other aspect of society advancing with the times, why wouldn't the United States government as well? For centuries, the United States has held elections, encouraged as many people as possible to vote and tallied those who actually did vote, to determine which candidate is elected as President. In most cases, citizens place their trust in a candidate who does not get re-elected into his second term, which starts the reign over again. Let's be realistic here. After a candidate is elected into office for their first term, common sense would tell you that they need at least a few months, spent getting accustomed to the bylaws, the inside information and the accurate factors in the issues the country faces. It may take several more months to accurately create an effective strategy and start implementing these strategies into place. The first year, give or take, of a new presidency is spent just breaking themselves into their newfound position.

At that point a US President has only three years to ensure their game plan is executed to perfection and creates a notable (long term) solution to current issues that American citizens can actually notice—such as a better quality of living or more resources that remain readily available. If a President cannot showcase such results within their first term, they are more likely to be voted out of their second term—leaving room for another candidate to step in and restart the process. At this point, what happens when the second President doesn't share the same insights or priorities as the first? More time will be spent reversing, so to speak, the actions and strategies which were previously put into place. And the cycle continues.

What would happen if the United States developed a new concept of government such as implementing an educated citizenry as the center political power figure? Would this strengthen our government and improve the economy? Currently the United Nations is responsible for maintaining the rule of law both nationally and internationally for the safety and security of the citizens. This means that for principle purposes, "that everyone— from the individual right up to the State itself—is accountable to laws that are publicly promulgated, equally enforced and independently adjudicated." (United Nations, 2004) If such a government did exist, and educated citizenry did stand as the backbone of the rule of law concept, would such laws be different from those instilled today?

Although the laws may not in fact, be all that different from within a democratic government to those within an educated citizenry; they do not have to be. As history stands to remind us, an educated citizenry creates a more proactive enforcement of these laws because the people themselves, can better understand the individual laws and their importance for the quality of living and standard protection. "⁶Americans have long believed that a healthy democracy depends in part on free public education. The nation's founders stressed that an educated citizenry would better understand their rights and help build a prosperous nation." (Smithsonian, 2004) This concept is exactly what the United States is currently lacking—the strong future of a prosperous nation! Although public schools are funded, in part, by local taxpayers and residents paying school taxes on their homes, this is an aspect of the education realm that could use some tweaking to maximize the benefits of citizenry education as a government option.

Today, to make the economy flow more smoothly, the community residents who live within each school district, pay school taxes accordingly (despite how many children from each household, if any, even attend the schools in the district). Community members vote each year on the school budgets to determine which schools will receive which percentage of those taxes to maintain the facility throughout that school year. In regard to the education realm of reality, this system seems to work out. However, how this system helps to balance the economy is a different story. For example, is it fair that one neighbor who has four school age children attending school while both parents work is paying the same amount of school taxes as another neighbor who does not have any children attending school and who is a retired senior citizen—barely making their bills with their retirement income? No. This is not fair. Taking this a step further, an entire neighborhood can be put at future real estate risk because if senior citizens cannot afford their home (or the taxes thereof), their home will eventually foreclose—decreasing the property values of the surrounding houses.

The cause and effect of each aspect of government all tie into each other in some way, shape or form. Yes, using an evolutionary approach to a new government concept, at this point, is vital. Using an educated citizenry as the main basis would help the cause—if implemented carefully and properly. As strange as it may sound, think of the concept as a whole as in the movie The Matrix. Before meeting Morpheus, Neo had survived in the "real word"— comparable to our everyday life in a democratic government— for years without danger or static from any Agents. However, after Morpheus and his team explained and introduced Neo to the world within the Matrix—an individual form of educated citizenry—he was awakened, so to speak. He then saw life with a different meaning and himself with a different purpose. This same concept is the same in our reality. If we instill an educated citizenry as the basis of our government, the citizens themselves would see the world's problems as they actually are and self-perception would be a vital, more powerful part of the solution.

The consumption driven Unites States society is lacking much needed resources which were once available in abundance. Oil, being the perfect example. The United Sates has been involved in overextended wars with oil resources as the underlying motive. Due to this lack of open oil flow from the Middle East, the price of petroleum in the United States has increased (and at times decreased) over the last few years. This has raised sub-issues as homes and many other buildings either being transitioned from oil to gas heating systems or drastically reducing heat usage altogether (risking an array of health issues). This has also encouraged carpooling and use of mass transportation—which in itself causes minor issues between traffic, crowding and public cleanliness from pollution. When analyzed on a global scale, these issues have all added their potency to the global warming issue we face today.

Financial Institutions

Financial institutes can flourish only in a secure and democratic structure. Without democratic political system in place, people do not have trust in financial institutes, and naturally they cannot grow or serve a nation independent of the government. People's participation in political and financial institutions is a mandate for economic growth and prosperity of any country. As an example, one does not need to go very far. Sluggish economic growth in twentieth century Russia, with hesitant foreign and domestic investments in the country, can be contributed to lack of democratic values and processes being exercised during Putin and Medvedev reign in power. Major foreign investment firms decided not to participate in the government's ambitious plans for economic growth and financial recovery of the country since 2008, due to many social and political restrictions introduced in Russian society, especially after the plight of funds from Russia to Europe by Russian investors and business community, indicating the lack of trust in political structure of the country.

In a democratic form of government, although private and independent banking system is needed for financial strength of the country, a strong central banking system, with people having shares or interests in that organization is needed to maneuver the mortgage system and support the major investments in the growing industry. Industrial developments cannot be left to the private banking system alone—as was witnessed in the financial crisis of 2008/9 in the U.S. and world at large. The role of financial institutes in democratic societies is to serve their respective nation as another infra-structure component for the economic growth and productivity. With such a strategy in placed, financial institutes can contribute and safeguard the democratic processes in capitalist societies. However, once their role is manifested with greed under un-regulated business environment, it leads to corruption and influence meddling not only in businesses, but also in the political structure of the society, endangering the fundamental health of the nation. Financial crisis of first decade of twenty-first century across the globe, resulting in financial collapse of a few institutes as well as many businesses, created financial hardship on many individuals as well as organizations all over the world. That was a clear-cut example of such disastrous policies, even in advanced societies. Extension of the corruptive arm of financial institutes in politics and their lobbying ventures are well pronounced and very toxic in most countries, destroying democratic values of respective nations.

Influence of financial and interest groups on law makers and government bodies threatens and eventually destroys democracy. In other words, influence of money and power exerted by interest groups will hijack the democracy, leading to corrupt capitalism and creation of a totalitarian system of governance.

The influence of the banking system and major corporations in the Western world on governments and local politics alike has tarnished the Capitalism, and hence democratic values of societies. Capitalism can work best in an integrated democratic structure, with absence of influence by any interest group, especially financial organizations, which are plenty, especially in the U.S.— on congress, government agencies, media, and policy matters at all levels of social and political arena. A government regulatory agency, representing the will of people, need to have a seat on the board of directors of any financial institute to monitor their activities, and control income level of their staff. In this manner, small businesses can be protected against larger ones, reduce discriminatory measures, and eliminate the influence of such institutes in the governmental affairs. This needs to be curbed, before the fundamental pillars of democracy crumbles, leading to social and economic revolts by masses.

Market Manipulation and Fraud Lead to Housing Market Collapse

Between 2008 and 2010 a financial calamity that had been over a decade in the making hit the United States and world financial markets with such force that it devastated national economies, financial institutions, and homeowners; millions suffered life-altering losses so a relatively few self-serving power brokers could profit. The seeds of this economic crisis began to grow in the late 1990s when large-scale investment banking set upon an unsustainable course of challenging traditional practices and constructs primarily to reap financial windfalls from a strong housing market. Risky investment practices that contributed to a system of banking that could not maintain itself included the lowering of credit and underwriting standards, the use of short-term financing for long-term investments, and high reliance on mortgage-backed securities among other things. Furthermore, government regulators ignored indications of a market bloated with risky investments, did not perform due diligence in oversight and monitoring responsibilities, and even contributed to the problem by imposing subprime lending quotas on Government Sponsored Enterprises (GSE) Fannie Mae and Freddie Mac.

Upon initial review one might conclude that the worldwide economic troubles, and more specifically those in the United States, that began in 2007 and continue to the present day led to home foreclosures on a volume previously not experienced. However, a more in-depth analysis reveals that self-indulging investors and politicians created an environment that did just the opposite. An over manipulated and under regulated mortgage lending and investment system caused an inevitable collapse—a bursting of the housing bubble—that adversely affected markets ultimately leading to mass foreclosures. In short, the root of home foreclosures was gluttony for self-profit by some. The decline of home values was predictable and avoidable and only a symptom of the underlying cancer of irresponsible market manipulation.

A robust housing market existed in the U.S. in the late 1990s because readily available credit fueled a strong national economy. To facilitate easily accessible credit, underwriters lowered rating standards, thereby opening the door for millions of new homebuyers to access loan financing. Additionally, politicians representing both major political parties, eager to influence favor with voters, encouraged lenders to provide easy finance options to low-income borrowers. In fact, between 1997 and 2000 the Department of Housing and Urban Development tasked Fannie Mae and Freddie Mac to increase subprime mortgage purchases to 52% of all notes they held.[7]

With so much credit available to subprime borrowers, the number of home purchases increased, thereby driving up property values; a classic case of supply and demand. Obtaining loans to purchase property became so undemanding that by 2005 four in ten home purchases were either as second homes or business opportunities such as rentals. [8]Less desirable loan structures in the form of higher interest rates, adjustable rate mortgages (ARM), and balloon payments normally accompanied the higher risk of subprime lending. This home-buying frenzy caused personal debt to rise at an alarming rate, and by 1997 Americans spent $1.27 for every dollar of disposable income they had. [9]More people with less money were purchasing more homes at higher prices than ever before. Investors responded by betting billions of dollars that this cycle would continue.

The practice of selling mortgage-backed securities (MBS) began in the 1980s and slowly gained in popularity. A mortgage-back security is akin to a selling a bond to investors who are then paid revenues derived from the mortgage payments of thousands of homeowners. This works reasonably well and is a safe investment so long as interest rates are low and borrowers keep up with their payments. However, problems arose when bankers bundled subprime or higher risk mortgage loans with prime loans. The mix of reliable mortgage borrowers combined with the higher interest rates charged to subprime borrowers provided an allure that spurred investors to devote ever-increasing amounts of capital into MBS opportunities.

Further complicating the matter, shadow banks, organizations that operate largely outside the boundaries of normal government oversight or interference, are often involved in high risk ventures such as hedge funds and lack the financial assets that could limit the negative impacts of bad investments. Investment banks commonly partner with shadow banks and in this manner expose themselves to the same vulnerabilities of high-risk speculation. Shadow banks often make use of short-term financing to purchase long-term assets like mortgage-backed securities. The consequence of this funding practice is that if the housing market declines, short-term funding becomes impossible to obtain and the system can collapse in on itself. The financial meltdown of the investment banking company Bear Stearns in 2008 exemplifies this negative cycle.

Bets, in the form of MBS investing, by most banking institutions, including Fannie Mae and Freddie Mac, hit a crescendo in 2003 when over $2 trillion in assets were issued [10]. As the housing market climbed to its zenith in 2005-06, gambles kept paying off, thus motivating investors to continue to pour money into MBS opportunities.

Notwithstanding the false hopes of investors, the volume of subprime loans drove home values to an unsustainable height, and high-risk borrowers began to default in ever-increasing numbers beginning in 2007. In the face of skyrocketing defaults, credit rules tightened causing home sales to drop off precipitously. Aside from declining sales, tighter credit restrictions also made refinancing nearly impossible for subprime borrowers, over 90% of whom in 2006 had relied on ARMs to initially obtain home financing with the expectation of refinancing to fixed-rate mortgages. [11]Over the next two years as ARM percentages increased, even more homeowners defaulted, accelerating the downward cycle of the housing market.

In the meantime, investors stepped away from mortgage—backed securities which resulted in less funding available to lending institutions that subsequently were unable to lend money, even to qualified buyers. The invalidation of the false assumption that the market would continue to rise for years to come, highlighted the interdependency of so many mortgage-based investments, all reliant on continually increasing housing values and sales. Treasury Secretary, Timothy Geithner admitted in 2008 that the "combined effect of these factors was a financial system vulnerable to self-reinforcing asset price and credit cycles."[12]

In 2010 nearly a quarter of all homes in the United States had a mortgage loan whose value exceeded that of the home itself. Many Americans chose to walk away from these upside down mortgages further exacerbating problems with the housing market.[13]

Rather than renegotiate interest rates, banks chose to foreclose on defaulted loans. Government watchdogs were no better. When warned of an impending housing market crisis in 2003, Barney Frank, senior Democrat on the House Financial Services Committee said "These two entities—. The more people exaggerate these problems, the more pressure there is on these companies, the less we will see in terms of affordable housing."[14]

Despite Representative Frank's statements, the housing bubble inevitably burst because of short-sighted, self-indulging, get-rich-quick investments that ignored all the warning signs. High debt ratios, large volumes of subprime mortgages, lowering of lending standards, and unrealistic expectations should have been noticed and heeded, but were not. In 2008 a report released by the G20 summarized the situation very well.

> During a period of strong global growth, growing capital flows, and prolonged stability earlier this decade, market participants sought higher yields without an adequate appreciation of the risks and failed to exercise proper due diligence. At the same time, weak underwriting standards, unsound risk management practices, increasingly complex and opaque financial products, and consequent excessive leverage combined to create vulnerabilities in the system. Policy-makers, regulators and supervisors, in some advanced countries, did not adequately appreciate and address the risks building up in financial markets, keep pace with financial innovation, or take into account the systemic ramifications of domestic regulatory actions.[15]

Using polished verbiage, the G20 blamed greed and a lack of due diligence by government at all levels for the false build-up of the housing bubble and its foreseeable, perhaps avoidable, crash. Because so much capital had been invested on the belief that the housing market would sustain unprecedented growth, the wave-sized ripples of the crash pushed their way into all the nation's and the world's economies. Mutual funds, retirement funds, the stock market, and other financial instruments often relied upon by everyday working folk lost tremendous value.

With higher debt, less credit, and lost investment value, millions of families across the nation cut back on spending as a means of coping with the economic crisis they found themselves in. Less spending translates to a diminished demand for manufactured goods, which in turn means fewer and lower paying jobs, less tax revenue to governments who traditionally pay to aid the unemployed. This, joined with unprecedented numbers of home foreclosures, has disrupted the social norms of untold millions.

Finally, unscrupulous lending practices led to "paper mills" wherein bogus loan documents are created by the thousands in order to legitimize foreclosure actions by banks that did not properly process loan paperwork during the peak subprime lending years. Today, so many of these "paperless" home foreclosures are in litigation that thousands of homes remain unsellable while courts sort it out. Sheila Bair, Chairman of the Federal Deposit Insurance Corporation believes banks should be required to establish a "clean up" fund to address this problem.16 Whatever the outcome, it is clear that unscrupulous practices led to the crash of the housing market and eventual foreclosures.

The democratic governments need to assist in creating jobs, using stimulus measures to assist the economy to grow, and that is beyond the capabilities of private banking system. Policies and measures for such a growth need to be executed at national level rather than private banking level in support of certain industries or business enterprises.

Adam Smith, the great economist of the18[th] century, in his masterpiece of 1776, The Wealth of Nations, is portraying the path towards prosperity for nations, leading to the fact that certain necessary measures need to be implemented in any society in seek of prosperity and economic development. He addresses the role of government and the rule of law as keys to national prosperity. Effective government safeguards property rights, which is the cornerstone of any economic growth. This is further enforced by a justice system to protect all that. Democracies, with a free press and protection of minority rights, are regarded as the most important measures for an effective government.

However, when the trust of people in any government is lost, the nation's ability to invest and own property, or for that matter, transact business, increase wealth or property value in the society in bringing prosperity to the country is diminished substantially. Uncertain environment and lack of trust or participation of people in industrial growth, or general affairs of the country, will raise credit risks and thereby increase the interest rates in the society, which in effect dampens productivity and limits the economic growth.

Although technology plays the main role in any development program to bring about further economic growth and prosperity to the society, it must be emphasized that full benefit of technology development can only be realized when the whole world population can benefit, if it can elevate their standard of living. In other words, expansion of technology will bring about major changes and expansion of trade and prosperity across the globe, if its implementation is planned properly within a democratic environment. Take the example of the Internet versus anti HIV drugs, the latter of which are controlled by pharmaceutical companies with limited market. It is very interesting to note that according to the observations made by Amartya Sen, the Nobel Prize winner in economics, ". . . no substantial famine has ever occurred in any independent and democratic country with a relatively free press." In an open democratic system, technology can be used to serve the people for job creation, economic development, and initiate innovative processes or products to bring to the market. It serves as a catalyst in the development planning, provided adequate educational system is in-place to support such a program.

Chapter III. Neither Communism nor Capitalism

Pragmatic Movements

The Soviet Union

December 1991 brought about the great schism that the world had been waiting for with bated breath. A sense of surrealism overpowered the intense reality and significance of the actual events taking place in the world. As fifteen new countries found naissance, the augmentation of one of what was one of the most powerful empires in the world crumbled, and the Soviet Union was no more.

This demise of the Soviet empire was at the time considered a victory for the west. This collapse was a symbol of freedom, the victory of democracy over the tight reigns of totalitarianism and unequivocal proof that a country needs a completely capitalist society to function and thrive. The United States was at the head of the celebration parade, as the empire that posed the biggest threat to them dissolved before their eyes. The long standing Cold War finally thawed out and the entire world went through a political makeover, reformulating economic, military and political alliances that had formed through the strife all around the globe.

The intentions behind the formation of a communist empire were not evil. The exploitation of the essential communist values created a distorted version of reality, plunging the Soviet empire into unfortunate dystopia, generating worldwide resentment with no outlet of expression. Russia adopted communism as a product of the Bolshevik Revolution in 1917, which slowly transitioned into the communist society as defined by the Marxist-Leninist school of ideology.

The state of Bolsheviks creation was supposed to overcome national difference within a single monolithic state. The state was supposed to be based on a centralized political and economic system, stressing upon equalitarian values. However, communism soon gave way to totalitarianism as the state which was supposed to be the product of the utopian revolution Marx predicted would be required to unseat the imposing bourgeoisie and put them at the same level as the proletariats they control.

The original values of communism were lost, as the Soviet Union adopted a panoramic propaganda campaign, which they promulgated through state—controlled mass media biased in favor of the single ruling part marking out a very specific cult of personality. The same methods were used to propagate total control of the economy and its regulation. Speech was restricted and monitored and the masses were under constant surveillance. The whole regime was fueled by unparalleled use of terror to buy subservience and submission.

The whole ideology was impractical from the start as the Soviet leaders were enamored by the idea of a socialist estate, without any practical knowledge on how to run and control a vast, accumulated empire. One of the major reasons for its ultimate failure was the crucial underestimation of non-Russian ethnic groups that were residing in Russia, making up more than fifty percent of the entire population. They did not count on the amount of resistance they would receive when they tried to group the ethnic minority groups into an all—encompassing Russian state, with unified language, culture and beliefs.

The second biggest underestimation on the part of the Soviet leaders was the effect of communism on the country's economy. Their economic strategies failed miserably when it came to fulfilling the requirement of funds needed for the smooth functioning of the state.

This was basically due to the torrid arms race they were locked in with the United States which ultimately brought the Soviet Union down to slow, torturous economic decline. With such political and economic unpredictability, people were not ready to accept the basic values proposed by communism, despite of the Soviet Government's best efforts. The constant failures to resurrect the economy even demoralized the little influence the regime had left over the population.

By the time Mikhail Gorbachev came to power, in 1985, the country was already falling apart. Existing in a situation of static and stagnation, the USSR was merely waiting to be pulled out of the gigantic rut it was stuck in due to the deep seated economic and political problems of the country and the general state of dismay of the population.

Gorbachev tried to gain redemption by introducing a new two-tiered reform policy, which included glasnost or freedom of speech, a luxury the nation had never been afforded before. However, he also simultaneously instigated perestroika, an economic reform that stands for rebuilding and re-establishment. Glasnost is seen by some as a severe misstep on Gorbachev's part as this completely backfired on him. The population finally had an outlet to unleash all the suppressed emotions and political resentments that they were forced to suppress for decades. Yet this might have been the objective and intent of Mr. Gorbachev, used as a vehicle for populous to steam-off for a major change. To top that, the economic reforms also failed miserably, despite of his reassuring predictions that it was the best method to resuscitate a dying economy, which was also met with severe criticism which the nation did not refrain from holding back given their new found freedom of expression. The society did not have the necessary infrastructure to absorb the economic change, and was not ready to receive the economic reforms.

The first signs of disintegration started in the non-Russian peripheries of the Soviet Union. The first reason to break free in the form of a mass, organized dissent was the Baltic region in 1987 with Estonia stipulating autonomy of state. Soon Latvia and Lithuania had joined in the same cause. Gorbachev was put in a precarious situation as the nationalist movements advocated by the Baltic republics were weighing down heavily on his glasnost policies, but he did not want to force the issue despite of the fact that it would be the eminent ruin of the Soviet empire.

The Baltic Region was the first link that managed to break away and other regions followed suit, as the Soviet empire fell prey to the domino effect and toppled, one country at a time. Nationalist movements in countries like Ukraine, Moldova and the Central Asian republics crippled the power of the Central Government. Paranoia was high and rightfully so as cooperation was wearing thin on all sides, and governments were subjected to high level espionage in attempts to bring it down by several different methods.

The final blow to the USSR came in August 1991, when a group of 'hardline' communists orchestrated a coup d'état by kidnapping Gorbachev. This group was founded under the implementation of glasnost and was prepared to hold on to the communist regime at any cost. The same group decided to publically announce on state television on August 19th 1991 that the leader Gorbachev was crucially ill and would not be able to perform his governing duties. The announcement was met with unprecedented pandemonium. The entire nation was in an uproar, and marched onto the streets staging immense protests in Leningrad, Moscow and various other cities of the Soviet Union.

The group that instigated the coup tried to exercise control over the chaotic rioters by bringing in the military. However, the soldiers rebelled themselves by claiming that they will not hurt people of their own country. The coup failed without military intervention or assistance, and the effort died out as the nation united as one to drive the instigators out.

The failed coup was the last straw in USSR's resistance, and the empire visibly crumbled under the state of political awakening. Both the people and the governing authorities accepted that the damage done is too immense to repair, as the 'August Days' demonstrations had clearly established. The nation would settle for nothing less than complete democracy. Realization sunk in and Gorbachev abdicated his position, admitting that he was no longer capable of leading the nation.

The world saw the emergence of a new entity named "Commonwealth of Independent States" as the advent of the New Year marked the end of the Soviet Union. From January 1992, the countries that had comprised of the Soviet Union all established themselves as independent nations. They maintained complete political independence while still holding out economic and military ties with other countries within the newly formed Commonwealth Republics.

The new elected leader of choice was Boris Yeltsin for Russia, who had served as the Chairman of the Russian Supreme Soviet from 1990, was eventually elected as the President of Russia in June 1991. Yeltsin employed his plan of action immediately after coming into power. He acknowledged that without the Soviet Union, Kremlin would not have Gorbachev, and in effect he winded up the USSR as a conjunction in collaboration of two other Slavic republics, Ukraine and Belarus. The manner of the disintegration of the USSR was completely new to the region. The Soviet Union simply disappeared within a period of six months. The inner echelons of the Communist Party had replaced democratic centralism with public debate.

The principles of what defines the party's basic role within the system was challenged by society, as new political organizations formed, ready and willing to make reforms. Ultimately, the Communist Party's manifesto of power was eradicated from the Soviet Constitution, obliterating the only formal recognition of the stark reality of the previous year.

The fall of the Soviet Union was unique because of the manner it was disintegrated. Throughout history there rarely has ever been such an intense authoritarian political system which had the military means to wipe out all life on earth have been subverted with such smoothness. The resistance wielded minor bloodshed and incidents of violence. Even if the newly created states had immense struggles in store for them in terms of their economic and political development, as well as the new system of governance in Russia, the way the resistance of the Soviet was taken down is a true example of political master class in the 20th century.

Dissolution of the Soviet Empire in the early 1990's was predictable and shortcomings were well pronounced in earlier years to the ruling elite in Kremlin, as well as managers, policy makers, intellectuals, writers and historians in the Soviet Union and the West alike. In other words, the collapse or dissolution of the Soviet Union as the vanguard of communism was not unexpected at all. It can be argued whether Communism would be regarded as a political system of governance for societies, or need to be defined as a political thought, or simply just phenomena in the course of economic-political development towards more prosperity for certain nations.

Over a dinner conversation in December of 1988 in Moscow between the author and Mr. **Nikolai Ivanovich Ryzhkov**, then prime minister of Soviet Union under Mr. Gorbachev, Mr Ryzhkov adamantly admitted to the fact that "   when Lenin introduced his Communism to Russia in 1917, we did not have much industries to speak of with a sizable labor force, or literate peasants to be effective participants in the revolution. There was a political vacuum under Tsar, with people frustrated under his (Tsar) suppressive rules, Lenin just filled the vacuum." This is exactly what is happening in many countries with recent "awakening movements". Without political institutions in-place and a political structure for people to participate in, there is a danger that they just change the guards—changing one dictator to another! Any uprising or social/political revolt needs strong, well thought planning for transitional period, as well as long-term system of governance after the revolt for people to benefit from their sacrifices. That's the only way they can succeed in their movement; otherwise, chaos will follow the "change", leading to another non-functioning government, with more suffering for the people.

Lack of such a preparation and disciplined political infrastructure will lead to opportunist and extremist forces to take over the society, resulting in more suffering for the masses— examples of recent Egyptian "change-over" or Afghanistan after defeat of communism, or Iran after the fall of Shah are only a few to name. In such circumstances, Communism or Moslem Brotherhood elements, with their pre-planning can fill the political vacuum, as was the case in Egypt of 2012 and Iran of 1979. After upheavals/Revolutions of Libyan and Egyptian societies in 2011, upon their overthrow of their tyrannical regimes, world was witnessing chaotic societies with no clear agenda and action plans to govern their societies—without pre-planning, organizing a disciplined mass participation for a genuine change, no movement can claim a success.

Again, it is the role of younger elites and new generations to get familiar with pitfalls of unprepared "change" to be able to control their destiny. The changing role of educated younger generations in shaping or transforming their societies towards a democratic form of governance can be very instrumental in establishing strong political and social infrastructure to build on. They can serve as true voice of people, and generally, democratic societies will not be attracted towards extremism or compiling weapons of mass destruction, including nuclear arsenal.

The Nature of Change

For better understanding of this argument, one needs to examine the nature of change in any society. In any technology and applied science, in the course of any sudden change—from a laminar stage to a different turbulent stage, even another level of laminar—a turbulent, unsteady phase can be experienced. Let's examine the rate of economic growth of various countries over the past couple of centuries. The degree of progress can be measured by an empirical value, "National Status Number" (NS), or a similar method being used by the United Nations in assessing the prosperity level of different countriels over the years. A number of factors affect the NS number—GNP, type of educational system, health care system, political structure, financial system, employment level, and the most importantly, faith of the people in their political system of governance, etc.

The following diagram reflects the empirical method of expressing the rate of economic growth, National Status number (NS#) of different countries versus time.

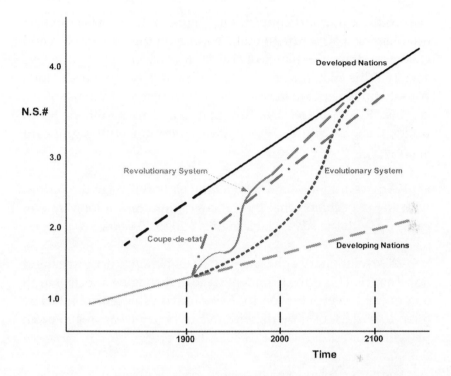

Change in Rate of Economic Growth

Countries such as the U.S. and Sweden with NS# above 3.2 and 3.4 respectively, or France, Germany and Britain with a range of 2.8 to 3.2 all enjoy a laminar, steady growth—technically as well as economic prosperity. Whereas, less developed countries with NS numbers less than 2.0, or even less than 1.2 suffer a widening gap in their economic growth and standard of living in relation to the prosperous, industrial nations, even though they might have a modest rate of growth against time. Countries experiencing this type of condition, with the desire to catch up, or reach to a prosperity level of more advanced nations—NS# above 2.8 or better—need to make a drastic strategic change, politically and economically. There are a number of options available to them, before this gap is translated into a social/political violence, or spark—called "revolution".

- With a military coup d'état, having a benevolent dictator, establishing a structure to make a jump on the growth path and exercise a dramatic change of policies in governing the respective society. This method has proven to be disastrous on the long run—Latin America governments in the nineteenth and twentieth century, Russia under Tsar and Stalin, and many others. Spain under General Franco was a rare exception with significant success.

- An evolutionary and democratic path to change the course, with the expectation that the process might take a long time to catch up with the advanced societies—20 to 40 years!

- A revolutionary upheaval with drastic change in the means of governance. This is the turbulent stage of managing a society until a minimum level of prosperity, NS# of 2.0 is achieved, followed by a laminar stage of growth, with evolutionary measures to catch up with the rest of the world—NS# 3 or better.

The latter form, which society passes through a turbulent revolutionary phase can be portrayed and be called "communism". In other words, once the respective country or society's NS# reaches 2, or better, it cannot afford to remain communist! This theory was presented in the 5th International Symposium of System Engineers held at Purdue University, U.S.A. in October 1972 by this author. Russia has just passed this stage. China today is experiencing the same phase as Russia did at the end of twentieth century. However, Chinese leaders are steering the society in a much subtle and evolutionary method to change the rate of economic growth, without allowing a revolutionary form of change to take place. As soon as an acceptable prosperity level is achieved, the Chinese society cannot accept and be governed under "communism". In other words, communism is just a transitional phase for societies under severe economic condition, in the process to get to a higher level of prosperity like the rest of the world!

The world, as we know it, is evolving faster than any of our current government types can keep up with. What seems to be smooth sailing in one country, has left indirect havoc on another. One of the main reasons for this increase in pace is largely due to the increase and freedom of the business realm. Is it possible to uniform the entire world under one government in attempts to gain balance? If so, which would be the most logical government to implement? These questions become much of an open-ended one since different countries face very different issues, aided by their type of government. However, in comparison to the different governances, some aspects of China's government seems to be effective.

China

Although communism might be the fastest way to instill a global fresh and equal start, the odds are because of the track record of the infringements of individual freedoms and human rights violations associated therewith, the populace would not be accepting. However, from the depths of the Communist Party of China, came the birth of the People's Republic of China; proof that reformists can make a huge difference. This was a country that controlled everything including crops, jobs, education, and business. Globally speaking, the world has much to learn from China on their education standards alone.

Compared to the United States, do you really think China would ever allow the lack of education of their youth to grow so bad that a "No Child Left Behind" law would need to be implemented? By simply placing more emphasis on education rather than business, the world would see a tremendous, productive difference. 17For example, research has shown that in China, ". . . education levels of household head and household members exert positive impacts on the likelihood of becoming middle class or upper class". This demonstrates the importance of human capital formation in this context.

When the economy in China failed to support even the most basic of lifestyles, the country, as a whole, reacted. But, who is to say that we would see the same positive results globally? Implementing a model of this type of government globally would be far more difficult due to the fact that some countries might actually revert from productive gains they might have made over the centuries. Some might need to sacrifice for the greater good of all. However, even now there is no country that currently stands as one hundred percent self-sufficient. No doubt though no matter what we do to change global direction, some loss of a few to safeguard the future of all, will be needed.

With the Rise of the People's Republic of China, the statistics of progression alone are impressive. [18] According to research gathered by the Asian Development Bank, "the People's Republic of China has achieved astonishing poverty reduction since economic reform began in late 1978. In addition, as a consequence of rapid economic growth, we see the rapid emergence of a burgeoning middle class, and more recently, a super-rich sub-population whose wealth rivals that of their counterparts in developed countries."

Compared to the United States, can one really think China would ever allow the lack of education of their youth to grow so bad that a "No Child Left Behind" law would need to be implemented? By simply placing more emphasis on education rather than business, the world would see a tremendous, productive difference. For example, research has shown that in China, ". . . education levels of household head and household members exert positive impacts on the likelihood of becoming middle class or upper class. This demonstrates the importance of human capital formation in this context.

Imagine how different your own life would be if not only you were financially stable, but if everyone was as well. On the very feeble side of the spectrum, social lives would be more productive. Productive social lives increase the businesses which host them—thus, greasing the wheels of the economy. On another note, this (newly found) universal financial stability has the capability to work wonders for individual self-esteem. A happy person recycles that positive energy right back into the world. How would this benefit us from a political perspective? People would have more faith in and support for their government if they felt that their government was acting in the people's best interest. Currently, that faith seems long lost in the political system of many countries. This is what we lack globally. That emphasis on our best interest as individuals first. The world has placed such a vast emphasis on business and money that we have subconsciously allowed business and money to dictate our overall quality of life. This is one of the main reasons that the People's Republic of China is such a fascinating government which the world could, and should learn a lot from.

The People's Republic of China was born, in essence, from the idea that change was much needed. By analyzing and learning from both the success and failures of other government types throughout the world, China was able to quickly (from an evolutionary perspective) turn their economy around— maintaining a more productive quality of life for the people. The Rise of the People's Republic of China allowed a revolutionary form of change to take place.

A key point to realize with this success, however, is that this progression came from within an already communist government. Would the results still be as effective (and rapid) if established within a democracy such as the United States, or a monarchy such as England? In other words, today's economy is so damaged that perhaps some form of communism or socialistic measures would effectively allow transition of the economy back to a stable flow across the world. This might be merely a transitional phase for societies under severe economic condition, in the process to escape from poverty and tyranny in order to achieve a higher level of prosperity, could be effective.

Considering the fact that China needed rapid economic growth in the country, their focus in early 21st century was to devote their major resources in providing vast network of infrastructure for masses across the country—roads, education, rails, communication, and more importantly, industrial planning. This policy created job opportunities, while businesses grew. However, having kept the wages low, the standard of living has not improved proportionately.

One of the major issues and concerns that the Chinese are faced with, is introduction of modified responsibility of capitalism within the country itself—state-by-state, or by province. The application of capitalism, without spoiling elements such as corruption, and financial greed starting from financial institutions are the main reason for China's gradual implementation method of "Open-Market" in a step-by-step technique, region-by-region policy to test and adopt a "workable" capitalism, tailored for their society. This is much like the needs of the United States and other countries which have let the strength of big businesses overpower the needs of the individuals.

Despite the different personal opinions one could have, it is undisputed that a worldwide change is overdue and imperative— at this point—if mankind is going to survive comfortably. Although for many countries, such as the United States which is used to a democracy, a restrictive society would be drastic and far from ideal for the people. The US enjoying a NS # greater than 3 cannot afford or does not need to adopt such a transitional method —"communism."

The middle class accounts for most of the world's population. "A look at the geographic distribution is striking. [19]In 2000, developing countries were home to 56% of the global middle class, but by 2030 that figure is expected to reach 93%." These statistics alone should be good reason enough to utilize the progression of the People's Republic of China in their efforts to stabilize their economy. "China and India alone will account for two-thirds of the expansion, with China contributing 52% of the increase and India 12%, World Bank research shows." (Wharton, 2008) Obviously, China has realized something that the rest of the world has yet to. Change starts within a group and becomes almost contagious to those surrounding.

Not to say that this type of government is the answer for the global economy, however, there are certain aspects that could serve as effective transitional tools—if implemented correctly and accepted globally. Much like China, a strong, new leadership is long overdue. [20] One that is able and willing to "stress the need of reform, an opening to ameliorate the life conditions of the Chinese population and to strengthen China's economy. But reform was not a political reform towards democracy as was demonstrated by the Chinese leadership in 1989." (Theobald, 2000) This statement expresses the further hardship that we would face implementing this republic within an existing democracy.

The Rise of the People's Republic of China has without a doubt been a long, vigorous journey, much like our noted process of elimination. However, this is just one country. To revert the entire world back their bare basics of political development seems to be the way to ensure any type of comfortable future. There is no reason that countries such as the United States should have so much political control and influence over certain nations in order to wage wars to safeguard their interests—such as in Afghanistan— while many countries in Africa and Middle Eastern region have citizens starving and facing a violation of their human rights on a daily basis. Yes, change is definitely needed. Communism is not the most appealing type of government, but the right leaders and statesmen would be needed to steer the societies towards a just and acceptable path throughout the world. There are some principles that could be effective measures in such a government model, while keeping or implementing respect for individual freedoms and human rights.

Many of the political and even management issues under communism do not work in a laminar, steady growth phase. Lack of efficiency and low productivity, or absence of incentives, or powerful and dominating central governments are amongst many deficiencies of this system. On the other hand, capitalism is not without faults either. Self-interest and influence of business enterprises in strategic planning of governments, unjust social values being experienced, and lack of attention to infrastructure services are amongst the deficiencies of this system.

Beginning with the end of twentieth century, pragmatism is replacing the dogmatism in both systems. East & West policies and tactics for running the respective societies are merging together, in search of a common ground, with the vision for "what is the best for society" at different stages, in a dynamic manner, leaving the *.isms at distant past—pendulum is moving to the Center! Recent upheavals in the Middle East are good examples of these phenomena. The world at large is generally realizing and attests to the fact that tyrannical systems of governance need to change to a more civilized, and democratic system, with a great respect to human rights. Eastern European countries were the first group of nations to re-structure their political systems after dissolution of Soviet Union. In the second phase, we are witnessing the wave of political changes across the Middle Eastern nations. Societies need to be served by their own people, curbing any corruption, focusing on job creation and economic measures to increase prosperity for all, and eliminate poverty. Development of democracies to guarantee the rule of law and safeguarding their political stability to be able to prosper in due course has become the ultimate aim of any political movement. What has become very important in either camp is the organization to manage their growth by adopting the most efficient method to achieve their objectives and potential success.

The factors affecting the success or failure of development programs include:

- Availability of Skilled Manpower; (M)

- Availability of adequate resources; (R)

- Adequate Space or facilities; (S)

- Effective Organization to perform; (O)

The relation between the above elements can be formulated as $(M+R+S)*O$ = Progress. Having adopted the use of high-tech and all essential technological tools in a dynamic form of management can produce successful programs for development.

The United States

The special case of the United States with the growing disparity between the wealthy, well-to-do, and the poor needs immediate attention and adjustment. The need for a review and analysis of the social contract as it is believed to exist in the United States.

The United States has led the way as a powerful economic force over the last century. By allowing a free market of capitalism governed by limited rule, industry, education, and technology flourished. The free market in the United States that helped fuel prosperity has also resulted in reckless consumption.

[21]Currently, the United States consumes almost twenty million barrels of oil daily. This is more than one fourth of the world's total oil consumption which results in an equal amount of the world's carbon emissions. [22]According to the U.S. Census Bureau, as of 2010, the United States makes up only 4.52% of the earth's population or about 308,000,000 people.

Predictions are that the United Sates will drain the country's own supply of oil in less than fifty years. Despite that forecast, the demand is increasing. There are three factors that cause the need for oil to increase; population growth, discoveries that cause new needs, and a boost in living standards. While the United States has been growing in population for several decades and continues to do so, the standard of living has been the major contributor for consumption increase. [23]By 1950 the United States reached the point of an average of one car owned per household. Within forty years by 1990 this had more than doubled to over two cars owned per household. Note: A household consists of an average of four people.

In addition, the design of U.S. metropolitan areas was supported by less consumption and lower costs of oil. People escaped residential life living in the cities as developers built the suburbs, although most of the time the industries and jobs did not follow them. This resulted in massive highway systems and a veracious increased appetite for oil to feed crowded work commutes. As affluence blossomed, free time and involvement in activities for families grew. As parents racked up miles on their automobiles chauffeuring children to events, the lifestyle became so common that vehicles were designed to accommodate them such as minivans and across the country terms like "soccer moms" were coined. With no economic obstacles, people developed a penchant for a flurry of activity that achieved a regarded status.

While cars are a major guzzler of oil resources, there is also the increased transportation of goods that goes hand in hand with the rise in living standards. Because of the sheer size of the U.S. and the fact that the prosperity was geographically distributed, the demand by the transportation industries for oil resources has also burgeoned.

Products beyond the imaginations of predecessors of just a few generations ago, were developed to serve the new so called needs of convenience. A television set spawned a remote control, a computer replaced file cabinets, an automatic transmission replaced the manual version, and kitchens became wonders of mechanization and computerization with automatic dishwashers, garbage disposals, wine coolers, electric can openers, and a host of gadgets designed to reduce physical exertion.

Where once people toiled in fields and grew their food or hunted game to survive, there are now fast food establishments that allow people to enjoy a meal while never standing or leaving their car. These advances allowed many people to become so sedentary that billion dollar industries were born to bring people back to physical condition. So, diets, a plethora of exercise contraptions, and health clubs sprouted in the suburbs like spring dandelions. Obesity became a national health concern epidemic as people gorged themselves with foods designed to please tastes with little regard to nutritional value in a competitive market.

The U.S. political system that governs capitalism is also dependent upon and addicted to the spoils of prosperity. In order to fully understand U.S. politics, follow the money trails. Big business drives politics with campaign contributions and lobbyists. Full development and maturity in political structure of any society, with the objective to serve its people, requires flexibility in the dynamic constitution of the land. The laws need to be tailored for the society based on their necessities of the time, status of technology, educational system, and the living standards of the people. Rigid and obsolete laws create an environment of resentment that social justice, democracy and political freedoms in the land would be threatened, leading to social unrests.

Law-making bodies of any society need to exercise an outreaching vision for improvement of social, political and economic health of the society, irrespective of any dogmatism lobbied by power groups or even political parties. It has been proven by many advanced and matured political systems in the twentieth and twenty-first centuries that political parties, in particular, can develop and present policies, and even groom or introduce their candidates to a political office. However, once the individual is appointed or elected to a position of responsibility within the government, he/she can no longer represent the interests of their associated party, rather, they have to represent the best interests of the nation.

Capitalism provides a fertile ground for innovations, new businesses to strive, leading to job creation. However, people involved in the growth and success of such enterprises need to be compensated in a harmonious manner with the rest of society they are benefitting from. Communism lacks this phenomenon. They need to adjust and allow free enterprise to flourish in respond to the need of their society. Participation of people in well-being, planning and economic growth of any society is geared to the political structure and environment in which businesses can thrive. Governments, without interference or influence of financial organizations or major corporations have the duty of formulating an acceptable and workable system of participation between employer and employees to safeguard the democratic values and free enterprise spirit, either by taxation, or limiting the greed in large corporations. Why a football player or basketball player need to get paid many times as a physician, or physician in some societies get paid ten times more than an educated, well trained industrialist, or educator? Limiting the gap between these two levels of earners is essential to reduce poverty and increase middle class for a stable society.

The Income Gap in the United States

Reading the headlines of different media in the United States early in twenty-first century, they all communicate a clear sense that there is a growing gap between the haves and the have-nots in this country. The Occupy Wall Street protestors are only the loudest and most recent group attempting to draw attention to this issue. If this perceived gap does exist, what factors are driving it, what are the implications for individuals and the nation, or its law makers, and what, if anything, should be done about it? There is a growing disparity between the rich and poor. Banks also need to become socially responsible and understand their responsible role to serve the societies.

A quick review of economic statistics gives an immediate indication that this perceived gap is quiet real. According to the Congressional Budget Office between 1979 and 2007, income grew by 275% for the top 1% of households and just 18% for the bottom 20%. [24] The United States Census Bureau also identifies a gap between the highest income earners and the lowest during that period. Census data goes further however, indicating that the gap between the highest income earners and the lowest remained consistent until the mid-1970s when the gap began to widen.[25]

This widening gap is even more pronounced over the last dozen years. Between 2000 and 2007, a time of economic expansion in this country, the top 1 percent captured two thirds of all income growth. [26] In fact, the gap between the lowest income earners and the highest income earners was greater in 2007 than in any other point in US history outside of the "Roaring' 20s" just before the Stock Market Crash of 1929 and the beginning of the Great Depression.[27]

Considering the evidence of income disparity in this county, and further evidence of the sharp growth of this disparity, it is worth considering what factors contributed to this situation. A look at past research indicates that contributing factors include tax policy, a changing economy, globalization, and decline of trade unions.

Tax Policy

There is evidence that tax policy along with some government regulation (or deregulation) may contribute to the income disparity between the rich and the poor. In the case of tax policy, the marginal income taxes of the wealthiest Americans have been reduced from 91% in 1964 to 35% in 2003 [28]. Perhaps just importantly however, were changes to taxing policies over the last 50 years that treat income exclusive to the wealthy differently. For example, capital gains taxes have decreased in the last 50 years. Estate and inheritance taxes have also decreased in the last 20 years.[29]

Concurrently, deregulation of the banking and financial industries, provided those who had it, greater freedom to use their wealth to get more wealth. [30] Government policy, purposefully or not, has tended to support the accumulation of wealth through all forms of income in the last 40 years.

Technology Economy

With the rise of the tech economy, a more highly skilled and educated workforce is required. The move towards more employment that requires higher skills leaves those lacking the proper training left behind. At the same time, the environment in which many low skilled workers work or receive training, the manufacturing setting, is on the decline and no longer provides this opportunity.[31]

Research from the early 2000s, indicates that the higher the educational achievement, the higher the average earnings for adult workers. [32] In fact, only college graduates have experienced any real median weekly earnings in the last 30 years. Those who have not completed high school have seen their real median weekly earnings decline by 22%.[33]

Immigration

Immigration itself does not cause income disparity but as indicated above education level has an impact. While immigration brings many college-educated individuals to the workforce (an equal percentage of the immigrant population is college educated as in the native population), it also brings a higher percentage of high school dropouts than the native population. As indicated above, educational attainment directly correlates with average weekly earnings.

Globalization

As noted, as the US economy becomes a more and more technology-oriented and the traditional manufacturing sector shrinks, there is less and less demand for low skilled workers. At the same time globalization and liberalized trade policies have opened up whole new labor markets. Low-skilled American workers are now competing for the few remaining jobs with workers from any number of nations across the world. Many of those nations are without workers' protection or other regulations that may increase costs, reducing the hiring costs, and making workers outside the US a more attractive hiring pool.

Decline of Unions

The last 30 years have seen a steep decline in union memberships; union membership went from 20% in 1983 to about 12% currently.[34] This coincides with declines in industries that are heavily unionized (manufacturing) as well as decreased union density (the percentage of workers belonging to unions). If we accept that, the collective bargaining power of the union helps its members maintain their wages than we can see how decreasing membership contributes to the income disparity.

There is also a case to be made, that along with declining membership, labor unions saw a reduction in their political power. This decline is evidenced by changes in federal law and political appointments that have occurred since the early 1980s.[35] This period of decreased political support also coincides with the period in which the wage gap grew.

Impact of Wage Disparity

Now that we have evidence of the income gap in the United States and an understanding of some of the factors that influence that gap, we next consider the impact of this gap. Does it really matter? There are those who argue that that the gap is not significant as long as overall income is rising. However, the impact of this gap goes beyond what is "fair" and has the potential to disrupt the fundamental values and systems of this country.

As we have seen in a number of countries in last year's Arab Spring, economic disparity can have a destabilizing effect on a country's population. In this country, the Occupy Wall Street movement has demonstrated the concerns of the "the other 99%"—presumably those not benefiting from the highest real wage increases. While this is an organized, nonviolent movement, it is reflective of a growing unrest and is wide spread across the nation. While any sort of violent overthrow seems of no interest in this case, it is not hard to imagine what impact a well-organized movement of citizens concerned about income disparity might have in an election year.

The longer-term impact may be even more significant. One of the principles the United States was built on was the belief that, through hard work and perseverance, every child has an opportunity to do better financially than their parents. As we have seen here, that is becoming less and less the case. In fact, an American child has less opportunity for economic mobility (that is "moving up the ladder") than a child from Canada or almost anywhere in Western European countries.[36]

And this pattern tends to reinforce itself. Income disparity influences where people live, the health care they receive, the schools they attend. Inadequate health care, education, crime, and homelessness contribute to long-term ills for the individual that makes it even more difficult to climb out of poverty. This self-perpetuating and real physical separation between those at the top and everyone else leads to ongoing class separation. This separation leads to rigid divides that become increasingly difficult to close. The wealthiest, those most likely to be in power, no longer have an understanding of the experience of the rest of the population. This lack of understanding places barriers to fixing the problem and removes a sense of urgency to do so.

In his essay in Vanity Fair in May 2011, Former Economist of the World Bank and Chair of the Council of Economic Advisors during the Clinton Administration, Joseph E. Stiglitz, describes what Alexis de Tocqueville observed about Americans at the birth of this nation:

"Alexis de Tocqueville once described what he saw as a chief part of the peculiar genius of American society—something he called "self-interest" properly understood." The last two words were the key. Everyone possesses self-interest in a narrow sense: I want what's good for me right now! Self-interest "properly understood" is different. It means appreciating that paying attention to everyone else's self-interest—in other words, the common welfare—is in fact a precondition for one's own ultimate well-being. Tocqueville was not suggesting that there was anything noble or idealistic about this outlook—in fact, he was suggesting the opposite. It was a mark of American pragmatism. Those canny Americans understood a basic fact: looking out for the other guy isn't just good for the soul—it's good for business.[37]"

It appears we, as a nation, are in danger of losing that "self-interest properly understood" that we once held in such abundance. It is yet unclear if a burgeoning Occupy Movement or a hotly contested presidential campaign can change our course and help us get it back.

There are the super-rich such as Bill Gates who admits he ruthlessly stepped on small businesses and people by stealing ideas with no conscience for their losses. Now he controls billions of dollars making decisions about who should benefit from his gains, and seeing himself as a great philanthropist. While his later humanitarian efforts might be positive, this brings into focus the question of who should have the power; the right to decide who benefits from capitalism and who does not. In this case the old adage of "he who has the gold" becomes the rule.

India

Despite India's government becoming a Democratic Republic back in the 1947—and currently being the largest existing democracy in the world—it is hard to fathom the country's high poverty rate. India, for the most part, has remained an overall poverty stricken country for centuries. However, the country has for six core export resources including oil, coal and steel—making the revenue continuously and readily available.

Despite democracy and profitable exports, India's poverty level remain on the rise, and there is a blatant unequal social and political status present amongst the people of India. Seems as if India has mastered the concept of cultivating the profit of big business without ever putting a dollar back into their own economy. The current political system in India makes this all too easy to continue to do.

India is considered by much of the world today, as an emerging new world power. This is a country that statistics show is home to almost one billion people, with a literacy rate of 74.04% and an average life expectancy rate of only 63 years old. (Ministry of External Affairs, 2011) For a country of this size, such a high literacy rate shows the education of the people—since nearly three quarters of the population do possess some type of literacy competency. However, with such a short average lifespan—one can safely assume that there is something wrong with some other aspects of life within the country's borders.

According to researched World Bank statistics—the quality of life itself for the people of India is far less than acceptable—most malnourished and hunger stricken. "The number of poor people living under $1.25 a day has increased from 421 million in 1981 to 456 million in 2005. This indicates that there are a large number of people living just above this line of deprivation (a dollar a day) and their numbers are not falling." (2011) this tragic fact would without a doubt affect the average lifespan of the people of India. The number of people living in these conditions, is far too obvious to go unnoticed by the political system in India—yet still nothing is done to improve the underlying issues.

If such a vast number of the people of India are living under these conditions—where is all of the profit generated from the major businesses being funded? Currently, India's political system is structured much like that of the United States—although certain aspects were adapted by other government types such as Britain's Parliament. That being said—why isn't the money being put back into the quality of living for the people—schools, community development projects, construction to further develop the country and job security? When analyzing the facts, the numbers do not add up! In the early 1990's, India adopted the "Open Doors" policy. Today, 56 Indian companies are listed among the Forbes Fortune 500 companies. (Ministry of External Affairs, 2011). As one can clearly see, statistics like this can only mean that India is home to nearly 10% of the world's most successful companies. Although the landscape represents everything, the Ministry also reports that due to present level of economy and quality of life in India, the middle class of the country has currently reached 350 million people. (2011)

Truly—this country has perfected—so to speak—how to continuously maintain and grow wealth while poverty continues to rise. The answers are in the statistics. For this reason, the events and developments over the last twenty years in India have been crucial—undergoing many high and lows—including the ongoing war in Afghanistan. Since the late seventies, "the demand for coal in India's power plants has rapidly increased . . . with power plants in 2005-06 absorbing about 80% of the coal produced in the country. "(Pew Centre, 2008) One would think that such a self-sufficient country would have a much lower poverty rate—not to mention, a smaller middle class—solely based on the reduction of overhead costs and surplus of jobs. Unfortunately, this is not the case in India. The profit is there. Proof of this can be found in nearly any analysis of the industry. For example, the future of the coal industry is factually based on the availability of the resource, but is otherwise, realistically recession proof. Sales will and have only increased since these statistics were released in 2008. So why has poverty level increased rather than decreased during the same time frame? Job security seems prosperous—since the future increase is expected to be steady and coal is exported by railways.

As the political system in India stands as a Democratic Republic, the overall party has more than a wealth of members. This aspect of their government causes a bit of conflict when analyzing the poverty rate of the country since so many blatant solutions stand overlooked. The Parliament itself consists of the Lok Sabha's 565 members and the 250 members of the Rajya Sabha— not to mention the Council of Ministers and the Prime Minister himself. For a political system this large—being this specific type of government—there should have been more progressions and decreases in poverty levels over the last ten or so years.

Consider the Reforms of 1991 as a vantage point. The landscape of India's land is agriculturally ideal to produce more than enough crops for export and food supply, as well as job stability for the locals. Instead, the economy grew more stable and the reforms "left the country with terrible inequalities, within cities as well as between urban and rural areas. [Being the ideal time] to tackle the causes of poverty in India . . . rural poverty." (Poverties.org, 2010) The political system chose business over the people's needs and quality of living—leaving the majority of population subject to poverty due to the migrations from the overpopulated cities. The fact of the matter lies that India remains a country that is so intellectually advanced that over the last few decades has not only designed and remained armed with nuclear technology—they have since tested their technology more than once! A bone chilling point of realization when a country defies the rest of the world—fully armed and ready for any opposition.

With facts such as these, it is not surprising that India is currently in the condition it is—home to multiple wars and battle grounds. India has become a country in which the loyalty of the peoples' faith in their leaders and their religion is so strong that generations after generations are born into the same path of extremist beliefs. Crimes and poverty in India are so high that people live in daily fear of these extremists, rebels and militants—scared of being caught next to a suicide bomber at the market or sending children to a school that could be bombed at any given time. These aspects of unimaginable torments are part of everyday life for some Indian people. A fact that has not changed over the last ten years—despite all the economic progress. As current headlines in India showcase, the people of India desire change and are willing to go to any level to accomplish as much. "Car Blast near PM's House", "Explosion in embassy car in Delhi, Israel sounds alarm bell". (BBC, 2012) The extremists of India are becoming more aggressive and tripling in numbers—rioting against the government and civilians alike to express the depths of their wants and beliefs. How much of this can one country survive?

With a political system as large and widely spread as that found in India, the conditions of the quality of life will never improve unless the government representatives dramatically alter their focal points back to the people. The resources in India's core products are vast enough to maintain themselves with the current production and exporting means while the government works to improve the poverty rate and appeasement of the people. Until focus is placed on the right underlying issues rather than those driven by residual income—the animosity will continue to grow. Even India's most recent headlined current events to attempt to censor Internet profiling and offensive content from social media networking sites shows how far on the downward spiral India actually is. Whereas the cyber world may be only an inimitable space that we must log onto, Senator Hilary Clinton—along with the rest of the United States—had to remind India that the people's rights and freedoms are the same in underworld as they are in the physical world.

The Role of Internet in Advancing Nations:

Rapid and open communications across the globe—thanks to the development of the Internet—has created a new dynamic environment for evolutionary changes in all societies, from East to West, and from North to South alike. Independent press and media can play a major role in safeguarding the democracy by playing their unique role responsible watchdog and pillars of governance. Independent Internet services and public communication system needs to be available to all citizens at all times and need to be regarded as another valuable element in support of democratic system. Therefore, a forth branch of government—Media & Internet—need to be recognized in modern dynamic constitutions. Blockage of Internet services for communications by many tyrannical regimes, denying access of their citizens to available facts and information has been exercised in recent political events. Acknowledgement of such arrangement in any society can protect the right of citizens against any abuses of power by the government. It can also promote world community to a higher level of human values and strengthen the political standing of the participating societies.

Starting in the late twentieth century and continuing in early twenty first century, more advanced and prosperous nations are undergoing a second industrial revolution, leading the way by the development of high-tech products—the Information Revolution, also sometimes called the High-Tech Revolution. Naturally, the advancing nations are benefiting from this revolution one way or another, by adopting policies towards implementation of democratic values, and taking a new evolutionary path towards greater prosperity level. The wind of dynamic changes in their political structures, with greater role of people in their own affairs and government is blowing all over the continents—from Africa and China to Eastern Europe and Latin America. However, there are still rogue states in the world resisting the changes, struggling to keep the status quo by applying the most brutal totalitarian system to rule over certain nations, even blocking the access to Internet. Although Internet and global communications have caused the awakening of these nations to realize the shortcomings of their ruling elite, their struggle for freedom and implementation of human rights values are revolutionary and severe.

Advancements in science and technology are moving fast in practically all levels of societies, in both advanced and advancing nations, with no boundaries or borders to limit knowledge transfer. This drive has made the out-sourcing of services possible, although the receiving society lacks basic infrastructure to support its serving people. Objective of parties for outsourcing are quite different. The motive for Host Company, operating on a short-term that is engaging in outsourcing is access to cheap labor, and increased profitability. Whereas the receiving party is looking for job opportunities and increased revenue to survive, or increased prosperity level for its workers. Although the Internet as a tool has helped globalization of economy to grow, however, the expected growth in both sides of equation has not materialized. Unless both parties can mutually benefit from such an arrangement, globalization of economy and Internet services cannot and will not deliver successful ventures. Take India as an example. Software companies are developing the most sophisticated and advanced programs for the U.S. market, while the living standard and conditions of living for most employees are still the same and easily can be categorized as primitive in nature.

Demand for improved levels of infrastructure in such societies are in rise, and the effect of Internet cannot be ignored or reversed, causing revolutionary movements in many societies, demanding better standards of living and people's participation in their government bodies. Unfortunately, certain high-tech products and their applications have been abused by some advancing countries, creating more misery and more suppression for the people, and even hindering their advancement towards higher rate of growth. Exchange of information between different societies have become instantaneous and in many cases have caused rapid changes in many societies.

Transition Examples in the Last Century

The latter half of the 20th Century saw some tumultuous changes in the world, with many long-time communist regimes falling by the wayside. Most of these changes were achieved through peaceful means and the population of those countries for the most part saw a positive change in their lives. The ones with the most positive changes adopted democracy and while the process has been painful in some instances; the change has come about relatively fast. Other countries have maintained what many regard as out of date government models such as Communism and monarchies, but still have become economic powerhouses because of abundant resources.

While some people could make an argument that people in socialist countries have access to better health care and other services, the recent troubles in Greece and other European countries have shown that any country with an aging population cannot afford entitlements without enough young people on the tax rolls to fund them.

The Czech Republic

One of the best examples in the last 20 years is the Czech Republic. The story of the country goes back to World War II, when it was absorbed by Nazi Germany in 1938. Ravaged and torn by 6 years of warfare, the Czech Republic, which was then part of Czechoslovakia, was first occupied by the Red Army of Russia after the war. A democratically elected government was overthrown in a coup-de-tat in 1948 and the country became a satellite nation of the Soviet Union with a puppet communist government ruling the nation.[38]

Under Soviet rule, the country floundered as free enterprise became almost non-existent. The government lacked the funds to provide social services and the infrastructure of the country suffered. Today, the Czech Republic has achieved the status of a developed country according to the World Bank. [39] It is also ranked highly in human development among central and eastern European countries and has one of the lowest infant mortality rates. How did this change from 3rd world country was transformed in a period of 20 years? A look back at the last two decades provides the answers.

November of 1989 saw the Velvet Revolution, which transformed the Czech Republic through peaceful means from a communist government to a democracy. [40] On January 1, 1993, the Czech Republic split apart from Slovakia and the new government immediately went to work on economic reforms with the intention of creating a capitalist economy. The infrastructure was strengthened and rail lines were built in the capitol city of Prague and elsewhere to create jobs and bring prosperity to all regions of the country.

The Czech Republic may be lacking in natural resources when compared to UAE and China, but a democratic government allows for free enterprise and the citizens there have embraced their freedom like few other people in the world.

Today the Czech Republic has one of the strongest economies in all of Europe. They have embraced the technology of the day as the country has the largest number of Wi-Fi subscribers in Europe, and several of its citizens use the internet directly or indirectly to make a living. [41] It is also one of the top tourist destinations in all of Europe as people from all over the world desired a first-hand look at its rich history and stunning architecture, after being secluded for years under Communist rule. Today over 110,000 people, or about 1% of the population is employed in the tourism industry.[42]

None of these astounding changes would have been possible under the previous government, and the surging Czech economy is made for healthy growth for the foreseeable future.

A Desert Gem in the Middle East

United Arab Emirates is a thriving country located on the Persian Gulf, and it borders the countries of Oman, Saudi Arabia, and Kuwait. It dates back to 1971, when a federation of seven emirates was formed after gaining independence. Its political system is based on a constitution which was written the same year. Each of the seven emirates has a monarch that has complete domain over his emirate along with a United Arab Emirates president who has domain over all. It is not a constitutional monarchy nor is it a republic. The constitution concerns the relations between the emirates and does not in any way promote a constitutional form of government.

The long history of UAE dates back to the time of the prophet of Islam Muhammad in the 7th Century. Over the past several centuries this region was a colony of first Portugal and then England. As recently as the 19th and early 20th Century, one of the main industries in the area was mining the Persian Gulf for pearls. That industry declined rapidly in the 20th Century with the introduction of the Japanese cultured pearl, and several difficult years followed for the people of this region.

That the United Arab Emirates thrive today, are product of the rich oil reserves they sit on and the close relationship with the west. [43] When the first oil revenues started rolling in during the 1960's, the rulers here invested heavily in schools, hospitals, and the infrastructure of the country. That the ruler of the nation fought strongly to improve the living conditions of his people speaks to why this monarchy thrives to this day, when they are very rare in most other parts of the world. While the UAE has one of oldest government systems in the region, the rulers there act in the best interests of the people and walking the ultra-modern streets of Dubai is no different than any city in the west.

The citizens here, regardless of living under monarchs, have freedoms that other citizens of Muslim nations can only dream of. Dubai is one of the most modern and beautiful cities in the world. [44] It features western-style malls that have extravagant extras such as ice skating rinks and hills with real snow that you can ski on. [45] It also features something you will not find anywhere else in the Muslim world, a horse racing track that hosts the richest horse race in the world, the Dubai World Cup. With its 6 million dollar purse, it attracts the best horses from all over the world. [46] Gambling is forbidden in most Muslim cultures, but the rulers of UAE are active in the horse racing industries and have long stated that their goal is to win the Kentucky Derby.

The UAE now has a thriving tourist industry that is supported by its very own airline, Emirates Airline. [47] One can catch a flight directly from many of the largest cities in the world including London, New York, and Dallas.

That the United Arab Emirates is one home to one of the most booming economies in Asia is of course a product of the oil that exports daily, but also the vision of the rulers to use this revenue to improve the lifestyle of all of its citizens.

China

And as discussed earlier, China is the most populous country in the world with over 1.3 billion citizens. [48] It has been fractured apart and reformed many times over its thousands of years of history and was a poor country as recently as the middle of the 20th Century. The big changes have happened over the past 20 years as leaders worked hard at modernization and bringing its peasant population out of poverty. China in 2001 joined the World Trade Organization and has one of the fastest growing economies in the world, exporting goods all over the planet.[49]

All of this growth has happened despite the fact that China remains a Communist country. But the government has been more open in recent years in allowing citizens to work abroad and allowing companies from other countries to move manufacturing options to China. [50] The fact being that it has such a large supply of workers and a relatively low cost of living, China is the ideal place for labor-intensive manufacturing processes and they are effecting competing manufacturing plants in other parts of the world who cannot compete with their prices. It is very common to go to a store in the western world and find many products that were manufactured and shipped from China.[51]

There is no one way to rise from 3rd world status. The fact is that there are a number of ways depending on what resources are available and what the leadership of the country is willing to do to promote growth. While there is still some turmoil in China, modernization has delivered many people out of poverty and improved their lives, though there are still some issues to be resolved ecologically to ensure the long-term growth of the country.[52] Time will tell if these countries have what it takes to sustain growth over the long-term while still providing good living conditions for its citizens.

Chapter IV. Technology and Politics of the 21st Century

Social Advancements over the past twenty Centuries

Humanity has come a long way during the past twenty odd centuries. Mankind has passed through many testing and decisive experiences—cultural shocks, wars, religious dominations, human sufferings faced with elimination or being eaten alive against opponents, renaissance, industrial revolution, colonialism, exercises of democracy and autocracies. Most recent experiences include the development of political institutions, leading to civil institutions, and technological revolutions of the 20th century, leading us into the 21st century. Not all these changes or developments have been through evolutionary processes—some merged as a revolutionary cause, or as a result of upheavals and struggles of nations against tyrants for change.

The struggles have been for prosperity, security and advancement of curiosities of man—which is the nature of human beings—seeking better or improved standards of living; for itself and the generations to come. There are still a few more centuries to go to reach a more advanced, matured and just society to live in. Naturally, mankind's expectations have changed from the first century to 14th or 15th centuries, or 19th and 20th centuries alike. Developments have been incremental, and reflective of the environment societies had been living in— proportional to time and their knowledge of other lands across the globe. On the other hand, more industrious countries and their ruling governments are being transformed too. Domination of other nations and colonialism has changed to neo-colonialism of other nations, resulting in suppression and eventual revolts within those countries. However, the process has come a long way too, understanding the nature of world order—assassinations, terror and invasions are transformed to acceptance of democratic form of governance for advancing nations. The West is gradually realizing that it is to the best interest of advanced nations to share their knowhow and democratic values with advancing nations in promoting democracy for all.

In reality, change is an inherent phenomenon of human nature; it is in its DNA. The question is how to bring about the changes to benefit humanity. It has taken about twenty centuries for mankind to realize that all the changes it desires cannot be applied in abstract, or within its own limited sphere and boundaries. Mankind is living in a global environment, and this fact has become more pronounced to him, as societies got closer to each other—thanks to transportation, communication and trade. These are the backbone of social and economic development, especially international developments. However, the speed of change or improvement in standard of living of mankind across the globe has been accelerating in most countries during the past two centuries, while a number of societies are still living and practicing in the medieval era.

The world community is divided in this respect into two economic camps of "Haves" & "Have-nots". It is the second group that is struggling for major change in their status. They are in need of technology, investment and other essential basic infra-structure services to come out of poverty. Although they can provide cheap labor, however, lack of support systems such as education or even political and financial systems does not help them in pursuing their goal, which is improving their standard of living. Available open communications and easy access to information, though beneficial in many respects, has increased the awareness and demand of "Have-nots" for better living conditions. Their desire, especially under suppressive regimes, can be translated into unrests and militant uprisings. Support of industrial world —"Haves"—to such regimes in order to benefit from cheap labor without attention to the need of engaged societies are creating violent reactions to their political and economic restrains, and resentment against the ruling elite. On the other hand, industrial countries (G20), in completion to win over the best economic deals from needy nations are stumbling on political and economic friction amongst themselves with restrictive trade measures. That's where all the conflicts start; no matter which nations are involved, either on trade issues, industrialization, or political structure of the societies at large. One day it is human rights, next day might be importation of bananas, or type of industry the advancing nations are contemplating to establish in order to create jobs at home and bring about prosperity and improve the standard of living for their own citizens.

The objectives and business tactics adopted by each group is different. The advancing nations are pursuing with measures to increase job opportunities to come out of poverty, whereas the host groups are pursuing with the aim to increase wealth. Focus of advancing nations need to be on elimination of poverty, creating internal industries and market for their goods rather than export. Social and political maturities of different advanced societies are indications of the degree of development those nations enjoy and prosper. It is reflected in the attitude and behavior of individuals in the respective societies—politicians, scientists, teachers or government employees alike. The speeches delivered on "celebration of life" of late Senator Edward M. Kennedy by his friends, and opponents alike in admiring the valuable contributions he had made to the society were good example of maturity of a nation; people look outwardly beyond their self-interest, focusing on solutions for any shortcomings of their society, rather than inwardly, working for their own self interests. In advancing societies, more and more one can notice that many politicians are active promoting their own personal gains or agenda, and political ambitions are geared towards personal interests, rather than the need of their society. All issues are personal rather than national. In other words, in many societies, day by day one can see the rise of politicians rather than statesmen to serve their respective nations. The degree of political maturity of any society can be measured in terms of the attitude of competing politicians—more advanced social order calls for statesmen to serve a nation. Contrastingly, in immature systems politicians tend to rule their respective societies. This is the root of corruptions, conflicts and shortcomings against any genuine social development—economically or politically. The first step for any nation to benefit from democracy is measures to curb corruption at all levels of government. Corruption at any level, or nature, will undermine democratic values and processes in any society, and will cause eventual down-fall of the governing bodies. Through an integrated and multi-level educational program, media participation, promotion of ethical principles and moral values, plus a strong judicial system, this social and political cancer can be removed from the fabric of any society.

Corruption leads to upheaval within the society and polarization within the country, and eventual collapse or destruction of the ruling system from within.

Role of Technology in Developments

Ha-Joon Chang, in his reviving book in 2008 titled Bad Samaritans, contributes the international development and prosperity of many countries in the past four centuries to restrictive trade regulatory measures, and the corresponding policies by respective governments. Whereas Thomas Friedman, in his book published in 2005 titled The World is Flat, contributing the progress and prosperity of different nations to ease of communications and the role of Internet. However, the accelerated growth of economic developments across the globe, specifically in many advancing nations and particularly during the past century, should be contributed to the many technological advancements of our time.

Technology, starting with industrial revolution of late nineteenth and early twentieth century, has contributed to bringing

86

prosperity to many countries, creating job opportunities, hence causing the standard of livings to rise in respective communities. As a matter of fact, development of technology and consequently leading to industrial revolution changed the social structure and fabric of societies around the world, identified social values and disciplines needed to manage societies, such as human rights and values of democracy at large. Technologies in nineteenth and twentieth century helped to create a social/political fabric for respective societies, bringing people together, working together, and develop urban life. Recent second industrial revolution, information technology, has made the societies even much closer together, affecting the political structures to get updated as well— for the benefit of mankind—to operate more efficiently.

The role of technology transfer in any country, or between different countries, which is very instrumental in any development plan, cannot be ignored. The term of "Technology Transfer" is quite controversial. Sometimes, very wrongly, it implies taking a technology from one country or company, and using it in another country or nation. In true meaning of the term, it refers to the process of devising a methodology—a step-by-step process—in developing a product or service, and delivering it to the end user's hand!

The process involves conceptual designs, R&D, detail designs, prototype building, production/implementation plans, marketing, resource allocation (including HR), financials, funding, promotion & sales, monitoring/audits, justification of budgets and training. This is a complete cycle of "Technology Transfer", from concept to delivering a successful product or technology to the end user, either within a country of the origin, or between multiple countries, contributing to international economic development.

Mankind, in seek of more prosperity, has realized its need for technological advancements in order to achieve its goals and objectives; either it is developed within their own society, or shall

87

be acquired from elsewhere. The global competition will sooner or later introduce some sort of technology to the advancing nations.

Change in Rate of Economic Growth

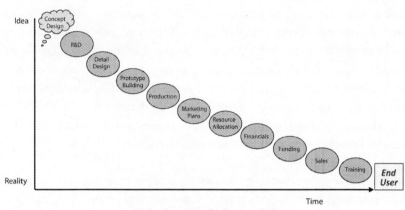

Technology Transfer Process Cycle

It is entirely up to the receiving party to decide and set their own acceptable standards for products and technologies they will receive over the years to come. They cannot keep changing the standards to please different competitive countries. Would that be in metric? Or British system of inches, foot and pounds? Setting standards are vital when a country decides on standards for aircraft support, ammunition, electrical communications, or even quality standards of their production facilities. There are international institutes to issue acceptable standards for different industries. Adopting certain universal standards can help the industries to enter into international market. Wrong standards can limit their trade capability or economic growth. Of course, adhering to a fixed standard by a particular country increases the potential of trade and exchange of technology between the corresponding parties.

Adopting such a cycle or policy by any society means engagement of the offering of a more advanced society on a long-term basis in their internal programs. The programs are quite involved and multi-disciplinary in nature. Many facades or different enterprises with variety of specialties may get involved in such a development program, from design architects and production engineers, to marketing gurus and financial specialists. Although most technologies are offered by private business enterprises, it requires deep involvement of the supporting governments. One cannot ignore the fact that the governments need to protect the interests of their constituents—individual citizens and businesses alike. Can we call this interference of politics in any international development program? The answer is quite clear: any government is obliged to protect the interests of its own citizens and enterprises. Naturally, they need to prepare and provide appropriate business environment for their constituents. Many nations, their vital interests and their existence depend on successful transactions across the globe and their ability to trade. Without that, their productivity and hence, employments at home will diminish and their economy suffers. Therefore, they need to promote their goods, technology and transfer them to certain receiving countries to benefit their industries at home. This cannot happen without a coordinated effort and precise planning between participating members of that society—government, industry, financial, and research or educational institutes, with a strong marketing arm to provide long-term visionary market strategy for the parties concerned. Close cooperation between industries, educational and financial institutes, with the government participation as a catalyst can guarantee long-term planning for entrepreneurial development, R&D and acceptable productivity level in a society to safeguard employment and economic growth.

Naturally, the role of government is guiding such a program, or act as a catalyst. In other words, technology transfer programs without participation of all the above partners, especially the government is not possible. It would be a fine line between the role of government and private industries that get involved in implementation of such ventures, or objectives of the government.

At this juncture, the political and economic values, long-term vision and policies that will be adopted in promoting host country's technology, business, standards, and political agenda will be under scrutiny of the receiving party and need to be well defined and set to benefit all parties for a long-term relationship. Joint venture arrangement between Germany and India to manufacture diesel engines in India under license and standards of German industry (DIN) for export to African countries, followed with support from India is a good example of such a long-term planning.

Three Components of Development:

Technology has played a major role in the development and raising the standard of living of many societies across the globe in the past 150 years or so. The question is what types of technologies have really contributed to this change. Technologies that are grown within the societies, or imported ones? Their impact is substantially different!

Secondly, for implementation of any technology, a proper educational—system as infrastructure for any development program—plays the major and decisive role in that society. Technology and Education work hand-in-hand to achieve the desired development level. A suitable infrastructure needs to be in place to be able to serve the society in the process of receiving, or benefiting from technological advancements.

The third component in any development plan is the media or environment in which the technology + education can breed and flourish – that is democracy. Democracy plays an essential role in preparing such an environment. In a democratic form of governance, with healthy political and economic infrastructure as a base, people can choose their desired and appropriate path to their prosperity, hence bringing solid economic development to their society. One needs a solid base to build upon. A democratic political system leads to a stable and fair economic structure that will enable the society to support the needed educational system, and accept or benefit from technologies. Democracy and free-market economy can help in economic growth and development. However, we need to define the term "Development". Development is not just the physical growth of buildings. The term is hidden in the social system, political and financial system, as well as culture and human rights.

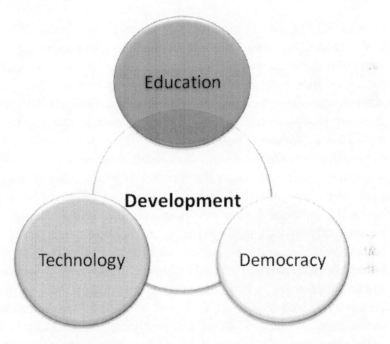

Let's analyze these three components in further detail. Before doing so, objectives and the best resource allocation of that society need to be analyzed. The nature, scope and direction of development need to be defined in order to identify appropriate technologies for such a society.

On Technology: Imported technologies can help to a certain extent in such a drive; however, they do not go far enough to provide secure jobs, and an environment of trade and assembly will prevail, it does not help to create solid and secure job base on the long run. Whereas technologies that are rooted in that society, backed by research & development to support basic industries as well as applied industries can benefit the society on the long-run, creating more permanent and secure job opportunities. Sharing the technologies between more industrial advanced societies and advancing nations can play a key role on long-term development programs.

On Education: Society needs a workforce with different levels of skills and expertise to benefit growing industries. Not everybody should have PhD's or university degrees to qualify for a job. In the process of technology implementation, society needs apprentices, technicians, skilled and non-skilled labor force, staff, engineers, as well as designers and scientists to develop the technologies further. They are all not only vital in implementing the application of technologies, but also instrumental in developing innovative techniques and the transfer of knowledge to the end-users. However, an acceptable, fair pay-scale needs to be developed and setup in the society for all participants to prosper. Economic growth can only be achieved if all participating members have equal opportunities and make an honorable, decent living without being forced to corruption and bribery to survive. In other words, the vast difference in pay rates between different levels of income, which dramatically affect the cost of living and affordability for lower income brackets, leads to bribery and corruption. Out of scale pay rates will create conflicts and many other social and economic problems in any society.

The delivery pattern or method of application of high-tech products in recent years is a good example of this: tech giants such as Microsoft, Oracle and Cisco train and certify enough support teams to back the products, before they are introduced to the market.

On Democracy: How can we blend all these requirements together? The common denominator is political infrastructure.

Prosperity of individuals can contribute to economic development of their respective societies. Their initiatives, risks they take and wealth they create are all part of general development of society and cause the standard of living to grow. This incentive opportunity to exist in a society is the key element in any development program. Therefore, a democratic form of government, providing equal opportunities for all, needs a solid, stable and populous political infrastructure with well-defined and coherent political institutions to serve the society, including financial institutes to support successful economic growth and development. One needs investments in the society to absorb the technologies and create jobs. Without a democratic system, people do not exercise any long-term planning in investment, or participate in the industrialization of the society. Even foreign investments to assist in technology transfer are hindered, or become hesitant in non-democratic environment, which would face risks.

All the above factors need to be considered in an integrated plan for a successful development program. In any case, technology is playing the major role in bringing job and prosperity opportunities to receiving countries, even changing the classical cultural values of respective countries—leading to an overall development on the social, economic, political and cultural aspects of the society. Sometimes it is beneficial and is for the good of that society; sometimes it is regarded very destructive and damaging, depending on the intentions of the offering enterprise, or the country for that matter. That's where conflicts start, and among other forms of resistance, terrorism starts brewing—protection against "status quos", cultural values or internal self-interests. The major question is what kind of technology is being transferred to advancing nations. Generally, at least in the Western industrial countries, it is not the government who takes the first step in transferring any technology. There is a distinct separation between the private and public sector. However, different countries have different setup and organizational structures to promote their international business—trade or otherwise. In the U.S., it is the

Department of Commerce that organizes visits and introductory programs in order to promote U.S. technology and business. Whereas in Japan of post WWII, MITI is in-charge of coordinated efforts on international market research, industrial design and production, education or research, and most importantly financing of all the above through private banking system to ensure a successful business promotion for the country, including technology transfer for their industries on long-term planning basis. China has recently entered the international arena on the same basis, creating the most competitive international market for all concerned. Since training is the major integral part of any technology transfer program, the advancing countries receiving such technologies are importing the language of transferring products too. In other words, long-term business and cultural involvement between the concerned parties need to be planned and established for a successful venture.

Gap between Innovations and Delivery Systems

Rapid growth and development of new products and services in the advanced countries, which are coupled with availability of necessary funds for research and business development, ensures superior products and continued enhancements. High Technology products are faced with unprecedented obsolescence issues and dilemmas to be confronted with—at government and international level. Patents and intellectual property rights of inventors are not always protected easily in many countries, making the technology transfer business more complex. The case of Siemens industries having a contract to build 60 Maglev train liners for China, and surprisingly getting their contract cancelled by the Chinese government in 2007 after the successful run of the first line, is a clear cut example of unsecured business and technology environment in the international arena. Could Siemens sue the Chinese government for not honoring their contract and risk their future potential business expansion opportunities in China?

Design and development of new products do not stop at the production line. Whether they are marketed in the U.S. or abroad, a detailed delivery system including training programs need to be designed and implemented to back the technologies, otherwise the success of the products will be compromised. Success of German technology—at home and abroad—is based on this vital principle of providing knowledgeable, well-trained and skilled technicians to support and deliver their technology at its most efficient manner in order to realize all its potentials. This mandate or requirement is the key for a successful program on trade and business development, whether it is offered to Africa, the Middle East, or any other advancing area, demanding any desired technology for their economic development. Establishment of trade schools, design and research centers, and training of needed workforce at all levels is needed in order to sustain and ensure the technological advancements and promotion of international development by means of technology.

Rapid growth of technologies and economic development in most countries are hindered due to the fact that there is a major disconnect between the technological innovations and delivery systems. In other words, the best ideas or products, well thought and produced can fail when the last link, which is the means of "transfer" to the end-user, is inadequate. That is happening in the U.S. as well as many other nations. Delivery systems are broken down, and subsequently, client dissatisfaction and failure of services are on the rise, and are every day's result. One can observe this in various scenarios: health care programs' poor standard of service and inability to communicate with patients due to the lack of trained nurses; bank customer support lines answered by automated machines that leave customers without any human contact or understanding of their concerns; instructional manuals bundled with the product box not accurately representing the product or service; or any service provider, whether at government or private sector, not being able to convey the information or take a responsible action. In such circumstances, the best programs or products can fail, although the initiators or designers had the best intention and design details in mind. In other words, the end-result is failure as far as the user is concerned. Clients or customers being disenchanted will result in failure of the technology transfer.

Chapter V. Infra-structure Issues: People and Societies

Education:

Educating the masses in a given society is for betterment and bringing prosperity to that society. Education can support the job opportunities being created. As a matter of fact, it is the level of education that attracts investment, and hence job opportunities in a given society. Its effect is long-term on a nation, involving generations to benefit from. The direction and strategies the nation can adopt is proportional to the nature and level of education. Therefore, it cannot be left to the private sector to design and operate it at its own private taste or desire. A nation, who is building its infra-structure, can benefit from the back bone of education, and it is obliged to tailor it to its need and objectives of the society. It needs long-term planning, with visionary strategies and objectives to benefit all, rather than a select group, or benefiting private enterprises alone. There must be a set standard and quality of education with direction for the society to be implemented by a common management—national visionary government. Operation of each entity should be independent, as long as the standard and quality is monitored by an independent non-profit body. Education needs to be regarded as investment of a nation on its development and future generations. Of course, education does not stop at writing & reading capability alone. It encompasses cultural, social, and political vision building for the society.

Structured multi-level education, similar to German method, to offer all citizens equal right and opportunity to benefit, and offering all individuals a slot in that program (nobody would be left behind—create an appropriate position in the system for the individual) is essential. General education till age 15, with an assessment exam to determine the desire and capability of students, to be directed to vocational schooling, with more practical applications and hands-on approach, or more theoretical disciplines towards university degree, with branching into more practical applications, versus more research oriented discipline for industries to benefit from. Creation of a common board consisting of industries, educational institutes, and central investment trust/banking (government representative) would guide such a system. There would be enough flexibility in the system for individuals to be able to take different paths to achieve their objectives in progressing towards a successful career.

Societies need to invest in their young, passing their experience to their next generation—bad or good—for change and improvement.

Leaving No One Behind in the New World Economy

The world as most people knew it has changed dramatically in the last decades. While there was always foreign trade and commercial interaction between countries, even in ancient times, the modernization of travel has done away with borders to a great extent, although time and distance offered a buffer to widespread foreign trade. Now, however, with the ease of transportation and the blending of the world's economic resources, it is becoming apparent that adjustments will have to be made if people will have the ability to earn a living in their home country. It is obvious that the wages of someone from Sierra Leone would not be adequate for a person living in the United States, so some means of assuring that those who live in countries where the cost of living is high will not be deprived of an income will have to form a part of this new economy.

The New World Order

The phrase "New World Order" has been in existence for quite some time, and most relevantly since the years of the First World War. The premise behind this concept is that if all nations follow basically the same governmental patterns—a representative government—the chances of friction either economically or as pertains to wars and other conflicts will be eliminated, or at least minimized. Ideally, a New World Order will foster an era of peace and prosperity for all.

At some level, a New World Order will require at least a cooperation between the various nations of the world. Some call for an abolishment of all borders and citizenship requirements, while other believe that a central power, such as the United Nations, should be what determines the economic and political reality for all countries. The International Monetary Fund, or IMF, has also been instrumental in causing adjustments to wages in countries that have made use of its monies for debt relief. Generally, countries that have needed the assistance of the IMF have seen a curtailing of wages and benefits for their workers as a requirement for restructuring loans.

If a New World Order is to be successful, the goal will have to be good wages, benefits, and working conditions for all people, regardless of where they live. It will also be necessary to establish guidelines so that low wage workers in more backward countries will not put higher wage workers in developed countries in the unemployment line.

Globalization

The concept of globalization and the New World Order go hand-in-hand. Globalization has actually been going on for centuries, although at a much slower rate than seen in recent decades. Today's globalization seeks to do away with any impediments to completely free trade and the exchange of ideas, skills, and culture. Although there are promises of a better life for all of the earth's citizens with the implementation of this idea, thus far it has caused job and income loss in most countries that have embraced globalization, oddly enough even in countries where wages are already low. The outsourcing of manufacturing and even many service jobs has caused unemployment in countries such as the United States, France, and England. Many who espouse globalization refer to the theory of 'comparative advantage', whereby each country will make the most money by concentrating on what it can best produce. Unfortunately, the free exchange of intellectual information means that most countries with any degree of development can duplicate, usually more cheaply, almost anything produced in countries with a higher standard of living.

Cheap imports have been touted as a hedge against inflation, and while they do reduce prices at the retail level, they also represent lost employment. When manufacturing and even craft work is outsourced to take advantage of cheap wages it means that a certain number of the importing country's citizens have been put out of work. It also creates a downward spiral whereby there are fewer people working good paying jobs to buy things, which will ultimately result in even the cheaper goods remaining on the shelves in stores.

It is also true that up to this point most of the world's trade is carried on by very large international corporations. This has resulted in a concentration of wealth at the top of the economic pile with many who are near the bottom becoming even poorer. The globalization of agriculture has also had profound effects on native farmers in developing countries—often the land will simply be given over to foreign corporations for use, leaving the former inhabitants only able to work as laborers on land they formerly owned.

The social issues of globalization and the New World Order must be addressed now—people need solutions to the problems that have arisen in the present, they simply cannot wait for a better life for themselves and their children sometime in the distant future. Promises of a brighter tomorrow will have little meaning if there is no food on the table for dinner.

Trained Workers Will Be Needed at All Levels

It is no secret that the time of the small scale manufacturing operation seems to be behind us, for better or worse. Large, multinational corporations are becoming the dominant economic force in the world, and although the need for highly trained, technologically sophisticated personnel will be high, there will also be a need for what might be termed support workers for these upper echelon people.

Any large firm is made up of dozens of different job classifications, and it is unlikely that CEOs could perform at peak efficiency if their offices or other workplaces were not kept clean and if not for the support of those who gather and collate the information that supervisors need. Any corporation is really similar to a jigsaw puzzle, where all the pieces are required to make the picture complete.

As the work force is spread out over the entire globe, it will also be necessary to make certain that those who have been displaced by the New World Order are not left behind to fend for themselves. Workers in developed countries with high living standards will have to be retrained in jobs that will provide them with a comparable income to that which they have lost. All too often now, those who have lost jobs that assured them of a middle-class income find that replacement jobs will usually pay only a fraction of their old positions.

Governments and businesses, especially those that have outsourced good paying jobs to countries where wages are low, will have to take on the responsibilities for progressive unemployment and lack of skilled personnel to further innovations and industrial growth in their country. Even re-training and introduction of newly educated workforce cannot turn around the bad economy quickly enough, without preventing social instability.

Why Fair-Pay Scale Is Important

The last few decades have not been overly kind to American workers, especially those involved in manufacturing. A great deal of America's manufacturing capacity was transferred to countries where wages and working conditions are far below the standards set here, or in any Western country. Regardless of anything else, it is simply impossible for an American worker to live on the wages paid in China; our cost of living is much, much higher than that which exists there. If lower wages become the norm in the Western countries, prices of goods, housing, and services will also have to fall. Third world wages will not be able to afford first world prices.

When Portugal was being considered for admission to the European Union, concerns were raised about the low wages in Portugal adversely affecting the wages of workers in England, Germany, and other EU countries. The solution was to place a tariff on goods coming in from Portugal that would raise the price of the item to what it would cost to produce in the importing country. In this way, wages in Portugal did not necessarily have to be raised, but the workers in England did not see their jobs evaporate.

Do We Want an Economy Based On Bribes?

One of the side effects of low wages is that they inevitably lead to a culture based on the bribe. This is not entirely to be unexpected when people simply are not paid enough to live. The quote from E. R. Edison, "Hard it is for an empty sack to stand straight" is all too appropriate here. Once wages are so low that the most basic human needs, such as food and shelter, are impossible to meet, it is only natural to expect that police, health workers, government clerks, and service people will want to receive a gratuity for performing their job. The habit of giving and taking bribes will inevitably corrupt a society from the inside out as everything is reduced to a monetary consideration. The answer to preventing a bribe-laden economy is to make sure that living wages are paid in each country. Imports from countries where low wages are the rule will have to be taxed or subjected to a tariff, and efforts made to raise the wages in the less developed countries, to make certain that everyone will be able to live with the dignity and security that all human beings deserve.

Health Care and a New World Order

Another common issue which affects the whole society, and its well-being and performance is health care. People do not get sick by choice! General hygiene or environment, as well as products or services being introduced to the society as a whole will affect the well-being of the masses. This service cannot be compromised by the greed of health care providers, or insurance carriers. Again, as an infra-structure for the society, for the nation to benefit from, health care, being a common service to protect the entire society must be offered by the government as a non-profit entity. It is not a profit making venture, rather than a common service for all, at the most affordable cost, to be controlled and managed by national government.

Having a non-profit, public entity—government in cooperation with public—need to offer national insurance, and regulate all hospitals. Healthcare providers can be independent, as long as they adhere to a standard and regulations set by this body.

The Health Care Debate Rages on in the United States

The health care issue and whether it should be public or completely private in nature has been a debate that has raged in the United States for over 20 years. While President Barrack Obama was successful in getting a government funded health care plan meant to make health care affordable for all Americans and reduce the millions of Americans who have no health insurance at all passed in Congress early on in his term, it has been under fire in the courts for 2 years now at this time. There are also a number of challenges to the constitutionality of Obamacare in individual states that are attempting to make their way into federal courts in an effort to get it repealed.

Problems Seen with "Obamacare"

The Patient Protection and Affordable Care Act was signed into law by President Barrack Obama on March 23, 2010.53 One of the focuses of this landmark act is to provide access to affordable health care for the estimated 30 million American citizens who have no health care coverage at all. Some of the criticisms of Obamacare as the health care package are sky-rocketing costs involved and lack of affordability for many in the United States.

At a time when the United States and much of the rest of the world are facing record budget deficits, critics claim the cost of the system could run into trillions of dollars and make a bad budget situation even worse for the foreseeable future. Others have criticized it for providing funding for procedures such as elective abortions. This lighting-rod issue will no doubt find its way into the debates, since many view this as an immoral practice. Many others have wondered about the cost and accountability of any system used to ensure that people have complied and bought the mandatory insurance that the plan provides for. Another problem many people see in this health care package is that employees or small businesses may not be allowed to keep coverage that they currently have and like, and will be forced to pay for a more expensive plan under Obamacare. Critics also point out that it will cause huge problems for seasonal employers, many of whom will have to pay a large fine, cut the hours of their employees, or lay off their employees.

Chances are, this will all play out in the American courts. Recently, the United States Supreme Court decided that it will consider hearing cases that challenge Obamacare on constitutional grounds.[54] Cases have been brought up in several states and it is far from certain that this program will ever be implemented in 2014 as it was intended by the Democrats.

A Look at Health Care in Canada

It would do Americans some good to look just north of the border to find a system that works. Canada has had a system in place that allows all citizens of the country to obtain quality health care regardless of their ability to pay.[55] It is publicly funded and in general is free at the point of use. The services are mostly provided by private entities and the entire process is guided by the Canada Health Act of 1984.[56] This act ensures that the quality of health care meets all federal standards. The government does not collect any information about patients, as that remains between a personal physician and the patient. The patient retains the right to choose their own personal care doctor.

Most of the funding for this health care system comes from the collection of income taxes. At this time, the government funds around 70% of the cost of the health care, though it should be noted there are still private insurances options available for people who can afford it.[57] The laws on private insurance vary from province to province, so you'll need to check out how the law applies to you based on where you live. The result in general has been a healthy population for the Canadians, but the system is not without its problems.

Criticisms of the Canadian Health Care System

One of the main criticisms of the Canadian health care system are wait times to see a physician. While emergency cases are dealt with immediately, within one day in most cases, those wait times are growing due to a number of factors.[58] One of the main reasons wait times are getting longer is the sheer volume of paperwork and red tape that comes with dealing with the government. Another problem most often cited by those in the profession are the growing number of Canadian citizens with chronic and complex medical conditions, and this can be attributed to a population that is aging. To complicate the process, fewer and fewer doctors are seeing new patients in the last few years.

Coming Up with Solutions

In 2007, the Canadian government announced that it will have Patient Wait Time Guarantees in place by the year 2010.[59] Priority will be given to people with cancer, hip and knee replacements, cataracts, and people who need diagnostic imaging. These new Patient Wait Time Guarantees apply across the board to all Canadian provinces and territories.

Investment has also been made to improve wait times across the board with technology. More and more patient records and requests for appointments have been moved to electronic media and computers, so information can be shared and relayed faster, cutting wait times and lost paperwork that can slow the process.

Computer technology is also invaluable as a tool for diagnosing emergency room patients who have pre-existing conditions and other information a doctor would need to know before performing care.

An Overall Look at the Effectiveness of the Canadian Health System

A recent study by Forbes magazine took a look at the 15 healthiest countries in the world, and delved in-depth into the reasons they made the list. The United States comes in 11th, while Canada checks in at number 8.[60] Despite having a low number of doctors versus citizens, Canada has one of the longest life expectancies in the world and would be ranked higher on this list if not for a relatively large infant mortality rate that can be attributed to some of the remote parts of the country not having immediate access to a doctor. So clearly, the Americans can learn something from their neighbors to the north, who are most certainly doing some things right while they work to improve their health care system.

In this day and age of modern medicine, the United States has almost 16% of the population without any health insurance at all, and has little access to quality and affordable care. This is a problem that will have to be addressed in the future, regardless of what courts decide on the future of Obamacare. The population of the country is aging, and health care costs have been skyrocketing for a number of years. And as the population ages, most of the costs of the system will be on the shoulders of a workforce that has not regained many workers since the recession of 2008 began.

Canada has decided that a national government funded health care system is an investment in the future of their country. They also believe that health care that is both effective and affordable is a right that all citizens share. The numbers at this point in time certainly seem to support them as the United States has many more doctors in practice than does Canada, but do not have as high of a life expectancy rate as their northern neighbors. The Forbes report also came to the conclusion that many of the countries who are part of their top 15 list are there because of government funded health care programs that make care affordable and accessible to all citizens regardless of their ability to pay. Other countries that rank higher on the list than the United States and have government funded health care plans include France, Austria, and the Netherlands.

Transportation

To implement an economic plan and growth policy for any nation, bringing prosperity to all members of its societies, — whether rural or urban—people need to be able to enjoy a common network of transportation system to benefit from, in a most modest, affordable system—to transmit goods or services on national basis. That creates a common national marketing pool for the society to benefit from, before export ventures are introduced into their society. Public transportation across the country will bring all masses together, increase commerce, provide convenience to all, and create productivity and job opportunities for all. Required national network cannot be planned, designed, or be manipulated by private sector. Creation of a national network for all nation will bring prosperity at all levels for population to benefit; again it needs to be planned, and implemented by national government, with the national objectives in mind—such as productivity, export, or disaster recovery measures. If government can provide highways, it needs to provide railroads too, as well as other public services to reduce traffic congestions, and increase the trade and commerce, which in effect will create more job opportunities. Operations can be private, whereas policy, planning and quality control needs to be managed by the government as another element of infrastructure development.

There are several countries that in the mid-20th Century laid out the blueprint for this economic plan, the United States and the United Arab Emirates are just two excellent examples. The United States Highway System was first created by the passage of the Federal Aid Highway Act of 1925.[61] Up until then, highways and roads were named by local governments and towns for the most part, and this act helped bring a uniform naming and numbering system to integrate them.

The Evolution of Public and Private Transportation Systems in the United States

Up until the 1920's, there was really no need for a highway system, as automobiles were expensive and only the very rich could afford them. This changed in the 1920's thanks to Henry Ford and his radical assembly-line manufacturing techniques that made the automobile affordable for the common man.[62] Now middle-class people literally had a vehicle that could make a difference in their lives, but the problem at that time was there were very few suitable roads for autos to drive on. The consequential decision that the federal government made in providing national accessible roads for the country would have dramatic results in the decades to come. It would fundamentally change the manner America did business in many ways.

The modern interstate highway system of America was originally conceived and funded by the Interstate Highway Act of 1956[63], which provided for a uniform numbering system across the entire nation, with north-south routes assigned an odd number, and east-west routes assigned an even number. Now people who had access to a car and a highway could consider jobs that were not in their immediate area for the first time in the nation's history.

The new interconnecting highway system had another effect that planners could have foreseen. Businesses grew up along the highway system, truck stops, gas stations, restaurants, hotels, and more to support the travelers.[64] It redistributed the population as well with people moving to meet these new opportunities and take lucrative new jobs that were springing up. The new highway system also made possible a new business, over the road trucking to compete with what had been mostly a monopoly in shipping, the railroads. In the years since the highway system became complete, delivering goods via trucks is one of the largest industries in the nation.[65]

And the highway system does more than just provide an economic stimulus function; it is vital to national defense as well.[66] A national highway system makes it feasible to move large numbers of troops, equipment, and supplies quickly and efficiently. This has long given the United States a strategic advantage and the military has evolved to be able to use this tool very effectively.

All of these benefits could not have been recognized without the investment of the federal government. While the railroads in the 19th Century started the transportation industry boom and was funded for the most part from private enterprise, the government saw the power they could wield during the American Civil War.[67]

The North had thousands of miles of railroad tracks which it used to quickly transport supplies and troops to the battlefields. The South had only a fraction of the rail lines of the North and never seemed to realize just how important logistics would be in this conflict, and that oversight cost them dearly at the end.

Private enterprise would have also had to coordinate with other private groups around the country to link up and coordinate the highway system. The federal government had the power to do a central planning, including all major cities of the day in the plan, and they had a way to fund the plan. It was funded by a federal tax on motor vehicle fuels, only a few pennies a gallon, but as traffic increased quickly, so did the tax revenues. First projected to be completed in 1975, the highway system was completed early in many parts of the country as revenues rose and businesses grew in response.

Another industry that the highway system helped to spawn, which was not largely planned for, was the tourist industry. Now middle-income families had an affordable way to load the family up and take a trip to almost any part of the lower 48 states. This industry grew quickly and gave rise to thousands of hotels, restaurants, tourist shops, gas stations, and more to support an industry that continues to grow to this day.

The federal planning and investment in the highway system has paid dividends several times over and was one of the main factors behind the unprecedented growth the country saw during the latter half of the 20th Century and is a driving force in the 21st Century as well.

Using Transportation Systems to Build Modern Super cities and Thriving Country— The United Arab Emirates Model

Until the 1960's when the oil business started a series of changes that go on to this day, the land that is currently occupied by the United Arab Emirates was mainly inhabited by people who had for hundreds of years mined the local waters for its bounties of fish. Pearling was also a big industry in this region until about the middle of the 20th Century. When oil revenues first starting flowing into the city of Abu Dhabi, the ruler of the region Zayed bin Sultan Al Nahyan directed a large percentage of the wealth to massive construction projects with the goal of making the region on par with the best facilities in the world.[68] He took the lead in transforming the country from the ground up, as he helped to assemble a functional government, created electric and water departments, municipal planning, police departments, schools, hospitals, and more. Major construction projects such as an airport and shipping docks continue to pay dividends to this day as the UAE is one of the busiest shipping ports in the region and in the world. The import/export trade surplus for the United Arab Emirate in 2007 was a staggering $55 billion.[69] Al Nahyan was also largely behind the 1971 merger of the 7 emirates into the United Arab Emirates that we recognize today and is regarded in the country as a national hero.

Today, the UAE can boast of over 1,000 kilometers of roads, all paved, modern airports, and two of the richest and most modern cities in the world, Dubai and Abu Dhabi. Both of these cities feature towering skyscrapers in the central city business districts, large multi-story residential buildings, large and amenity-laden shopping malls, and wide boulevards. The architecture of the region is Arab-Islamic in design and roadsides are adorned with date palm trees. Having such a strong infrastructure has also, like the United States, spurred a new travel industry with millions of people using Emirates Airlines to visit the region and experience the sun, sand, sea, and sports the region has to offer.[70] The region is popular for its many golf courses, home to a Professional Golfer's Association tournament every year, and the best male and female tennis players in the world converge annually here for a million-dollar tournament.[71] Both of these events draw tourists from around the world to the country.

While the United Arab Emirates is not by any means a democracy, but it can be said without question that the vast physical progress that has been made in the last 50 years was the result of a strong central government, in this case a monarchy, that utilized oil revenue to make life better for all citizens and put the country in a strong position to grow into the future. Since the United Arab Emirates is largely a desert area, the seven emirates were able to concentrate their resources on the coastal city-states and build a transportation infrastructure that makes commerce and trade within the country possible. The modernization of the country's ports have made it a global trading power and they have been a member of the Global Trade Organization since 1996.[72] The monarchs in charge of the seven emirates have continued in the tradition of the country's founder Al Nahyan and continued to develop the infrastructure and make life better for its citizens to this day. The unemployment rate in the United Arab Emirates in 2010 was reported at 4.3%, as opportunities for its citizens abound in many fields and workers from across the world are also a common sight in the emirates.[73] None of this phenomenal growth would be possible without the roads, modern business centers, and ports that were constructed as a result of central government direction.

With such a strong transportation system in place thanks to strong central governments, both the United States and United Arab Emirates are poised for long-term growth and prosperity. With this system in place, trade within both the countries and exports can continue to flow and bring wealth into these countries at an ever increasing rate.

Industrialization

The economic growth for prosperity of a nation needs to be guided and managed in such a way to benefit all the citizens alike. Although the operations and management of such ventures need to be rested with private sector, however, due to the amount of investments required, or risks involved, or even the direction certain societies may decide to take, it is beneficial for the national government to provide the vehicle and road map for success, such as financing, product identification, marketing strategies or guidance, and research or development on necessary technologies. Therefore, involvement of government in long-term planning will affect the growth and job opportunity creation across the board. Successful industrialization is coupled with research and development. Therefore, it is the government on behalf of entire nation that can plan for research centers, provide budgets, and direct the nature of research to benefit the industry. Cooperation or link between the two sectors—education and industry—can be provided by the government.

Government can invest in needed industries—mother, and basic industries—in partnership with private sector. After 5 years, reaching a profitable level for any entity, the government can sell its shares to public, or employees of the entity. An overall planning guidance can help competitive business development, as well as export potentials for the society as a whole. Policies being adopted by the government, on behalf of the nation, can protect the businesses in that society, establish acceptable quality standard for the country to benefit. Foreign investments need to be tailored for this need, with proper relation to benefit the masses, rather than creating economic slavery, and hence political domination and suppression!

Planning for a successful industrialization in a country is very critical and involved. Creation of financial institutes to back such a growth, with adequate protection for investors and public alike is very crucial. The financial infra-structure guarantees the security as well as economic growth rate of society. However, without secure and democratic political infra-structure one cannot expect to be able to create the necessary financial infra-structure. In other words, no investor would dare to risk in a non-democratic, unstable political society. Even a powerful dictatorship or totalitarian system cannot protect the long-term interests of any investor. Therefore, all nations need to provide a long-term blue print for industrialization of their respective societies, based on type of products or services, educational and research to support such policy, marketing and healthy financial system to back all those planning or objectives.

A strong central banking system in partnership with people (50% government, 50% shares/investment by public — not businesses or interest groups) need to be established, separate from normal consumer banking system, to invest and even launch different industries. This independent, yet government supported and regulated entity will guarantee the economic growth of the society.

For all advancing nations, with lessons learned from financial crisis of 2007-2010, they need to keep their governments in check and hold them accountable to adhere to a balanced budget at all times, and not get strangled by international banking vultures that are trying to lend them funds, knowing very well that at the end the receiving parties will fail!

Government - Business Partnerships — the Past, Present and Future

The cliché "Government-Business Partnership"[74] is a revised version of the centuries old notion. This mutual setting was also known as "Public-Private Partnership" in the late 20th century.[75] Do governments establish such partnerships with a good intention— for the benefit of the overall society, including the government, businesses and citizens—or for the benefit of a specific strata of the society? In an effort to create good earning jobs in any society, with vision for industrial development and economic prosperity, governments cannot only rely or concentrate on adjustment of interest rates for the banks, or indirect attempts on manipulating available cash for businesses to operate. They need to exercise bold and participative actions in partnership with local financial institutes, industries, marketing companies, and "people's council" in creating solid, long-term and productive job opportunities for their constituents. Their involvement in major projects, especially infra-structure projects are essential. Assisting banks, or bail-outs of certain large corporations with the wishful thinking of "trickle-down" economic effects do not solve any problems for the unemployed.

How the present system of trade has allowed some countries to prosper while others remain in poverty?

Before analyzing the current multilateral system of trade and its possible repercussions, we would like to reiterate the history of economic systems implemented in different parts of the world.

History[76]

The Economic discipline dates back to the ancient times of the Greeks or more significantly Aristotle. Back then, economics was part of philosophy. The debate focused on the different forms of political systems and the dilemma of public and private property.

Then came the Middle Ages where the foundations of modern Mercantilism and trade were laid. The stringent shackles of Feudalism also compelled man to explore and discover new lands. When the power of Feudalism started to wane, Monarchy quickly took over and Mercantilism was born.

The economic theory in the 16th century was to use the state's resources, especially military to safeguard existing supply routes and to explore and conquer new supply grounds. Thus, the seeds of Colonization and inequality were sowed. Even though International Trade was implemented, all countries could not benefit because the medium of wealth—gold, was in limited quantity and thus could not be shared among all countries.

Moreover, the Colonizers bore a mindset to extract as much wealth from the colonized land and remit to their home country. Very few colonizers invested for the betterment of the indigenous population.

The mid and late 20th century saw a clash of various economic and political systems. With Japan following an Autarky or Closed Economy, the West converging towards Laissez-faire or Mixed Economy, and Russia & China marching with Communist or Socialist economies.

The latter half of the 20th century was rife with struggles towards achieving a single economic system throughout the world.

Present System of Trade and Economy: A Global Multilateral Economy

Before moving on to the question, "Why some countries prosper while others remain entangled in poverty despite a Free-Market Economy?" we should define the present system of trade and economy.

Multilateral Economy

A Multilateral Trade System[77] is based on the concept of Globalization[78]. This loosely translates into Free-Trade or gradual removal of Trade barriers to ensure non-discrimination and fair competition.

World Trade Organization (WTO)[79] was established on 1st January 1995 with the intention of supervising and promoting liberal international trade. WTO replaced General Agreement on Tariffs and Trade (GATT). Almost all of the trading nations are members of WTO, with some exceptions. Therefore, the system is named as "multilateral" and not "global" or "world".

The intention of the creation of WTO was to ensure a level-playing field for all nations. It was a fact that less powerful nations previously had very little direct influence on trade proceedings. Moreover, countries also discriminated between trading partners—significantly altering trade conditions such as quotas and import restrictions for different trading nations. Even though WTO is recently established, the multilateral trade system is well established with over a half century's record.

Why has the Present System of Trade created unequal outcomes?

Capitalism[80] has often been criticized as supporting those with the most resources. Even though it has accommodated a large number of individuals, it has virtually failed to provide equal opportunities and comfort for everyone. The mechanism of capitalism promotes innovation and development, but it also answers to the one with the most power and resources.

Structural Adjustment Programs [81]

Majority of the developing countries are in debt. These loans have been structured through international organizations such as International Monetary Fund (IMF) and World Bank (WB). Many critics have pointed out towards the increasing dependence of developing nations on rich countries through debt. Thus, many poor countries face difficulties in repaying the interest and principal components of these loans. As a result, developed countries enforce Structural Adjustment Programs (SAPs) to ensure debt repayment. These SAPs lead to fundamental changes in the economic policies of a developing country, such as reducing subsidies and government expenditure on the welfare of the state. As a result, inflation and cost of living increases, thus making life more miserable for residents of an already impoverished country.

Brain Drain [82]

The concept of brain drain has achieved quite some popularity in recent times. Many under-developed nations invest immensely in a tiny part of their population through health and education. Yet these learned individuals are often attracted by developed nations. These able and educated personnel often denote the prevailing poverty and corruption in their home country as a reason for emigrating. The reason is simple—better future and prospects. These developed nations virtually enjoy a form of subsidy.

Protectionism vs. Free Trade [83]

It has often been discussed that developed countries need to have developing nations remove all barriers hindering free trade, yet these rich countries themselves employ protectionist practices.

- The West has quite often been criticized for heavily subsidizing their own agricultural sector and their farmers.
- Yet the same Western countries argue over removing inefficiencies and subsidies provided by developing nation's government to their farmers and manufacturers.
- Discriminatory trade restrictions by rich countries are still practiced. e.g. a Bangladeshi textile manufacturer would be taxed 20 times more for importing its goods to England than a textile manufacturer based in UK to import similar goods to Bangladesh!

How the world's resources could be better shared between countries.

It is astonishing to note that less than ¼ of the population residing in developed countries, not only in the west but also in the east, consumes more than 80% of our planet's resources. More interestingly, the 450 million of the sub-Saharan Africa share roughly the same amount of resources as consumed by the 10 million who occupy Belgium [84]. More facts include:

- 1 billion of the Earth's population lives on less than $1 a day
- 3 billion live on less than $2 a day
- This is more than half of the World's population. These individuals do not have access to sufficient healthy food, safe water, proper housing, or health care.

Our planet requires immediate changes to revive our economic system, which is based on the values of _competition_ and *self-interest*. Market based approach and global resource allocation can be improved and build upon to save 50,000 people from dying every day. Surely, *overconsumption* and *commercialization* needs to be curtailed in order to save our planet from the brink of destabilization and dramatic climatic changes.

Some of the key problems need to be addressed before highlighting the solutions:

- Our present economic theory puts profit over people and operates through the values of competition and self-interest.

- Privatization shrouds the exclusive control and monopoly of resources.

- Multinational Corporations (MNCs) are often at an advantage to extract excessive benefits and maintain monopoly across borders.

- Rampant export-orientation has compelled governments and organization to overlook food insecurity.

- Overconsumption and Commercialization has resulted in grave environmental challenges.

- Policy-makers have often failed to account for poverty and inequality, and leave these pressuring issues to market forces.

Steps towards fighting Poverty and better sharing of World's Resources

Micro-Enterprise Programs[85]

The initial step is always small in stature, but it is the harbinger of change. Micro-enterprise programs represent small loans to impoverished people to help them stand on their feet—establish their own business. Self-help groups are formed by international institutions. These groups manage money and provide the necessary training to initiate and operate business. A very famous example is of Grameen Bank. The founder of the bank, Professor Muhammad Yunus, brought a sweeping change in the micro economics of Bangladesh by delivering credit facilities to rural poor men and women.

Economic and Structural Revival

The first step towards a fair resource allocation would be to bring about a change in the exclusive controlling rights over natural resources. A new mechanism under the auspices of United Nations (UN) should be created, which ensures the management and distribution of natural resources on behalf of the global community. However, these plans are more long-term and strategic in nature. For a short term solution, emergency relief distribution should be planned and executed. Additionally, a global committee or organization could be setup on the grounds of democracy to ensure conflict-free distribution of natural resources. For non-essential goods and services, a parallel structure of free-market mechanism can be pursued. These suggestions have long been advocated by economists, policy makers, environmentalists, and various justice movements.

International Cooperation: a solution for Fair Resource Allocation

Even though majority of the nations are gathered under the umbrella of United Nations (UN) since 1945; but the alarming rise in poverty and inequality sketches an entirely different picture. The demarcation line between developed and under-developed countries needs to be erased so as to address basic universal human needs: food, water, shelter and healthcare. This effective cooperation can only be ensured through a major reform and upgrading of current international institutions, and by establishment of new institutions and a framework based on democratic principles.

Ensuring basic human rights for everyone on the planet

Our modern day economic principles are based on notions of a human being who is inherently selfish, individualistic, and competitive in nature. If humanity is to be saved from extinction, new ethical paradigms and principles based on collective values and priorities—ending poverty and hunger, and ensuring basic human needs, should be forged.

How countries could better measure their current resources available and their future needs for the next 19, 50, and 100 years?

Our current economic measures of progress, namely *Gross Domestic Product* (GDP) fails to account for the current and future state of natural resources. In fact, GDP measurement encourages the depletion of natural resources.

Revised Measures of Economic Progress

Index of Sustainable Economic Welfare (ISEW) / Genuine Progress Indicator (GPI) [86]

ISEW was revised and renamed GPI, and uses GDP as a foundation. However, it incorporates the fundamental component of sustainability. It takes personal consumption data as GDP, but makes deductions for income inequality, crime, environmental degradation and loss of leisure. The crux is to measure sustainable economic welfare rather than economic output alone.

Green GDP[87]

Green GDP specifically accounts for environmental degradation and depletion of natural resources into national output.

International Trade[88]—Import and Export

International Trade is of utmost importance for the economic survival of a society or nation. We cannot simply blame Nature— for blessing one nation with a unique resource and endowing other country with an entirely different natural wealth. Instead, "Man" has to "Manage the Sharing process" of natural resources with each other in a modest and practical manner. With the dawn of Globalization and the interconnectedness of all countries and nations into a Global Village, no country can survive without international trade—import and export[89].

We can view this international exchange as a vital instrument of mutual benefit and for improving each other's economies. It is a harsh fact that without a balance international trade, many people would starve and the world economy would lie in shambles and disequilibrium.

Every nation has something in excess, which they can export, and import commodities, which they usually lack. However, it should be noted that countries, which possess a strong export base, are at some advantage as compared to countries, which have to keep importing. Such importing countries often struggle to provide a better quality of life for their citizens and must resort to generating export quantities to restore the balance of trade.

There are some instances where certain nations are blessed with a specific natural resource but usually lack in other aspects. e.g. the Middle Eastern countries are endowed with the natural wealth of oil, but they are below par in other areas. Such nations should not just accumulate the foreign exchange from oil into their treasuries; rather they should focus on developing alternative methods of revenue generation. They should invest in equipping their citizens with the wealth of education and a healthy lifestyle.

Quality is another aspect to be emphasized upon. Various exporting nations often export crude raw materials without putting due emphasis on value-addition. It should be noted that a certain nation cannot achieve expertise in "Value Addition" overnight. Rather a systematic plan of investing in social development and education will equip the nation with the required technical expertise.

It should be noted that various countries are willing to pay higher prices for high-quality products. The only solution for export-deficient and importing nations is to develop and invest in their social infrastructure. Healthy and skilled workers translate into high-quality products. Delivering high quality of health services and world-standard education to their citizens will provide a nation with bargaining advantage.

Top Ten Exporting & Importing Countries

Countries usually export when there is a demand for their products. Additionally, countries produce more than they can normally consume. Exporting countries export a wide variety of their resources. The world market is a composition of major nations exporting the bulk of world output, with smaller and less developed nations exporting relatively a minor proportion of the total world exports. It should also be noted that when countries export more they also tend to import a larger amount of resources.

Top Ten Exporting & Importing Countries in 2008

	Country	Exports
1	China	$1,897,000,000,000
2	Germany	$1,543,000,000,000
3	US	$1,511,000,000,000
4	Japan	$800,800,000,000
5	France	$578,400,000,000
6	Netherlands	$576,900,000,000
7	South Korea	$558,800,000,000
8	Italy	$508,900,000,000
9	Russia	$498,600,000,000
10	UK	$410,300,000,000

90

	Country	Imports
1	US	$2,314,000,000,000
2	China	$1,743,468,000,000
3	Germany	$1,339,000,000,000
4	Japan	$794,700,000,000
5	France	$684,600,000,000
6	UK	$654,900,000,000
7	Italy	$541,200,000,000
8	South Korea	$525,200,000,000
9	Netherlands	$514,100,000,000
-	Hong Kong	$493,200,000,000
10	Canada	$459,600,000,000

91

Analysis[92]

One cannot make much sense to the data. Consider the amount of imports or exports on the basis of population. Measures such as *Per-Capita Exports* and *Per-Capita Imports* can provide real insights, as it balances out the differences in population. For example Germany exports $ 1.542 trillion with a population of approximately 85 million people. This makes the per-capita exports for Germany of about $18,152. Whereas the biggest exporter in the world—China exports around $1.897 trillion with a staggering population of about 1.35 billion. This makes the per-capita exports for China at about $1405.

Such measures need to be applied to break down the absolute values and gain more insightful information.

International Cooperation amongst All Countries on New Energy Sources[93]

Energy is one of the most controversial subjects on planet earth. Much of the contention and wars have been fought over this delicate natural resource. Scientists even predict that the future might hold a gruesome struggle over controlling water. But we should care for our present first. Developed nations should exhibit some responsibility by devoting only a small percentage of their resources to developing alternative sources of renewable energy.

We have been hearing about *Solar Energy* for a quite a while. For 3 billion people living on less than $2 per day, cheap and clean energy would only be a dream; until and unless countries work together to develop new sources of alternative energy on large scale. We have experienced certain individuals and NGOs making efforts for inventing and promoting solar energy in less-developed countries. But we have yet to see a joint effort by all nations.

We as responsible citizens should realize that most of the citizens of Third World Countries do not have easy access to even electricity. Therefore, these impoverished individuals resort to practices such as cutting trees recklessly.

By promoting and developing International Committees and Organizations on the likes of United Nations (UN), we will ensure our future. Such a world-wide organization should put aside funds and knowledge for developing cheap and clean sources of renewable energy. Bio gas and Solar energy[94] are potential prospects which are yet to be implemented on an international level. Continents such as Africa[95] and Asia, where the majority of the under-developed countries lie [96], would prove to be very successful in providing such products.

As we have seen, any freebies or projects hugely subsidized are often short-lived and filled with inefficiencies. There is dire need to add a certain level of commercial sense to the Alternative Energy Project. An appropriate financial model incorporating subsidies and return on investment would make the project a viable international solution. But to make this happen, cooperation between ALL countries is essential.

Implementation: Relationship between Businesses and Government.

In a Global context, International Organizations can fulfill planning and development of various projects. But for a ground-level and grass-root implementation, there should be a working relationship between Businesses and Governments.

A *Public-Private Partnership* comprises of a venture which is funded through a combination of government and private partnership. Various countries, notably Britain, Canada and Australia have successfully implemented PPP ventures. Government and Private ventures can bring long-term investment in infrastructures and other viable projects, thus promoting social developments. For example, a nationally owned and operated insurance company, in collaboration with government and public —as an independent entity—can provide adequate and alternative insurance policies and plans to the public—for coverage on a universal health care, unemployment, or general protection needs of society; very similar to the proposed plan for banking system.

Such projects also contribute towards creating employment opportunities. But the dilemma is that the governments of under-developed countries are usually strained with financial deficiencies. Many international organizations thus provide long-term loans for such social developments. But the aid is usually consumed half-way through government bureaucracies or is intended to obtain certain international desires.

Therefore, the need is to develop an **_International Organization_** with the mission to plan, execute, coordinate and monitor such Public-Private Partnership projects. However, it should be noted that predesigned projects would not be beneficial and the projects should be customized to every nation's specific needs. Additionally, the role of this Internal Organization should not be to enforce its own agenda, rather facilitate the regional process between governments and businesses.

Chapter VI. Management Policies for Industrial Growth, Education and Research

Management

Philosophy of government: When a group of people are making living in a region or occupying a land, they need to be able to manage their needed common services. However, in a realistic world, people don't want to have a large monstrous entity governing over them that eventually will lead to a totalitarian system of governance and suppression of the society. Only an efficient small common body to protect their interests, even as a nation, would be adequate. This body—the government—can formulate general long-term visionary strategies and policies for common good of the society.

As mentioned earlier, industrialization leads to job opportunities and prosperity of the society. While political stability, democratic form of government, and healthy financial infrastructures are regarded as the backbones for industrial and eventual economic growth, certain other tools of business are also mandatory for its success. Applied research, coupled with an educational system to prepare the necessary workforce for the industry is essential. Consequently, training programs at all educational levels need to be regarded as infrastructure for such a society. All other industries, though being operated privately, can enjoy common guiding policies offered by their government—in areas of statistics, market information, standards and financing. This leads to the fact that government needs to provide satisfactory and strong infra-structure and establish a central banking system to support the business enterprises, large or small, in support of masses. Money is regarded as a tool for the growth, rather than a commodity.

A well advanced society with high living standard and fully functional and developed political, economic and social systems needs integrated and advanced educational and technological systems in place. The ills of any society are correlated to the lack of education, or knowledge in a nation – either in the form of drug distribution/use, or any form of violence, or addictions. Even in support of entrepreneurial business or technological developments, the society needs to create an environment for such a growth, with equal opportunities for all its citizens to benefit from. Therefore, a common advanced infrastructural systems need to be established for the good of all citizens. Planning and providing necessary water, sewer systems, energy, and security, network of communications for roads, rail roads, ports, plus health care services, financial institutes or educational systems that would benefit all citizens and assure a healthy and secure growth for the society is the responsibility of all the people through their elected government. It does not mean that all these services to be operated or managed by the government. They can be structured by local cooperative councils, involving different sectors – public and private with regulatory policies.

Future generations of any society owe their success or failure to their predecessors' efforts in providing opportunities or measures in that respect. Leaving behind Trillions of debts, or a sound healthy society, or flourishing environment, or a successful integrated educational system in collaboration with the growing industries for advancement of technologies and businesses alike, are all the responsibility of present generation.

The banking industry needs to be regulated with a series of checks and balances to provide funds for growth and avoid making money itself a commodity that invites corruption such as predatory lending. Funds for business lending must be made available on a level playing field between countries and businesses large and small. Seed money must be earmarked for entrepreneurial projects, research and development. Agencies are needed to collect and gather data to forecast growth areas to plan future funding commitments.

From High Rises to the Street: The Crux of the Occupy Movement

The Occupy Movement gained worldwide attention in 2011, when young people took to the streets to protest the corrupt systems that had influenced economic wellbeing and financial solvency of different countries, especially the U.S.

The first major occupy movement, Occupy Wall Street, was initiated by Ad busters, which is a Canadian group of activists inspired by the Arab Spring. The movement is united under the slogan, "We are the 99%" and organizes using the #Occupy format on websites such as 'Occupy Together'. This movement has been used as a democratic awakening for the conscientious youth of the world who want to shed their image of contentment with the system to bring about some conscious political and economic changes to the structure of the world, which can improve lifestyle prospects for them and future generations.[97]

The first Occupy Movement which received worldwide attention was **Occupy Wall Street** in New York City's Zuccotti Park, initiating on the 17th of September 2011. The popularity for this movement and its objectives spread across the nation and over ninety-five other countries where protestors have set up camp to stay until the government decides to listen to their civil protests.

The initial two months of the protests saw tolerance from the authorities towards the movement, but the attitudes of the authorities transformed in mid-November that year, when they started to clear camps across the US and the Europe. As the year 2011 came to an end, so did most of the major camps set across the country. The last remaining camps which had any influence were cleared in February 2012 but there are still several locations where protesters are staging demonstrations.

The protesters gathering up for the Occupy Movement were ridiculed initially for having no clearly defined goals or any clue as to what they were actually supposed to be protesting. Several newspapers released mocking articles, interviewing protesters who do not have established careers or had set up 'quirky' camps and were exhibiting characteristics that led the newspapers to stereotyping them as 'hipsters' merely protesting a cause for the sake of sounding intelligent and aware of the political and global environment.

One major demand that was finally issued from the protesters was for a Robin Hood tax, which was supposed to be implied around the world. Representatives claimed that the protesters had clear demands on what they wanted to protest, which mainly circulated around the corrupting effect of money on politics.[98]

The New Yorker magazine portrayed the movement from the viewpoint of the protesters. The New Yorker made a statement claiming that the protesters wanted specific changes in the policies of the government. These changes were concerning the banking-industry regulations along with the banning of high frequency trading along with the arrest of all financial fraudsters that bought about the 2008 crash of the market. On top of that they wanted a Presidential commission to investigate and to prosecute all corrupt aspects that were ruining the integrity of the nation's politics.

The protesters were out there because they wanted better career prospects and better jobs. They wanted equal distribution of income and bank reforms to keep corruption at bay. They demanded a reduction of the sway of corporations over politics and a separate political structure not dictated by capitalism.

The concept of the movement was to denounce the abused values of capitalism. However, these demands have been countered by criticizing the very idea of shaking up a functional society over half-baked demands over an idealistic utopia. The logic behind the counterarguments is that if you shake up the foundations of capitalism, you are basically legitimizing the same power structures that you seek to challenge.

In late November of 2011, the Occupy Movements in London released their initial statement on corporations which demanded reforms to put an end to tax evasion practiced by rich corporations. The reason they cited for delaying in putting forward an articulate demand was that they took time to reach a final consensus so that they can come up with a proposal which was agreed upon by everyone through the somewhat impedimentary process of participatory democracy.

Other occupy groups around the world are still working on establishing an official agenda for their demands to issue a global statement. They are also working on reaching a general consensus so that they can provide a final demand that the movement can assemble under. All of these efforts are showing classic examples of the world's effort to reinvent politics, to revolutionize mindsets and to establish a functional utopia in the twenty first century.

Occupy Wall Street movement is being held in a manner reminiscent of the revolutionary movements held back in the 60s, each heavily influenced by pop-culture and the individual mindsets of the protesting youth today. The New Yorker even gathered up and composed a protest soundtrack[99] for the Occupy Wall Street protesters to listen to when they are out picketing places like the Fox office and Rupert Murdoch's house. While classic songs like Nina Simone's Rich Girl have been playing regularly, the movement has inspired quite a few songwriters to create their own songs influenced on the movements which have swept the indie music scene, and have been played at the heart of the movement, which are favored over the songs that were created back in the 60s such as music by Bob Dylan.

Some of these songs include Jeremy Gilchrist's "We are the 99%" with lyrics like:

"But there's a rising on Wall Street
I am you and you are me
We are the 99%'ers on the right side of love and history"

Another popular song that has been played frequently at the movement is by Johnny/ from the Tropic of Entropy's "Occupation Blues" which goes like:

"I ain't got no million
no hundred thousand
I ain't even got ten dollars
to my name
All I got
is a handful of nickels
hoping to the lord it's enough
to buy me a bagel"

Music aside, there were attempts by the protesters to show that the movement is a peaceful protest and that they would do their utmost to contribute to the betterment of New York City to make sure that the city is not inconvenienced in any way during this movement.

Hence the "clean up Wall-Street" operation[100] was initiated in which the protesters tried to clean up the mess they made in Zuccotti Park. But were stopped by the authorities stating that the cleanliness of the city was not a matter of civilian concern and the proper sanitization authorities would clean up the park when they wanted.

A protester commenting upon their lack of freedom stated, "Apparently cleaning up horse poop of the officers of New York is official business and cannot be done by good Samaritans" when he was stopped from cleaning up behind a police carriage.

Many people showed support for this movement from across the nation even if they were not physically coming to participate in the protests and sit-ins. Donations for food such as pizza were sent in for over eight thousand dollars for the protesters. Some franchises also donated food for the protesters such as McDonalds and Ben and Jerry's Ice-cream. Some franchises however, also have shown their disapproval such as Burger King which refused to sell food to the Occupy Wall Street protesters.

The method the Occupy Movement was orchestrated, it seemed as if the protesters and the sympathizers had no other option but to keep on repeating their demands till they are finally heard. The only option that they had was to resist intimidation by the authorities and not cave into the media's myopic views.

The message behind "We are the 99%"[101] was easy to understand. One needs to accept that status quo is not a fixed law of the universe. There is a dire need for pointing out the obvious, like the child in Emperor's new clothes, before anyone takes notice of what is going on in the world today.

For those who state that the demands of the protesters are unclear, all they have to look at is the unifying slogan, "we are the 99%". Then they will be able to see that the one percent that is left out is the disproportionate level of the people who hold all the power in today's society.

These people are the very example of a failed constitution as they are deeply undemocratic and the very example of living in a masked plutocracy. The slightest amount of contemplation upon this would make the meaning behind the protests crystal clear, which should generate a larger understanding and appreciation for what the protesters out in Wall Street are trying to change and improve for the world.

Educational Reforms

A major reform and planning is needed at all levels and disciplines of education in many industrial nations, as well as advancing nations, addressing the ever changing nature of societies and industries serving them. The main purpose of this revision is to produce strategists, thinkers, and multi-skilled management and technical employees and leaders. Inclusion of basic ethical values, mathematics, social and political, economics, arts and culture, computer, and communication skills will enable students to deal with multi-varied situation. Additionally, the curriculum should be revised frequently to match the developments in the industry. Many existing training programs, which were satisfactory in 20th century, cannot address the needs of 21st century environment, especially considering the overwhelming cost of education that many cannot afford, and the courses that are obsolete. That is the reason we are witnessing many university programs, even in the West, to be about seven to eight years behind their serving industries!

Education in the Less Advanced Nations.

What can and should be done in advancing nations is creation of local councils comprising of industrial, educational and governmental bodies whose central purpose is to support and implement job creation activities.

A better future for developing countries depends greatly on what that country is doing at this moment in education. A better educated population means more jobs as the economy of the world is going more global. There are role models in the world for developed countries to look to. India is a great example of a large country once relegated to 3rd world status. Today, they have an educated workforce and many companies from the United States and other countries have outsourced information technology and other jobs to that country.[102] But, to fix a problem, the sources of the problem must be identified and manners to fix them must be examined/considered.

Some of the Problems Facing Less Advanced Nations Today in Education

At the moment, there are very good reasons why children in less advanced countries complete fewer years of schooling and learn less than their counterparts in more developed nations. They are much more likely to come to school hungry and are fed less nutritious meals.[103] Study after study has shown that kids that are malnourished perform much more poorly than their counterparts who do not suffer from it.[104] Children with malnourishment are also much more likely to miss time from school with an illness. Other major problems range from lack of adequate transportation, or income levels of their family, forcing the child to become bread-earner in their family for their survival.

Other problems include rising birth rates as contraceptives are not readily available for most of the population of these countries. This only adds to the problem as families cannot feed the children that they already have. In many of these countries where the head of the household works as a sharecropper or migrant worker, children are needed at an early age to work alongside their parents to help make ends meet for the family, taking more days of education away from the children. Until these problems are addressed, any other changes to curriculum or anything else will not be effective.

As a result of poverty and low levels of income in less developed countries as opposed to those who are industrialized, people in these countries have either no savings at all or very little.

Savings are needed for investments, and with no investments in capital, it is almost impossible for a country as a whole to climb into the world economic picture. Capital is needed in the form of machinery that could boost the productiveness of workers and without it, an economy will remain stagnant and non-productive and its people will remain poor and impoverished. This is a sad cycle of poverty that is hard for any country to break out of.

German Model of Education

A look at the German model of education and what message or information can be gained for the developing nations and the United States. A different view of the "No Child Left Behind" policy of the United States.

The educational policies of the United States have long been a subject of much contention and consternation. The latest No Child Left Behind Policy (NCLB) has not exactly put the debate to rest. Under this policy which was enacted in 2002, academic standards were supposedly raised and measurable goals were established in an effort to improve education.[105] It had sweeping changes on what students are taught, what tests are administered to them, and how teachers are trained. It was designed to benefit students in many ways. Children could leave under-performing schools and move to a better school within their area. Children having problems with certain subjects could also receive free tutoring from a professional. A school could also receive grants to help them to attract better teachers and start new educational programs.[106]

Most of the criticism around the No Child Left Behind Act centers on the approach it takes. They argue it is a one size fits all solution that is not practical for all children. Other criticisms center around the testing methods, and believe that teachers are not allowed to teach other than to "teach to the test."[107] Standardized tests taken under the same conditions by all students are part of the policy and are the tool used to determine if the student and the school as a whole is performing to federal standards.

Some states have rebelled against this initiative and filed lawsuits with various degrees of success.[108] The main complaint of the states in these lawsuits is that the federal government requires school districts to pay for testing and other programs without being provided any funding for them. Also, many schools and students are not receiving the full benefits of the provisions of NCLB simply because they have not applied for them. The United States Department of Education lacks the resources to make sure all schools comply with all of the regulations stipulated by the NCLB act, and depend on parents to pressure their schools to provide all of the options available for their children. Teachers have also weighed in on NCLB with many of them bemoaning the entire educational approach of the initiative and believe it goes against all we know about how children learn and develop.[109]

The results of the NCLB initiative have been mixed at best, and many people are looking for better ways to educate children.

The German Approach to Public Education

Clearly the NCLB laws need some amending, and the Americans and developing countries would do well to study the German public education system. The German public school system has one overall objective, to prepare a student to have a job when they graduate.[110] Schooling is mandatory in Germany for all children from the ages of 6 through 14. Under the German educational model, all students have the same curriculum until the age of 10. Germans attend kindergarten through 4th grade as a group just as in the United States, but this is where the similarities end. Tracking of German students begins in the 4th grade, and their performances determine what educational opportunities will be available to them going forward. Starting with the 5th grade, German students are distributed to varying schools based on the abilities they have shown. More practical-minded achievers will be sent to vocational schools, where they will be taught trades and take on apprenticeships to prepare them for their jobs after graduation. High achieving students have the option of attending a college prep school and may later attend a university. There are also other routes a student can take including technical schools. The schools a child has attended in the past will determine what educational opportunities are available to them to go forward.

This system makes much more common sense than the American public school model of one high school for all. Germans recognize that not all children have the need or ability to study academics and instead prepare them to become productive members of society with real world skills that will serve them long after they have left public schools.

Criticisms of the German Educational System

The German system is not perfect, as it has some of the same problems as the American system. Children of immigrants and poor families have less of a chance than a German native to receive a good education.[111] Discipline has also become a problem in urban German areas just as it has been in the United States for some time now. Just as in the United States, many Germans think the educational system needs reform, they just can't agree on what needs to be done. Many people think the 4th grade is way too early to determine if a child is going to be a good learner later on in life. Immigrant children who do not have a good grasp of the German language often do not have the language skills to be deemed worthy of an academic education, while at the same time they do have other skills that would make them a good achiever.[112]

Despite having some problems that need to be addressed, performance of German students in the math and sciences are superior to American students almost across the board. German students and American students tested in grades 4 and 8 are close in scores, with the Germans having a slight advantage.[113] But by the 12th grade, the Germans have a clear advantage over the average American student. Some people seem to think that American scores are dragged down by underachieving students, but the facts say otherwise. When only the most gifted American students are compared to similar students from Germany and many other countries in math and sciences, there is still a significant gap.

A Common Sense Approach?

Very few people dispute the fact that academic study at universities or in middle and high schools are not for everyone. There will always be a demand for trade workers such as plumbers, electricians, auto mechanics, factory workers, and yes, even garbage men. Is it really necessary to teach those skills or information they may never use in their adult lives? Wouldn't it be better to teach them job skills while they are young that will prepare them to function as productive members of society? Also, by using this method, students who are not interested in academics are not in class to distract those students who are prepared and interested in this type of education. This could help to improve their performance as well.

The United States and other countries looking to improve their educational system would do well to imitate at least part of the German model. The same tests, the same education, and the same curriculum are not right for every child. Recognizing this fact will go a long way in fixing what ails the American system of education.

Another change in the system that needs to be made are standards for what is acceptable in teacher education and experience. In Germany, teachers are state-employed and enjoy high salaries and are considered important pillars of the German society. Professors at German institutes of higher learning enjoy a status that top business executives enjoy. In America, teachers often have to undertake a 2nd job just to make ends meet.[114] There is no doubt this situation has an effect on the people who may consider teaching as a career. The low salary drives away people who are more qualified to teach and ends the careers early of many who leave to take higher paying positions in other fields. While this has long been a problem, it is not easy to address raising teacher salaries at a time when many states are facing a budget crisis, and are facing record deficits.

In the end it may take more than just changing an education system, an entire overhaul of a culture may be needed to place more emphasis of the role of the teacher in society as well. Pay for teachers will need to be raised to attract more qualified teachers, but that is another debate about who will fund it, the federal government or the individual states. Also, while the German model is to be admired for many reasons, it also relegates children by the 5th grade to either vocational or trade schools, or a track to a college education. While the educational system in the United States may leave a lot to be desired, it does provide more opportunity for all students to achieve a college education. The solution may be a hybrid system that takes some of the very best of the German model and incorporate them into a new system that can suit all nations.

Finding a Way Out of the Vicious Cycle of Poverty

Because of the costs involved, these less developed nations will need considerable help to pull themselves out of the vicious cycle of poverty. Even if economic gains are made, an increase in the population of the poor will negate them quickly. Local councils and government bodies must make a concerted effort to educate their citizens on birth control and the proper use of contraceptives. There are some case studies that have already proven successful. In Indonesia, rural clinics have contraceptives which are given away free on request.[115] But free contraceptives are not the answer in and of themselves. Education must also be part of the plan if any sort of industrialization is to take place in the future.

Taking the Next Steps Out of Poverty

There are a number of areas that are seeing some improvement in formerly dismal educational regions. One such example is Afghanistan and some inner-city schools in the United States that were once performing at a poor level at best. There schoolchildren are being introduced to technology through the use of laptops.[116] Computer literacy is taught through the use of graphical user interfaces and the response from the children has been overwhelmingly positive. More and more jobs in this global economy rely on a computer in some way, shape, or form, and the sooner children become acquainted with them, the better.

Reaching Out to Independent Businesses and Charity Groups

There are institutions in the United States and other countries along with industry giants such as Microsoft who have the power to help regional councils and governments to get cheap laptops for children. By reaching out to one or more of these companies it is possible to get laptops for use in schools that will go a long way in educating the youth of 3rd world countries. And the success stories are not limited to Afghanistan and inner-city America, students in Africa and South America have seen their educational institutions improve with the introduction of laptops.[117]

Laptops can also do more than just teach children how to use a computer. Any number of professions can be introduced through the use of a laptop. Government, industry, and community leaders must join together to develop programs that teach useful skills that children can use to get a job once they have left school. If national resources and local industries are not the solution to break the cycle of poverty, government, industry, and community leaders must devise a strategic plan on developing businesses that can compete in an increasingly global marketplace.

Working Together as a Team to Explore a Strategic Plan

Some examples of growing businesses that should and can be explored are translation services via the internet. With the exploding growth of the internet, translations between almost any native language and one of the major languages such as English and Spanish are a lucrative niche to explore.[118] Languages are best taught while children are young, and by learning a 2nd or 3rd language, a child will have a tool they can use for a lifetime whether or not they use it to make a living. Another very lucrative market that can only be reached with a higher education is information technology. More and more businesses in the United States and other developed countries are looking for cheaper methods to operate their information technology departments. Entire data centers have been outsourced by companies in the US and other developed countries to countries such as India and the Philippians.[119] But again, to be able to compete in this increasingly competitive market, it will take both capital expenditure and an educated work force to be able to staff it.

Jobs in web programming are now outsourced by companies all over the world, and the ability to learn these programming languages is readily available on the internet. Some of them are even free if one does enough digging around.[120] Once one of these mostly web-based programming languages is mastered, all it takes for anyone to go to work is a computer with an internet connection. There are several brokerage sites such as www.guru. com that match people with jobs to outsource with people who are looking for work.[121] People from Europe, North America, South America, and Asia have made the switch to starting their own businesses and working their own hours, and web programming skills are not the only skill that is outsourced. People with expertise in transcriptions, writing and translations, virtual assistants, and more use these sites every day to make money and secure their futures.

Coming up with Comprehensive Solutions

The problem with less developed countries, as is the case with the U.S., is getting their citizens up to the educational level that is needed to compete for the 21st Century jobs. To the objectives, it will take a concerted effort from both federal and state governments, as well as local officials to develop a mutually beneficial plan. Some kind of school lunch program will need to be set up to ensure that kids have the nutrition they need to be able to learn and grow. The same officials will need to take a hard look at the available resources and decide if local industries are the answer to future employment needs.

If they are, educational tracts for trades or other skills need to be a part of the local school curriculum. If they are not feasible solutions for the present and future, more options need to be explored. Third-parties such as large corporations and charity groups need to be contacted to see if they can provide reasonably priced technology items such as laptops and smart phones so students can be exposed to some of the latest technologies that no doubt will play a large part in future job growth.

There are no hard and fast answers, but a comprehensive strategic plan need to be implemented from the time children start school to level desired to enter the job market can play huge dividends in the future. The global job market has probably evolved more in the past 20 years than it has in the modern industrial age, and there are no signs that is going to abate anytime soon. Workers in this century need modern skills to be able to compete on an employment stage that is more global in nature with every passing day. Multi-level education system is needed to support any growing industry.

Partnership between Industry and Educational Apparatus

There is a dire need to revive and build upon the relationship between the industry and the educational setup. Frequent integration of faculty and professionals in a company should be designed. In this manner, the teachers will be able to deliver an integrated and holistic combination of classroom learning and the practicality of industry to their students. Advancing nations need to take appropriate measures to safeguard their political and economic growth and prosperity derives by creating productive industries to serve their internal market, which will affect their standard of living.

Establishing a Relationship Between Industry and Education

The global scenario is rapidly changing. The advent of the *World Trade Organization* (WTO) has significantly contributed to the process of *Globalization* and shaping the interconnectivity of various cultures into a coherent *Global Village*.

Despite of all the protests and conspiracy theories related to *Globalization*, WTO and NWO; nearly every country desires to enhance their contribution to the *International Trade* and emerge as a substantial trading nation to benefit from global partnership. The 21st century can surely be regarded as an era of increased international trade.

But, are the nations fully prepared to embrace such a change? Significant social and cultural reshaping is required to tactfully tackle and prepare for this transformation. However the governments usually resort to superficial changes, such as providing more support for their farmers and manufacturers in the form of subsidies and improved infrastructure. Rather, a more profound and deep-rooted approach is the need of time.

Governments should recognize that not every nation can survive for long on the basis of natural resources. Additionally, with topics such as *Climatic Changes* and *Sustainable Development* securing centerpiece in every debate, nations cannot rely solely on industrialization. Therefore, the governments world over should focus on nurturing the required workforce for the Tertiary Sector and especially a *"Knowledge Society"*. This can only be achieved by redesigning and reshaping the educational systems. A working relationship can be established between the industries and the educational process so as to better train the candidates for the needs and challenges of the New Age: the age of New World Order. Integrated cooperation between industries, educational, financial, research institutes and a government agency as a catalyst would suffice the need of today's technologies.

United Nation's Global Educational Program

The UN's Global Education Program is regarded by analysts as the first real step towards creating a *New World Order* (NWO). The basic intention behind this project founded by Robert Muller is to ensure that every child on the planet Earth completes a standardized primary education. There have been much debates and discussions over reaching a consensus, but the primary aim is to create a comprehensive and holistic educational process that prepares individuals to readily participate in a globalized world. Much emphasis is placed on:

- Mastery over multiple languages.
- Respect and knowledge towards individuals belonging to varying cultural background.
- Possessing skills so to enable an individual to work effectively in cross-cultural environments.
- Awareness about various global issues.

Business Schools are not enough

Even though various Business Schools are quite excellent in fulfilling the demands of the corporate world—leadership and responsibility, but certain changes need to be made at the grass-root level. Business Managers are well equipped to handles the challenges of the revolutionized world, but hundreds of millions of workers are entering the workforce every day. This workforce needs to be better trained with a hands-on and practical approach to serve their industrial drives.

The increasing gap between rich and poor and staggering income inequality compels individuals to take up jobs and bread-earning responsibilities right after their *High School*. Various individuals do not complete their graduation—due to exorbitant prices by universities, and enter the workforce without any clues about the corporate world. Only after gaining experience, they get an idea about the corporate sense and the practicality required.

Reforming the Educational Process

The educational system in the West, especially US has received severe criticism from social workers and educators alike. Even though the governments are investing massively in the educational system or equipment, these efforts are dubbed as shallow. Repetitive reforms have failed to produce the desired results and there is a continuous decline in student's achievements over time. The task at hand is surely insurmountable but not impossible. The goal is to scrap the entire education system and replace it with a modern structure based on less conflicting values and philosophy—spending more on quality educators rather than expensive equipment for tools of delivery.

Mr. Robert Muller, former Assistant Secretary-General (UN) envisioned the dream of Global education. His words are a great source of inspiration and enlightenment, *"We need a new education system for the world. Global education, which is the education of learners in the universal home of the global village, is making good progress. But we should proceed beyond this point. We also need cosmic education, which is advocated by religious leaders such as Mary Montessori. We need a holistic educational system in which the relationship between our planet and the universe is taught".*

Reinventing the Classroom

The classroom lies at the heart of an educational process. But sadly the word 'classroom' we know of is synonymous to a traditional place where teachers compel students to rote memorize facts and figures. The structured nature of this learning process is marked by the absence of innovation and creativity. The reinvented classroom should rather be an unstructured and flexible learning system where the role of instructors would be to 'facilitate'. The main highlight of this overhaul would be to provide children with the option to pursue their interests. In this manner a child will be able to initiate the courses at school according to his or her own preferences.

The revised curriculum will not encompass futile and unnecessary books. Rather the process will be to enable students to initiate and work on projects that involve the creativity and ingeniousness of students along a loosely structured path. Students will undergo a meticulous and detailed exploration of local, national or international issues and finally come up with an objective result at the end. However, it should be noted that the books are simply not discarded away, rather the projects will be built on a variety of disciplines, including: mathematics, languages, social sciences, and philosophy to give students a broad vision on humanity and international affairs or development.

Students will not just be graded over the group's achievement, rather significant mechanisms will be developed to ensure that the student is assessed over his or her contribution and involvement in the project.

'Philosophy' as a Pillar of Our Educational System

Additionally, 'Philosophy' will be incorporated as a fundamental pillar in the reformed educational process. Universal truths and questions such as 'Where did I come from and what responsibilities I bear?' will ignite the imagination process. Such philosophical notions are not included to bring the debate pertaining to religion and God into the learning process, rather to facilitate and stretch the inquisitive nature of participants.

'North-South' Divide

Even though the 'North-South' divide is quite evident in our present situation, there is no place for such a distinction in a truly globalized world. Teachers and students alike are increasingly familiarized with this discriminatory distinction and often use such terms intentionally and unintentionally. The 'North' is used to denote countries with industrial, economic, and advance social welfare prowess; while the 'South' is coined to refer to Third World and under-developed countries with famine, hunger and economic difficulties. Such an increasing 'We-Them' thinking is detrimental to the universal idea of equality and peace.

'Exploitative' and 'Self-Centered' Thinking

At present our educational, economic, moral and social values impeccably revolve around the 'Self'. This exploitative nature of human being has led to a further strengthening of the North-South divide. We have clearly witnessed this exploitative nature by corporations which extract all natural wealth from the 'South' part of the world.

Solutions

The solution to such problems is to revise the entire curriculum and to incorporate multi-faceted values and establish classrooms comprising of students with different ethnic and social backgrounds.

If we perform a careful analysis of Robert Muller's vision, the attributes of 'tolerance' and 'open-mindedness' are quite evident. The purpose of this reform is to cultivate patience towards different values and religions within the context of nationalism. Equality for human and physical life is the defining belief. Children should be instilled with the principle that every living being should be respected and protected, and that all forms of life should be considered primary in order to safeguard the ecological system of nature.

Moral and Spiritual Values

Such an educational structure also caters to the increasing concerns about Mother Nature and the ecological well-being of our planet. Further investigation of Muller's words reveals that there is a pressing need to educate our children about the relationship with their brothers and sisters, our planet, sun, and the cosmos. There is a dire need to break through the shackles and boundaries of materialistic and scientific disciplines. It should be noted that the intention is not directed towards advocating the elimination of scientific and materialistic values. The purpose is to embrace and incorporate moral and spiritual values along with scientific and materialistic notions in our everyday life.

Eliminating the 'North-South' Divide

The curriculum, teachers and students should interrogate questions such as, "Why is there a North-South divide?" The answers to such harsh realities will provide results that a

North-South divide is simply an imaginative geographical distinction. The major problem is the unequal distribution of political and economic wealth. The debate and awareness amongst our children will pave the way towards reconciling such differences by 'Thinking globally, act locally'.

Children will then be able to answer questions such as, "How can we eliminate the North-South Divide?" an improved understanding will promote mutual cultural respect and tolerance. The Northerners will be able to learn from the Southerners and vice versa in an environment marked by trust, mutual respect and relationship. A global culture of amalgamated values will emerge that will promote the interests of human and other physical life in a globalized world.

Rid Ourselves from the 'Exploitative' and 'Self-Centered' Thinking

Attention should be focused on delivering solid social-corporate responsibility and concrete steps should be taken to improve the social and economic conditions of humans residing in third world countries. The initial step would be to educate the children of North with values so that they can exhibit patience, tolerance and a helping attitude towards the children in the South; whereas the children in the South should be better equipped with knowledge and technical skills, so that they could compete on an equal footing.

Only after such major educational reforms, the citizens of this world will be proud to live in a multi-cultural and interconnected global village.

Creating a Link between the Industry and the Educational system

Apart from the absence of ethical and moral values, students face a number of difficulties when they enter the workforce. Problems such as a lack of practical understanding and absence of hands-on technical know-how have been the major concern for employers.

Educators and employers have increasingly voiced their concerns for developing a stable relationship between the Business Community and the Educational System. Various workshops, seminars and technical institutes have been conducted and established, but the problem still persists.

There is a dire need to incorporate industry-based education in the curriculum. At present, it is only at a later stage that Business graduates learn how businesses operate. A revised curriculum comprising of technical and operational skills pertinent to small, medium, and large corporations should be implemented and followed across the board from the 'Secondary-Education' phase. Increasing participation from industry experts and alumni is highly recommended. Consistency in skills and knowledge competency is another aspect which requires improvement.

Industry representatives and educators have agreed upon the following areas of improvement:

- **Compulsory skill set:** including English as a second language and mathematics to contribute towards technical literacy skills.

- **Critical-thinking skills:** including identifying the problem, planning and the appropriate decision taking power.

- **Interpersonal skills.**

- **Communication skills and tolerance towards workforce diversity:** in an increasingly diversified world, cultural awareness and patience towards different values is highly essential.

- **Ethical education and practical training:** various soft-management tools to be taught, focusing on ethical management practices and leadership skills.

- **Compulsory Computer Literacy:** hands-on experience with basic computer and internet knowledge is the need of time.

- **Practical and Hands-on Training:** this is the most necessary condition. Technical and management skills according to the specific needs of the profession should be included in the revised curriculum. 'On-Job Training' is also essential.

- **Revision of Educational Curriculum** linked with improvisations and developments in the Industry.

Vocational Training

Developing a Better Prepared and Trained Workforce for the 21st Century

Part of the reason behind the world-wide debt and recession problem is a lack of skilled workers in new industries. There are few college courses for the most part for new high-tech industries and skilled trades. And these are high paying jobs that will be in demand for the foreseeable future.[122] The future economic health of both the United States and other countries around the world depends greatly on having the right workers with the right

156

skills, at the right time, at the right place. With an economy and workforce that is becoming more global in nature by the day, it is imperative that a work force has the right education to be able to fill these essential jobs that play a major role in maintaining and building the infrastructure of their country.

For years in the United States and other countries, vocational training was only given to those students who were failing or falling behind in traditional academic courses.[123] For years the key to economic growth was believed to be preparing high school students to attend college to obtain the highest possible wages and best jobs. Now with many college graduates not being able to find jobs in their fields or being underemployed[124], a few states and school districts are rethinking to develop a new educational and training program to address multi-level of education, including research, specialized programs, executive training as well as vocational programs. New attention needs to be focused in this area so that the essential jobs are filled with trained people who are ready to go to work straight out of high school.

Based on the need of the society with respect to industrial development planning, the skill sets can be planned. There needs to be better ways and programs to assess the skills of participants and point them to appropriate program, including vocational training. This will require school counselors, in cooperation with local "people's council" to go beyond their traditional roles and keep tabs on the current and future state of the job market.

The Present and the Future of Vocational Skills Training

There are programs in the US that are having success by pairing core subject teachers with vocational education instructors.[126] One school district in Michigan pairs teachers with diverse yet very similar talents to show students how math skills can be applied to a trade such as carpentry. An important aspect of carpentry is determining the slope of a roof in order to correctly install it.

These classes go a long way in training youths in how math and other academic course can apply in the real world, and this can a long way in helping youth decide on which career path is right for them.

This type of training can do more than just give students hands-on skill or training experience, it can also be good for the community as a whole. Some of these classes in Michigan take students through the entire process of building a home, from the foundation up. Once the class is completed, the home is donated to the charity Houses for Humanity, a non-profit organization that provides homes for the needy, a win-win situation for everyone involved. This is most certainly a program that needs to be adopted not only across the United States, but across the globe.

Perhaps the very best example of this kind of training is the Van Buren Technology Center in Michigan.[127] Here high school students receive one on one instruction in academics, technical instructions, and career tutoring. It is a magnet type school that is open to students from all over the area and gives students experience in real world work experience situations. It is of little surprise that students who attend this school and excel are ready on the day they graduate to step into a high paying technical or trade job, with excellent pay. Some of the training available here includes automotive mechanical training, technical training including computer repair, and traditional trades such as plumbing and electrical training. Students not only receive traditional education from a textbook, but actually get out in the field with real professionals and get an up close and personal look at what a normal day on the job in their particular profession will be like. Armed with this powerful knowledge, it is much easier for a student to decide if this is the profession they want to work at for the rest of their lives.

The Role of Community Colleges in Training Workers for Today's Jobs

For the past 20 years, many junior or community colleges in the United States and other countries have filled a vital role in teaching vocational trades to people of all ages. In just two years, students can graduate and step in jobs in lucrative positions such as registered nurses, physician's assistants, heavy equipment operators, computer technicians, and learn the basics of several other trades. It is a much more affordable option than a 4-year university. Community colleges have also been very proactive in consulting with local business and industry to design their programs to prepare graduates to be ready to work upon the day they graduate.[128] Most every community college in the nation has a number of success stories involving people who were laid off, downsized, or had their jobs outsourced who found new careers by attending a community college.

Big Challenges to Far Eastern Countries to Keep Their Growth Going Strong

Getting enough skilled workers to fill vital positions in today's work force is by no means a problem that is limited to the United States, there is an even bigger problem in the Far East, where changes have been fast in transforming those societies from an agricultural economy to an industrial one.

In China for example, the booming growth of the last 20 years has been a result of companies who are globalizing their operations in an attempt to cut operating costs.[129] But the vast majority of these jobs have been labor intensive manufacturing jobs that do not require many skills that cannot be taught on the job. Regardless of the skill levels needed to work in these manufacturing plants, they have been essential in improving the lives of their citizens.[130]

The challenge that faces China today if they want to sustain the economic boom of the last 20 years is to migrate more jobs from the low skilled manufacturing section, to skilled trades in order to help modernize the infrastructure of their country. The same thing can be said of other countries in this region including Laos, Thailand, and Vietnam.

Stepping up to the plate to educate badly needed workers in this sector are trade schools and other community colleges.[131] However; without the proper educational background in many subjects such as math and science, these efforts will prove futile. Government officials in these countries are going to have to encourage people to stay in school longer to get the background in math that is needed to perform many of these jobs.

Changing Perceptions

The stigma that was attached to trade jobs has to be changed to help the global economy bounce back from several years of stagnation and in many countries, being close to collapse. But at this time change may be coming from some very unlikely sources. In his State of the Union address before the United States Congress in February of 2012, President Barack Obama called for radical changes in education, proposing a budget of almost 70 billion on education with a strong focus on boosting vocational training in both high schools and colleges.[132]

The centerpiece of this bill is an 8 billion dollar community college to career fund with the stated intention of training up to 2 million workers in the next few years to work in fields such as clean energy, heath care, and high-tech manufacturing jobs.

The bill also intends to encourage community colleges and local businesses to work together to find out what skills are currently in demand and for the colleges to develop the courses that are needed to train those workers to perform those jobs.

But like many government programs in the United States and other countries, politics play a large part in funding. There is a great need for individuals to shoulder responsibility for the future of education and the benefit of their fellow countrymen and mankind.

Research

Innovations through research in new technologies have become so sophisticated that the old manner of higher education training leading to research opportunities—either in small private sector companies, universities, or large institutes—cannot respond to the everyday demand of the industry and market alike. Well-trained personnel, with appropriate expertise and background in applied research, are essential for the continued growth of any industry. Therefore, institutes of higher learning need to establish a discipline at master's level to offer training in conduct of research projects. The graduates will be absorbed by industry for specific task of conducting research, not the business or the administration sides of industry. This can be a parallel track, similar to MBA or Technology Management, with emphasis on conducting research programs.

Research, which is the backbone of any industrialization or economic development, needs to be structured, guided and managed by a team comprising of educators/scientists, industry reps, and business/government. This team would guide the growth, finance the projects and provide job opportunities, creating an atmosphere with vision for economic and social growth and prosperity of any society. Therefore, educational institutes need to provide appropriate training programs for their students to benefit in either: (a) Clinical/industry application at various levels including apprentice, technician, or professionals and masters, (b) Research, (c) Technology Development, including business finance and management. This cooperative body can be established in concert with local civil societies in every segment, town or county, with networking system with central chamber of commerce to create a harmonious planning and growth, participating the local population in all aspects of their life, step by step.

Chapter VII. Roots of Upheavals and Revolutions

International Business Development

Business enterprises in most advanced countries have reached production saturation due to high economic prosperity level their societies enjoy. In order for their stocks value to appreciate, and hence return on investments be satisfactory for their shareholders, naturally they need to expand their market from home to international. They do not expand the production or decide to export their goods because of their love for receiving countries, or their need for development.

Of course, the receiving countries need to have reached certain economic base to be able to afford the goods or services from the advanced countries. In this case, international business is developed between advanced and advancing nations, with all kinds of business relations—joint ventures, trade, production facilities, and exploration and marketing services. All the creative arrangements are established on two purposes. First, assisting the exporting country with their economic growth, and second, assisting the advancing country at the receiving end with their need for economic development. It is a two-way street, but the motives are very much different. That's where the role of technology transfer becomes apparent.

What technologies are being traded between the advanced countries and advancing ones? Naturally, labor-intensive old technologies, i.e. mostly the classic ones, are passed to needy advancing nations, keeping the high-tech emerging technologies at home. Since new technologies are instrumental in operating the classical old ones more efficiently, the receiving country is always dependent on the exporting country to run their business, and they cannot operate alone. Manufacturing advanced bulldozers, machinery, or for that matter, production setups, all need sophisticated electronic devices and software to operate in the most efficient manner, which are made in advanced countries. Even rockets or airplanes, military hardware that are being traded across the globe have their own built-in sophisticated software to operate, track, monitor and evaluate the effectiveness of the device. Missiles are equipped with tracking software, and their signals can easily be jammed by other super devices at the time of need. Simple cars that are being produced today require sophisticated control and memory boards, with advanced micro-chips to produce the necessary commands of operation on certain tasks or devices (*electro-mechanical devices*).

Not all sophisticated devices are readily being produced by receiving countries. They need to employ expertise and critical components from the exporting country forever. Such transactions are beneficial for the advanced exporting country as a whole: they benefit from less expensive labor and their production costs decrease, increasing their profit margin. It is also beneficial to the receiving country to the extent that some local job opportunities are created. NAFTA is a good example of this arrangement, which has not lead to the increase in the standard of living of the receiving parties, contrary to what was expected or promised. Outsourcing, especially on long term, has proved to be disastrous for the exporting country in general, while it has been beneficial for the business entity on short run.

While outsourcing may or may not meet expectations of the countries and people involved, there is little doubt that it is increasing as a business practice. A recent study surveyed over 500 global corporations and found that between 1998 and 2005, their outsourcing grew four fold, and that trend is likely to continue.[133] And, there is a very good reason it will continue, the tremendous savings involved for the companies that are outsourcing either labor, technology, back office, or other facets of their business. Many studies have shown that manufacturing and other costs can be cut by up to 60% by outsourcing facets of a business to China or India. It also reduces risk on the part of the outsourcing company as they do not need to risk investment to have those tasks done on-site. Other value added benefits are faster start-up and development when new tasks or special orders arrive, avoiding a crunch on your human resources department, and the ability of a business to concentrate on their core functions while outsourcing those which are not.

Definition and Short History of Outsourcing

Just what is outsourcing? It is defined as contracting with another person or another company to do a business function.[134] In almost all cases, the function that is outsourced is not core to the business doing the outsourcing. It has long been a part of the business world. As an early example, some businesses such as an insurance company, may outsource its janitorial services to a private company that specializes in that function. In the 1990's, it became common to outsource many information technology facets of a business, and there are many top providers in that area in the United States including IBM, EDS, and Cap Gemini. Now the number of companies doing these business services and more multiply by the day and are available in parts of the world where they did not exist even a decade ago thanks to the internet. And the companies who can benefit from outsourcing now are just as varied in size as the companies offering services. Specialized services such as information technology and accounting are now readily available at a reasonable price for even the smallest of businesses.[135]

How The Internet Changed Outsourcing?

The internet changed the scenery of outsourcing significantly starting in the 1990's. The internet made it possible for small to medium-sized businesses to take advantage of outsourcing to build their companies more quickly and focus on core activities.[136] Some of the business processes that were outsourced for the first time were help desk functions, network management operations, and call centers. Developing countries like India were able to offer significant value because workers there earn less than workers in the United States, and are willing to change their lifestyle since it involves staying up a good portion of the Indian night to deal with American companies during their normal business hours. India also can boast a large and educated English-speaking work force that has proven over time they can get the job done at a great price.

Technology also had a major role in the development of the outsource market. With communications tools such as smart phones and iPads, and software tools such as instant messaging, chat, video conferencing, and high speed internet connections, outsourcing eliminated one of the main problems it had before the advent of these technologies. Directions and specifications that once took hours to relay to the contractor can now be done in real-time, resulting in even more savings in time and money. It doesn't matter where you are in the world, with the internet, you can talk to anyone in real-time and conduct your business.

Some of the Direct Effects of Outsourcing in the United States and for China

The effects of outsourcing in the United States have been numerous. If you look at where items are made next time you go to the local big-chain retailer, chances are half of the items or more are made in China. A recent study of outsourcing in the year 2004 showed that over 46,000 jobs were outsourced that year, with over 10% of that total going to China.[137] These jobs had a negative effect on middle and lower-class Americans, as many of these people were the ones losing their jobs. At the same time, China experienced an unprecedented boom in their economy and it has created something that China has really never before had in its long history, a middle-class that mostly works in the larger cities of the country. It has also driven China to the verge of topping Germany for the 3rd largest economy in the world. China is also on the verge of overtaking outsourcing world-leader India, with some estimates saying it has already happened as of 2011.[138]

Beginning in 2008 in the United States, outsourcing became a source of unrest for those who had lost their jobs, and the new college graduates who were also not able to find work. While many companies can offer savings that they often say are passed on to the public in the form of lower prices by using outsourcing, many in the US remain skeptical at best. {the savings never passed to consumers; the companies made their profits off-shore and kept it outside, without paying taxes.} There has also been a great deal of backlash against companies that sell products from China or outsource jobs. This will be interesting to watch as the past has often shown that the thumb of the governments on businesses has not always had the best consequences, and many times have had very bad unintended consequences.

There has been a price to pay for China's surging economy, and the environment has taken the hit in this country, as has the health of some of the residents of their largest cities where smog and pollution are exceedingly bad. The Chinese government has long considered it one of the prices that must be paid for modernization of the country, but lately a few top officials have been speaking out.[139] While the air pollution levels in many of the big cities vary with the winds, many days the blend of factory emissions, vehicle exhausts, dust, and aerosols can choke the cities with a cloud of smog that is hard on the eyes and the lungs, and studies have shown that repeated exposure to an environment such as this can have devastating long-term health effects. {Causes of low quality services}

In the days before the Summer Olympics in Beijing in 2008, things were so bad that government had citizens stop the use of cars in the weeks leading up to the games in an attempt to clear the choking air pollution in the city. Many companies have moved operations to China because of their lax pollution laws and you can expect that trend to continue until the government steps in and does something about it. It's also a great place to manufacturing labor-intensive products with a work force that is cheaper than most in the world. But at some point in time, when health problems start to overwhelm the health care system, the government of China will have to step in and provide some sort of regulations for pollution by manufacturers. And with the number of automobiles owned by the citizens of China increasing annually, some regulations on car emissions will be needed at some point in time as well.

There are also ongoing complaints about the quality of work that is done in China. There have been recalls with many products such as toys that were discovered to have lead contamination. And there have been claims that Chinese companies have outsourced jobs to other Chinese companies without informing or seeking the permission of their clients. This has caused problems with many companies in the US as recalls cost a large amount of cash as do lawsuits that can result from defective products.

Hope for Impoverished Citizens of China

But things are changing in the country of China. With more and more factories opening up, and American companies more dependent than ever on Chinese labor, what was a dream just 10 years ago is now a reality for many people in China. Working at a factory used to be a hard to attain dream, now there is competition in China among factories for the best workers, and as such, some of them are facing having to raise wages and benefits to attract them. This could also lead to better working conditions for Chinese workers in a country that remains Communist in name, but is started to work much like a capitalist country from the west in order to drive their economy into the 21st Century.

As companies in China have to pay more for talent, this is driving up their costs which in turn will affect prices of goods being exported to the US and other countries.

Many people also look for China to move towards acquiring more expertise in information systems so they might compete with India for that lucrative market niche in the near future. China is already using some of the money they are making from outsourcing to improve their infrastructure and technology. In the last few years, a few Chinese companies have taken the unprecedented steps of outsourcing IT work to a domestic firm rather than one in India or the United States, and you can expect this trend to continue as the Chinese begin to see the power of technology working for them.

Trends in Outsourcing

Outsourcing is not just for the Fortune 500 companies anymore, many companies in the last 20 years have gotten started from the ground-up with the help of outsourcing.[140] There are "human cloud" resources on the internet where you can get any number of tasks done while starting a business so the owner can concentrate on his core activities. Some examples of these "human cloud" resources are elance.com, guru.com, oDesk, and Freelance Switch. These sites feature people with a number of specialized skills such as writing and translations, web programming, database design, and many more. You can post the job you have on one of these sites, and people will bid on them over a period of time. You can research the job history and qualifications of each of the bidders and the select the one you feel can best do the job for you. This form of outsourcing has been growing in popularity for many years now and you can expect that trend to continue for the foreseeable future. These contract workers also come with no overhead such as insurance costs, rises in electricity bills, and they command absolutely no benefits making them the perfect solution for small and medium-sized businesses. With the internet, people have the ability to work from anywhere in the world where there is an internet connection, and this is another reason you can look for more outsourcing with businesses of all shapes and sizes.

Other trends in outsourcing concern the information technology process of a business. Now with a wide range of services available including off-shore data center hosting, back office work, mainframe and web computer programming, and virtual assistants, there is almost nothing outside of a business' core functions that cannot be outsourced to a 3rd party. The cost of manpower is considerably lower which makes for a better bottom line.

Top Countries for Outsourcing in 2010

141

Rank	Country
1	India
2	China
3	Malaysia
4	Egypt
5	Indonesia
6	Mexico
7	Thailand
8	Vietnam
9	Philippines
10	Chile
11	Estonia
12	Brazil
13	Latvia
14	Lithuania
15	United Arab Emirates
16	United Kingdom
17	Bulgaria
18	United States
19	Costa Rica
20	Russia

How Outsourcing Will Change the Way We Work and how Industries Operate in the Future

Outsourcing is one of the ways that a true global economy now exists. That retailers can use the internet to hawk their products to a world-wide market is another part of the equation. With competition from foreign as well as domestic businesses, today's industries are always looking for better ways to work and improve their bottom lines. And with a steady supply of college graduates in China, India, and the Philippines who have the expertise to do the work, are more than willing to work hard, and do it for roughly 1/5 of what an average American worker makes, more and more companies are taking the outsourcing plunge.[142] In the past, it was mostly blue collar workers who faced the ax that outsourcing could bring. Now white collar professionals in information technology, accounting, and more also face the same threat to their jobs.

The Bottom Line for China and Other Developing Nations Hoping to Grow Their Economies

No doubt, China is headed in the right direction in a number of ways to achieve sustainable growth for the next several years. More of the income from outsourcing needs to be invested in industrial machinery, education of the population, and a strategic plan to regulate population in the larger cities and beyond. Regulations like those in the United States for all vehicles, corporations, and more need to be explored before the situation gets too far out of hand. Beijing already has some of the worst pollution in the world.[143] Another strategic plan needs to be place to move the country from its labor-intensive manufacturing focus to another that involve more high technology jobs and more specialized product production. Capital needs to be invested in making internet connections available for more of the population at a reasonable cost, that move alone could give employment to millions more of their citizens as outsourcing jobs abound on the internet and that trend is not ending any time soon.

By making the right moves, China could provide a blue print for other countries in the region looking to grow their economies and provide a better quality of life for their citizens. Countries such as the Philippians and Thailand are also seeing a rise in other outsourcing besides the traditional labor-intensive manufacturing jobs and could use a template for success from their neighbor. China has a unique opportunity here to provide a keystone which could be used by other countries in the region to provide for a 21st Century boom in their economies.

How Japan, the United States and Other Developed Countries Can Stay Ahead in the Game

Many companies in the United States and other developed countries who have not experienced any of the benefits of outsourcing and globalization most typically have managers who either do not understand the power of these options, or do not understand just how it all works. Colleges and universities in these countries need to incorporate a course on outsourcing and globalization as part of the curriculum for all business students, especially those with a marketing or management career tract. All students in high school should not leave those institutions without a clear understanding how to use a computer for purposes of using it to work and/or find a job. It would also not be a bad idea for the government agencies that deal with the unemployed to let them know of the opportunities that are available to them as contractors, and have a few programs that can help train people to fill these positions. Just as outsourcing is changing how people work in China, the effects on workers in the US and other developed countries are just as profound.

And these countries will have to do this while facing federal government budget deficits, an aging population and a shrinking workforce, and in the case of Japan, an economy that has basically been stagnant for much of the last 2 decades. No to mention having to fund the re-building and recovery of the northeastern shore area of the country that was devastated by the massive earthquake and tsunami of 2011.

The challenges on both sides are abundant and actions taken now will have some serious repercussions on future events.

Outsourcing has both a micro effect on people within countries and a macro effect on large corporations and governments. Its effects and benefits need to be explored by anyone who wants to compete in what is becoming more and more every day a global economy. It would also not be a bad idea for the federal government to fund a study on the effects of outsourcing on the economy and what can be done to help ready for the workforce for changes that could be coming quickly.

Globalization and Outsourcing Help to Usher in New World Order

There is indeed a new world order on the horizon, and it could very well mean better lives for people in impoverished countries and more challenges for people in developed countries such as the United States who can no longer expect to work for one company for all of their professional lives and retire in the manner the previous generation did. The next decade will entail many changes for people all over the world, and the people and governments that evolve and adapt the fastest will emerge on top.

Those that react quickly and decisively will be the ones that reap the rewards of a global economy that will continue to evolve and change over this decade and beyond.

A Case for Government Intervention in Creating Employment Opportunities across All Economies

Every society needs to create job opportunities for the survival and betterment of its citizens. Individuals and businesses alone cannot plan or set measures for the country as a whole to create jobs. It is the role of the government to devise and direct appropriate measures to ensure such requirements for its citizens.

Although it is important to note that the government by itself is not going to establish all businesses or setup entities to create jobs, however, it takes devoted statesmen to plan and design a program for national interest of their country. It is obnoxious for politicians to be heavily influenced by business enterprises, especially lobbyists of any particular international company or entity. Such an activity is only beneficial in the short-term and is often proven to be contrary in the long-term aspect of national interest—including corruption, disparity and eventually leading to anarchy and revolution.

The information age (Media and Internet) has increasingly resulted in conscious masses, well aware of the consequences associated with the decisions made on their behalf by the government. Suppressive actions by the government can avert genuine demands in the short run, but will lead to protests and violent confrontations in the long-term.

If *Globalization* is to be implemented in its true essence; business expansion, industrialization and job creation in different regions can be designed in a more harmonious and fair basis to benefit all. The prevalent disparity and inherent problems can be alleviated by understanding the role of government in long-term planning of a society's development.

History of Government Intervention

The 21st century is characterized by a world, where *Globalization, Democracy* and most importantly *Capitalism* have become pervasive in the economic thoughts and policy making. The economic philosophy of 'Capitalism' signifies minimum government involvement, no taxation and absolute leverage for private investment. This 'laissez-faire' form of governmental concept was at the heart of American society in general and strongly rooted at the start of the 20th century.

But the Great Depression of the 1930's brought upon a significant change in the overall mindset—the role of the government was established to be essential in creating employment and eventually stimulating the economy. The academic validation for government spending and its subsequent role in revitalizing the economy was provided by the book *"The General Theory of Employment, Interest and Money (1936)"*, authored by John Maynard Keynes.

However, the role of government was again despised by the advent of the economic crisis of the 1970s, which was triggered by the Oil Embargo. Criticism quickly followed to disapprove the role of government in generating employment in a period of stagnation—high unemployment and high inflation. Strides were made against a free-market economy. Nevertheless, the Global Financial Crisis which ensued from 2007-2010 led to an unending debate and harsh criticism of free-market economic thought.

It is worthwhile to note that the role of government is not restricted to policies in times of economic or financial hardships. Governments' world-over, especially the US government invested ingenuously in basic science. This has led to exponential advancement on multiple fronts, including cure against cancer, satellite communications, and microwave oven and most importantly the advent of the internet.

The government has not only invested in scientific advancements, it has also assisted new and innovative ventures through *Small Business Administration* institutes and programs. Companies we now recognize as global corporations were struggling at one moment and were rescued by the government FedEx Corp., Apple Inc., and Nike Inc. are some of the few powerhouses to name in a long list of government supported organizations.

Apart from the literary skirmishes between academicians and economists regarding the appropriate form of economic policies, an increasing number of politicians are announcing their economic policies centered on job-creation. This writing will discuss and establish the fact that there is an urgent need to include long-term vision and planning on the government's end to cater for the labor demands. It has been proven that complete dependence on private sector to create jobs could prove fatal for the whole society. Long-term visionary policies adopted by the governments can and will create professional jobs at all levels. Leaving this undertaking to private sector alone will result in the growth of service industry, and low earning rate jobs, rather than manufacturing or productive jobs. Richard Wolff, in his book titled "Capitalism Hits the Fan" blames the economic crisis of 2008 on private capitalism* and the whole system. Further examinations reveal the fact that abuse of capitalism, destroying the democracy in capitalism is the major factor leading to the economic crisis. When Goldman Sacks, an investment bank, pays well over $16 billion in the form of "bonuses" to its employees, and $50 million to its chairman alone just before the collapse of the company, or Pfizer, the drug manufacturing company, pays $200 million "severance package" to its resigning chief executive—all at the expense of tax-payers, indirectly affect the balance of wages in society. This widening gap between wages of different sectors of society is deepening the economic crisis, leading to transformation of US policies, and hence global financial structures. Job creations, and the nature of jobs being created all depend on the income level of participating wagers and earners and the gap between the top earner and skilled labor.[144]

International experiences and statistics prove that job creation backed by government planning and subsequent spending, surely creates business and employment opportunities. This phenomenon is not only successful in a crisis ridden situation but is also worthwhile for the long-term development of a society.

Until recently, large corporations and multinational companies seemed inert from the growing problems of unemployment at home—simply, because they had a goldmine of foreign customers and global resource mobilization. This meant that companies could possibly sell their products and services abroad without having to worry about job cuts and unemployment at home. But with the financial crisis engulfing the international scenario and economies world over in turmoil, corporate managers have realized the importance of a strong domestic economy.

Nonetheless, it is futile to rely heavily on a false notion that the private sector possesses the ability to absorb labor to ultimately end the unemployment crisis. However this writing does not undermine the importance of the private sector, instead it will focus on the government's role in leading the change in collaboration with the private sector.

Understanding the Mechanisms of Labor Market

Like any other market, the labor market is established from a complex interplay of demand and supply. Businesses can toggle between labor, capital and machinery to achieve output that will maximize profits. The key point worth attention is that full employment is not a mandatory option for businesses. In the technologically driven, globalized world, businesses strive to keep their personnel structure at a minimum. Organizations will not compromise on profits, if they can substitute labor with automation. Therefore, there exists a case for government intervention in spurring employment.

Governments can respond in two different manners. In the first case, the government can generate employment opportunities by devising microeconomic policies for specific economic sectors or by influencing the macroeconomic scenario of the economy. This also includes the fiscal and monetary policies and subsidies directed towards incentivizing private companies to hire workers. The second solution pertains to direct involvement by the government and comprises of an explicit approach of hiring unemployed individuals to perform national projects.

But what lies at the heart of government intervention is the absence of profitability when hiring or creating employment. This has led economist Hyman Minsky to coin the term "Employer of Last Resort" for the government in the 1960s. There are multiple instances of successful government intervention across the globe in countries such as Argentina, Bangladesh, Cambodia, Chile, Ethiopia, Ghana, India, Korea, Peru, South Africa, Sweden, and United States.

Long-term Planning

Long term effect of a recession cannot be ignored on industries as well as many other businesses alike. Various businesses and corporations strive to maintain their survival by cutting on their budgets and laying off employees. If a government can plan efficiently to intervene in a timely manner, it can possibly avert the unemployment crisis by effectively preventing recessions. This needs close cooperation between the government and industrial sector, in concert with educational institutes to provide re-training of needed staff, as technologies change.

Additionally, various investment experts and policy makers have emphasized on the need to invest in growing industries. Renewable energy sectors or biotechnology can prove to be major employment generators in the future.

The Need for a New Model of Employment Generation

There seems to be an apparent harmony amongst economists and academicians over government's interventions in creating jobs, but what is the appropriate method of creating employment opportunities is a dilemma. Traditional policies of stimulating investment and spending through *Fiscal* and *Monetary* policies have not significantly materialized, apart from short-term fixation.

To put it more simply, government incentives and subsidies on large infrastructure projects and massive bail-out packages for the private sector have resulted in miniature outcomes. The existing unemployed labor force is pressurized by the exceeding number of new labor workforce entering the market. Government's world-over should place due emphasis on catering to the increasing number of college graduates entering the labor market for a future period of at least 10-15 years.

Governments must work with high school counselors for career planning. More and accurate information that forecasts the future needs of the labor force is required to avoid flooding the human resource pool with valueless degrees or too many applicants for a particular sector. Many out of work graduates without opportunities in their chosen fields turn to menial jobs such as taxi drivers or worse yet become involved in crime.

The new framework is centered on incentives and support to young entrepreneurs by equipping them with the capability to generate new jobs. This policy is not the traditional 'Silicon Valley' venture capitalism, rather an innovative concept of fighting unemployment with micro-entrepreneurship. Such a drastic change is not achieved overnight, rather requires unfaltering commitment to a gradual process. Such a revolution requires:

- Fundamental transformation and revision of the educational system to support their cause.
- Formation of local "Cooperative Councils" with guidance from governments on the type of products or services being offered and forecasted.
- Nurturing a society composed of individuals who are ready to embrace the risk-taking attitude essential in entrepreneurship, with proper incentives and tax reliefs
- Removing any disparities inherent in the system, such as access to capital and gender inequality

- Encouraging innovation and rendering creativity a sustainable aspect of private and public life
- Promote resource conservation and self-sustenance through role models and behaviors set by the governing bodies

With the global economy rapidly evolving into a knowledge-based society, it is imperative for the governments to plan and execute long-term vision and goals for including soft-skills for their citizens. Apart from equipping individuals to meet the challenges of a transformed world, it becomes mandatory for the governments to assist and engage in supporting local "Cooperative Councils" at national level to effectively utilize talent by providing adequate tools and mechanism (finance & marketing) to create employment opportunities.

Poverty as a Disruptive Force:

In order to succeed in curbing the terrorism, one must investigate the roots of the problem rather than confront the symptoms. Poverty is cradle for terrorism. Investigations into the roots of social upheavals, revolts or terrorism shows very clearly that all unrests, which eventually leads to a major change in the respective societies, are related to their education and poverty levels. The conflicts start with continued poverty and lack of education in societies breeding terrorism. Mankind, in search for prosperity, in order to come out of poverty takes drastic actions, especially if they are suppressed politically. Poverty, lack of education and political suppressions in any society are the instruments for people desiring change to confront the establishment. Street protests are the mildest form of confrontation; with added frustration, it will lead to harsh conflicts, even taking up arms to get out of their embattled situation—they have nothing to lose! Although they might be branded under a specific religion or cult to create pseudo-legitimacy for their cause, they are all rooted in their desire to upgrade the standard of living. Failure of political institutes or parties that have not been able to address or fulfill for them. Political doctrines, philosophies, or dogmatism of the past are no longer responsive to the need of unprivileged members of many societies. With the world population growing, advancements in health care and improvement on environment, societies are faced with a serious challenge in improving the standard of living of their citizens, fulfilling their aspirations, and curbing injustices.

Although multi-national business enterprises that influence their respective governments in protecting their interests are the main source of injustice in receiving countries, it is the role of the local governments to remedy the economic gap, improve living standards and educational level to reduce this danger.

The solution does not rely on military might, or propping dictatorial or totalitarian regimes. Even the role of international institutes such as World Bank, United Nations, etc. need to be changed drastically to respond to the realities on the ground. Their continued support for the agenda of a few advanced countries at the expense of many under developed or advancing nations need to change. Obviously, injection of capital for economic growth or insertion of educational system alone will not curb the situation; unless political meddling of more powerful governments, on behalf of their interest groups, in the affairs of poverty stricken nations are totally eliminated.

It is the prime role of advanced industrial nations in cooperation with democratic advancing nations to identify and formulate solutions to improve the economic prosperity level of developing nations, by focusing on elimination of poverty in that society. This could be achieved by introducing democratic values and measures to defuse social upheavals and confrontations. Participation of people in all affairs of their society—planning, execution, monitoring of finances and educational programs—will guarantee development of democracy in their society. This should be accomplished before the individuals or groups in the receiving society turn to more radical and unlawful means for achieving their social or economic objectives. Business intrusion and slavery of people by international enterprises are also one of the prime instruments for creating unsatisfied and frustrated individuals in any society. Injustice, no matter where and at what level, will create frustration and dangerous atmosphere for the extremists to advocate armed struggle, and makes it easier for them to recruit from the unsatisfied and desperate population. It does not matter whether it is economic injustice or political; in either case the situation would be explosive and it would only be a matter of time before it is turned to a violent upheaval, no matter how hard the ruling group try to curb the situation by force.

Recent uprisings in the Middle East proved that future uprisings and confrontations with local authorities are not going to be on ideological grounds, rather on demands for democratic form of government to serve them best in curbing the corruptions and bring them out of poverty. Consequently, form of confrontations that in many cases are leading to wars, are changed dramatically. Mass armies cannot win unsophisticated Taliban in Afghanistan, or popular uprisings in the streets of Egypt or Libya. Air strikes alone might cripple the governing bodies, however, they are not effective in street battles, as was the case in Iraq and elsewhere. Therefore, the most useful tool would seem to be to win hearts by assisting nations to participate in their own affairs to gradually develop a democratic system of governance for themselves in order to prosper.

Perspective

According to the most recent statistics, nearly 25,000 people die every day of hunger or hunger-related causes throughout the world. (This equates with one person about every three and a half seconds)[145]. In the African Republic of Niger, nearly 93% of the population lives below the poverty level[146]. Even in the

United States—the richest of all the industrialized nations in the world—15.1% of Americans don't know where their next meal is coming from[147]. But, what exactly do these figures mean from the larger, global perspective?

As history is providing the evidence, poverty (most often manifested as people without enough to eat) has played a pivotal role in societal development throughout the course of human evolution. In fact, famine—resulting from severe climatic shifts (mini ice ages to prolonged droughts), volcanic eruptions, earthquakes, floods and tidal waves, epidemics, wildfires, and insect infestation—has been the primary motivator for most of humankind's great migrations. Archaeological evidence even suggests that food scarcity was most likely what spurred the exodus of early humans out of Africa and into the rest of the world between 400,000 and 800,000 BP[148].

Throughout history, natural disasters have resulted in human populations not having enough resources to sustain life (and subsequently impacted societal development). But, in many cases, it is by human hands that poverty most often persists. Though often the result of war or social upheaval, poverty is ultimately a product of societal inequity and exploitation—tyrannical rule, religious persecution, class discrimination, hegemony, or simple indifference. And while the existence of hunger within a given society does not in itself define poverty (and is most often indicative of a much larger, systemic problem regarding access to resources), it is often the primary motivator behind subsequent societal behavior[149]. Behavior that often serves to perpetuate poverty's destructive forces.

The Culture of Poverty

One of the most frequently-referenced articles ever written on the subject of poverty, "The Culture of Poverty," resulted from two extensive cultural studies conducted between 1959 and 1961 by renowned cultural anthropologist Oscar Lewis, culminating the two classic anthropological treatises, *Five Families* and *Children of Sanchez*. In "The Culture" Lewis addresses the so-called "cycle of poverty" socio-economic hypothesis, asserting that poverty is not just a matter of economic deprivation, it involves a variety of subsequent behavioral and personality traits. It is his conclusion that once people adapt to poverty, attitudes and behaviors that had initially manifested in reaction to their economic status are then passed down generation to generation through socialization— even if their social status subsequently has opportunity for improvement[150].

Citing some seventy characteristics of "The Culture of Poverty" Lewis writes, "The people in the culture of poverty have a strong feeling of marginality, of helplessness, of dependency, of not belonging. They are like aliens in their own country, convinced that the existing institutions do not serve their interests and needs. Along with this feeling of powerlessness is a widespread feeling of inferiority, of personal unworthiness." Thus, while poverty is often viewed as a localized or temporary societal setback reversible by sufficient economic growth, long-term, cross-cultural studies show a much different reality. Not only does poverty become an insidious, culturally-based institution that establishes behavioral patterns that effectively undermine attitudes and behavior for generations, it can even cross the cultural lines. As longitudinal sociological studies have shown, the so-called "Culture of Poverty" is an adaptation representing efforts to cope with feelings of hopelessness and despair from the realization that their condition is unlikely to improve soon enough not to negatively impact their lives and those of family members; not just day-to-day existence, but their foreseeable future[151]. Thus, what begins as adaptive measures intended to serve as temporary, ad hoc solutions, quickly become behavioral patterns adopted by entire families—and as is often the case, extended families. And that's just the beginning.

As poverty persists, families essentially begin to function as individual subgroups within their own social group—effectively isolating themselves not just from mainstream society but from others of their social strata. And while these subgroups may form alliances of mutual convenience—and even display a general sense of community—they more often become self-contained, tightly-knit survival units. Typically, children born into such units will adapt the basic values and attitudes of their subgroup by the time they reach six or seven years of age to the extent that they are not psychologically geared to take advantage—or even notice—opportunities that may arise to improve their circumstances (6).

From the extensive list of characteristics Lewis attributes to the cult of poverty, modern sociologists derive four specific attitudes, values, and traits they believe come to define the impoverished; adopted first by the individual, becoming the fundamental worldview of the impoverished family unit, then ultimately coming to characterize impoverished communities as a whole:

1. Over time, the lack of integration into the larger social structure of a given society becomes one of the more critical characteristics. The result of a combination of factors—cross-strata discrimination, social stigma, fear, prevailing suspicion, apathy—the marginalization of the poor creates a self-perpetuating and often, self-fulfilling set of circumstances.

    Instead of societal interaction involving normal commerce (property ownership, accumulation of savings, stockpile of food reserves) involving participation in the larger economic system, there is a high incidence of pawning of personal possessions, borrowing of money from informal sources, procurement of secondhand clothing and furniture (which is often sacrificed to obtain essentials), and the acquisition of food as opportunity presents itself.

Additionally, while the culture of poverty typically espouses institutions such as church and marriage, men with no steady work and no foreseeable means to increase income typically choose to avoid the inherent expense of formal marriage and divorce, opting instead for temporary relationships or "free union" marriages. Likewise, many women offered traditional marriage prefer a consensual union because it gives them the freedom to legally claim their children should they decide to leave their partners. In short, relationships are perceived as temporary, destroying the social fabric and values in their societies.

2. The second common characteristic of the culture of poverty is housing conditions described as over-crowded, socially gregariousness, and with a general lack of organization beyond the basic family unit. (It is this lack of greater cohesion that makes them vulnerable to neighborhood gangs and aggressors—particularly pimps and drug dealers in the slum and urban setting.)

In Mexico City, San Juan, and impoverished areas of South Africa, such districts are segregated by walls or other physical barriers, further isolating the poor from the remainder of society— and further adding to the social stigma. And while housing is generally kept affordable for those living within the segregated areas, this usually means that no low-income housing is available outside that area, making it virtually impossible for the poor to graduate to better housing.

3. On the family level, the primary major characteristic of the culture of poverty is the relative negation of childhood. Often forgoing formal education altogether or forced to quit school at a very early age to help contribute to family resources (through trade, theft, drug sales, prostitution) children of "The Culture" typically have an early introduction into sex and subsequently fall into the cycle of consensual marriages and high incidence of

abandonment of wives and children by men—or men left for those who can better provide. As a result, there is a high rate of female—and mother-centered families with no male role-models or father figures, as well as a general lack of privacy, a strong predisposition towards authoritarian parenting (where the parent's word is law and questioning leads to corporal punishment), constant sibling rivalry, and ongoing competition for food, material assets, as well as maternal affection.

4. On the personal level, the major characteristics of "The Culture" are a pervasive sense of inferiority, marginality, helplessness, and interdependence, with members seldom having a sense of personal history or ethnic background. Individuals raised in this culture are generally aware of little beyond their own struggles and way of life, and lack the perspective to see their plight reflected in others around the world who share their societal limitations. Having no sense of identification beyond their poverty, culture members are easily drawn to any outside group that promotes membership into a larger group—be it religious, activist, or pacifist. But perhaps most insidious, the culture of poverty typically lacks close maternal interaction, suffers low self-esteem and distorted body image, and often experiences sexual identification confusion. Additionally, members typically lack impulse control, are unable to defer gratification, lack the ability to formulate long-term plans, carry a prevailing sense of resignation and fatalism, maintain a fundamental acceptance of male superiority, and believe that a degree of mental illness is "normal" (6).

Poverty and Child Abuse

Although partner/spousal abuse has undoubtedly existed since the beginning of human history, only in more recent years have efforts have been made to document the frequency and contributing variables (5). According to national surveys conducted in the United States in 1975 and 1985, while spouse abuse stayed relatively constant over this ten-year period, a striking decrease in domestic murders among Black women beginning in 1976 (the vast majority of whom reported their status as below poverty level) attributed to the increased number of shelters for battered women beginning in the mid-1970s, drew attention to the shockingly high numbers of Black, impoverished women and their children who had for decades fallen through the cracks of the American welfare system.

As worldwide cross-cultural statistics now show, aggressiveness and violence between partners typically translates to child abuse; behavior magnified several fold when poverty is a factor. According to Professor of Psychology Jay Belsky of Birkbeck University of London, "Poverty is undoubtedly the major risk factor for child abuse and neglect"[152]. Exemplified by the 2009 article "Pakistani Children's Condition the Worst in South Asia" appearing in *Business Recorder*, according to the Global Organization for Human Empowerment and Rights foundation (GOHER), not only do more than eight million Pakistani children suffer from malnutrition, nearly 23 million have never been to school, routinely drink contaminated water, and regularly suffer physical and sexual abuse.

In the Punjab area alone, an estimated 30% of the children have fled their homes due to domestic violence (associated directly with financial difficulties), with over 150 reported cases of child abduction, rape and ransom. In all, over 30,000 children under the age of 15 live on the streets of Punjab—choosing the streets to the physical abuse suffered at home. Additionally, as of 2009, there were more than 4500 juveniles imprisoned in Pakistani jails, 66% of them housed with adults—leaving them vulnerable to sexual and physical abuse—and as many as 360 children known to have been smuggled out to be used as camel jockeys throughout the Middle East.[153] These numbers support statistics published in

National Catholic Reporter in 2006, estimating that as many as 860 million of the world's poor children are subjected to "nightmarish existences" that include sexual exploitation, prostitution, AIDS, war (recruited for small-arms operations), forced labor (handling dangerous machinery and toxic materials), and then ultimately, abandonment.[154]

While one may reason that children of abusive conditions would be less likely to perpetuate such behavior, the connection between childhood violence and adult violence is well documented[155]. Like many other behavioral patterns adopted within the culture of poverty, studies show that children who witness violence or who are themselves abused, are more likely to continue the "cycle of family violence," either inflicting abuse on their partners or children, or in some cases, permitting themselves to become victims of intimate violence. Additionally, children who have been sexually abused (either by strangers or through incestuous parental or sibling contact) are statistically more likely—though not inevitably—to sexually abuse children or consider incest a sexual option[156]. Thus, as poverty results in a greater and greater number of abused children throughout the world, the number of abused escalates exponentially from generation to generation—and spreads outward through intercultural marriage and unions.

The Feminism of Poverty

At the heart of the American and British Feminism movement (a concerted effort seeking reform on women's reproductive rights, domestic violence, maternity leave, equal pay, women's suffrage, sexual harassment, and sexual violence) is the Feminist Theory, the philosophical model aimed at gaining an understanding of gender inequality. Grounded in the reality that women of most societies are traditionally relegated to subordinate roles, it examines women's social status, rights, interests, and issues, promoting gender equality while rejecting discrimination, objectification (especially sexual), oppression, patriarchy, and stereotyping[157].

But one needs only to consider the last 3000 years of documented history to recognize that poverty is intimately interwoven into most of these issues, and one that affects women's lives far more profoundly than those of men.

Throughout recorded time, men have governed nations, commanded armies, controlled wealth and assets, and ruled over individual family units—sometimes, multiple generations. Thus, when it comes to access to even fundamental resources, men have always held the proverbial purse strings[158]. And although certain ancient cultures permitted woman to own property and function independently, the vast majority have always been patriarchal (also patrilineal), male-dominated societies where men—husbands, sons, brothers, and even son-in-law's —decide a woman's access to food, water, clothing, and other necessities. It therefore comes as no surprise that throughout history, woman (and by association, their offspring) have been deemed expendable—sacrificed for individual male gain and the "greater good." (Ironically, in most scenarios where women have risen to positions of political power, they have assumed male, hegemonic roles, ignoring the poor as well as the plight of their impoverished female counterparts: When Queen Marie Antoinette learned that the peasants had no bread to eat, she is quoted as saying, "Let them eat cake!")

As Ann Whitehead explains in *Failing Women, Sustaining Poverty: Gender in Poverty Reduction Strategy Papers*, a report published in 2003 for the UK Gender and Development Network, while it's true that both women and men suffer from poverty, a disproportionate number of women comprise the chronically poor, particularly in "heavily indebted" developing countries such as Tanzania, Bolivia, Malawi, and Yemen. Whitehead writes, "Poverty is more complexly gendered, as men and women are often poor for different reasons, experience poverty differently, and have differing capacities to withstand and or escape poverty. Gender inequalities and gender power relations interact with other inequalities and power relations to produce these differences"[159].

As most world authorities now acknowledge, not only does poverty have a greater impact on women in general, women are also more susceptible to persistent poverty due to worldwide gender inequalities regarding distribution of income, control of property, gender-bias in labor markets, and their comparatively limited access to credit, loans, and other institutional relief.

With this in mind, since 1999, international financial institutions (IFIs) have required "heavily indebted" developing countries (a list of 40 nations that also includes Afghanistan, Haiti, Nicaragua, and Ethiopia) to formulate nationally owned, participatory Poverty Reduction Strategy Papers (PRSPs) aimed at reducing the enormous burden of poverty carried by poor women, as a condition of receiving debt relief and low-interest loans from the International Monetary Fund (IMF) and World Bank. However, as *Failing Women* explains, economists recognize that in order to make an impact on poor women specifically, poverty must be reduced as a whole. Thus while even these mandated efforts seem like a step in the right direction, they will ultimately help perpetuate the inequity—a "Catch-22" as it were—that currently exists (15). In reality, after so many centuries, most of the world's institutions are designed to keep men at the top of the resource chain—and women at the bottom.

Poverty and Deviant Behavior

For well over a century now, economists have promoted societies' need to concentrate their efforts on eliminating poverty— not for the good of the individual, *per se*, but for the good of their respective societies. From Karl Marx (*Das Kapital*, 1867) to Henry George (*Progress and Poverty*, 1879), Charles Booth (Life and Labor of the People, 1889) to Willem Bonger (*Criminology and Economic Conditions*, 1905), it has been widely accepted that poverty is the root of moral decay, resulting in most of the vices that infect the world. Marx went so far as to say that crime, prostitution, vice, and moral evil are primarily due to poverty produced by capitalistic systems[160].

In that, the majority of criminals (both young and old), alcoholics, drug abusers, mental patients, and suicides come from the poor sector of society, it has long been assumed they are invariably the products of a life of poverty (16). And while worldwide studies have sought to comprehensively prove a cause and effect scenario, the best sociologists will currently claim is that a clear correlation exists. This seemingly lack of conviction, however, is more a matter of a lack of scientifically-conducted studies than belief that a causal relationship is not present. Even from a basic human instinctual perspective, individuals forced to obtain the basic necessities of life—food, water, shelter—through whatever means available to them, will logically do what is necessary to survive[161]. And while prostitution, petty theft, and a number of other everyday crimes are perpetrated by all socio-economic sectors of society, it's impossible to ignore that the vast majority are committed by "street people" constituting those living in poverty.

The Global Picture: Breaking the Cycle

It is often said that the first step to finding a solution to a problem is recognizing it as a problem. Poverty, however, is an issue far more complex than most. Institutionalized since at least Paranoiac Egypt and increasingly politicized through the centuries, it is one of the most misunderstood yet frequently manipulated aspects of any society.

For example, according to a recent *Washington Post* article, North Korea is about to suffer yet another major food crisis due to a poor harvest[162]. Though not expected to be as severe as the famine of the 1990s which left 2.5 million people dead, the US is preparing to send 240,000 metric tons of food for the children to North Korea. And while this humanitarian effort seems the compassionate thing to do for the wealthiest nation on the planet, it would be naïve to consider this a purely altruistic act. In reality, this "gift" is essentially a bargaining chip. A good-will gesture intended to give the US leverage regarding North Korea's use of nuclear weapons. And while some may say that quid pro quo is only fair, this exemplifies the inability to separate politics from world poverty today.

As one of the most misunderstood societal conditions, poverty is often erroneously equated with lack of food. In reality, the world produces more than enough food to feed everyone—but not everyone can afford it. Considering the fact that in many occasions, transportation or delivery system is the bottleneck to provide any needed commodity to the needy. As the World Health Organization (WHO) describes it, millions of people are caught up in a seemingly endless cycle: lacking the money to buy enough food to nourish themselves they become weakened—making them more susceptible to illness and disease. Increasingly less able to work, they become helplessly poorer and hungrier. This cycle continues for millions of people until death[163].

According to the UN, 24 of the 25 poorest countries in the world are located in Africa. The ten most desperate are: Niger, Ethiopia, Mali, Burkina Faso, Burundi, Somalia, Central African Republic, Liberia, Guinea, Sierra Leone—each with at least 80% of its population living in abject poverty. (And one need only follow the news to know that tens of millions of people live in deplorable living conditions in various other parts of the world including Haiti, Pakistan, and Indonesia.)

But it would be misguided to assume that leaders of the African nations necessarily want their people freed from the bondage of poverty. In fact, numerous times throughout the past decade, UN aid workers have delivered tons of food to these impoverished countries only to have their leaders refuse their people access.[164] As unreasonable as it may seem, many African dictators would rather their people starve than be indebted to any outside entity. Their rule is absolute. And this attitude is shared by many rulers around the world.

To most of the wealthy, affluent, and powerful, "poverty" is at best an abstract concept; simply something they are not. Since it is most often erroneously considered a disease of the lazy, uneducated, and the weak-minded, there has been relatively little done to eliminate it from the global scene. Simply put, the very people who are in the best position to help eliminate the problem or initiate social change are blind to the realities of poverty— economic, sociological, psychological, cultural, and otherwise. Thus, poverty remains shrouded in misconceptions, ambivalence, and apathy as its destructive forces continue to run rampant.

Chapter VIII. A Workable United Nations

United Nations is an international organization built upon the basic premise of providing all member nations with a single global platform to raise their voices and coordinate actions directed at solving mutual or individual problems and challenges. The foundations of this second multi-purpose global organization were laid on 24th October, 1945, after the cease of World War II. United Nations, which is more commonly referred to as UN, succeeded the League of Nations.

The United Nations was established with the aim of preventing future wars, by assisting in conflict resolutions between different countries. It was supposed to represent **nations**, with their democratically elected representatives—governments—sitting on the United Nations board. On theory, all nations were supposed to have equal voice and vote. In practice, this has not happened. Nations are not represented; only governing bodies, whether they are democratically elected body or not, they are all represented. Decisions on war and peace are not based on fair judgments; it is primarily based on the desire of a few dominating powers! The resolutions passed are not effective, since the UN body lacks the power and coherence that was designed to do. It has become a redundant discussion body without any effective base or mandate to be obeyed by any nation.

One or two countries cannot, and need not to police the world order. Their own national interests would be in conflict with the fair judgment or resolutions of conflicts in many instances. Therefore, in order to reduce tensions across the globe, and provide an effective arbitration for the world community, UN needs to have clear and powerful mandate to enforce the values of human rights and to keep peace between nations or their respective governments. This means to have an independent standing force (military to police) to become a powerful and meaningful peacemaker, with adequate budget; similar to NATO. More importantly, it needs to represent nations, and their democratically elected governing bodies that are elected under the observation of the UN; otherwise, the non-democratic ruling governments must be barred from attending decision making processes of the UN. Any government that uses tactics of terror and systematic annihilation of its citizens in order to rule the nation, has no legitimacy to govern or be represented on any world body.

United Nations Charter of 1948, established values for human rights and democracy in respective social and political structure of member states. Those values need to be converted into deeds. According to the adopted Charter of the UN General Assembly, the Security Council and the membership in the UN should comprise of representatives from **democratically elected** governments that are truly elected by their people. Any nation, not meeting the standard values on human rights and democracy—Articles 5, 18, 19, 20-1, and 23-3 of UN Charter on Human Rights—must be barred from participating in the decision making processes of this body, and its membership must be suspended. In this manner, this international body would become authorized to implement the rule of law and respect for human rights at all levels for its members.

In other words, memberships at the UN need to be limited to countries that have democratic form of government representing their people. Security and prosperity for all nations need to be observed and elevated by such an independent strong body with revised charter and management structure; it should be involved in all economic planning to reduce poverty on global scale with strong, effective mandate and appropriate tools to be able to implement such programs and objectives, without being influenced by a few powerful countries, and closing their eyes on many aggressors or injustices.

Experience of early 2011 with regard to the Middle East uprisings and lack of effectiveness by the United Nations or NATO in safeguarding innocent people against their tyrannical rulers was a lesson, amongst many lessons of twentieth century (Rwanda, Balkans massacres, Israel's aggressions and many others) to be learned, while the industrial West paid lip service to the cries of millions! Even lack of common vision and cooperation amongst the allies in the case of Libyan massacre of its own people was pathetic. It would be the time for civilized free world to re-structure the United Nations, and arming this institute with adequate tools and power to be able to translate its mission for defense of humanity into deeds.

The United Nations is empowered with 4 major tasks or purposes:

1. Ensure and maintain peace throughout the world
2. Encourage and promote nations to develop friendly ties and settle any ongoing disputes
3. Assist nations in developing mutual cooperation in order to reduce poverty, illiteracy, malnutrition, and diseases. Promoting respect and tolerance for each other's freedom and rights.
4. Serve as a central platform for harmonizing the actions of countries to achieve the above-mentioned goals.

Initially 51 nations agreed to form the United Nations and committed themselves with the goals of ensuring and maintaining international peace, promoting friendly ties amongst nations, and achieving social welfare through persistent efforts. These efforts were aimed at improving the living standards and avoiding any human rights violations.

With the passage of time, United Nations achieved accolades and support for its efforts and now comprises of 193 nations. The United Nations is currently headquartered in New York, but also has regional offices in Vienna, Geneva, Nairobi and other major cities. The UN charter recognizes English, Arabic, Chinese, Russian, French and Spanish as the official languages of communication.

The roots of United Nations are embedded in World War II and the subsequent failure of League of Nations to prevent another global war after the First World War. It is also important to note that the word "United Nations" was first used by the American President Franklin Delano Roosevelt. The US president suggested the word to British Prime Minister Sir Winston Churchill. The word was subsequently adopted to refer to 'Allies' in World War II.

But before proceeding to explain the origins of United Nations, it is essential to note why League of Nations is often referred to as the predecessor of United Nations and how did the League fail to prevent World War II.

The League of Nations (LON) was established by the Treaty of Versailles after the Paris Peace Conference in 1919. The League of Nations served as the first truly global institution and was created as a result of the First World War. It was tasked with the simple goals of sustaining global peace and curbing any future possibilities of World War II.

The League of Nations did have some success, including admirable achievements on the social level. Teams were dispatched to various countries to assist medical professionals in eradicating numerous diseases. Wells were dug, significant strides were made in elevating the status of women, child labor was reduced, and drug addiction to certain extend were reduced.

But various historians and analysts often overlook these social successes when highlighting the political failures of the League. On the political front, the League failed miserably to settle disputes amongst nations and as a result, World War II broke out. The

League of Nation was finally disbanded in 1946 after the end of World War II.

However, one of the fundamental arguments in favor of the League of Nations is the absence of its own armed peace keeping force. Thus, the organization was totally relying on the major powerful nation members to enforce its resolution and provide any sort of manpower.

With the failure and subsequent demise of the League of Nations, and the culmination of World War II, the global community felt an urgent need to establish an effective international organization that would avoid the possibilities of a Third World War. Another driving factor was the horrific and devastating effects of the war experienced by the humanity. Therefore, an effective international institute was the need of time.

The initial idea of the United Nations was prominent in the declarations agreed upon and signed in the *Moscow Conference* and subsequently in the *Tehran Conference* during 1943. A year later, various representatives of prominent nations, including China, USSR (Russia was formerly USSR), US, France, and UK met at the Dumbarton Oaks Conference held at Washington, D.C. to discuss the creation of United Nations. The conference was a huge success with consent on the purpose of the United Nations, hierarchy and structure of the organization, and viable arrangements on maintaining international peace, and economic and social welfare goals. The *Yalta Conference* also marked a positive step towards the creation of United Nations and discussed the membership of various nations.

Governments, educators, numerous intellectuals and non-governmental bodies, including Lions Clubs International and Rotary International received invitations to discuss and draft a proper charter for the UN at the *United Nations Conference* on *International Organization* in San Francisco on 25th April, 1945.

The drafting process was marked by arduous discussions and stretched over a period of two months. The next four months encompassed a strenuous process of ratification by member nation governments and consequent acceptance and signatures over the UN charter. The United Nations was officially created on 24th October, 1945.

Legal Footing

The legal proceedings of the case: *'Reparations for Injuries Suffered in the Service of the United Nations'* and the simultaneous legal opinion by *International Court of Justice* (ICJ) established the UN as an international legal person.

This legal decision empowered the organization with the powers and rights to file a claim against a government pertaining to injuries and harm. Additionally the powers vested in the Charter enables the organization to take action on a wide range of issues and achieve the goals mentioned above.

Hierarchy and Structure of the Organization

The United Nations adopted various components and structural guidelines from the League of Nations. The purpose, functions, and structure of the League of Nations inspired the United Nations to a great extent. The UN's core body and auxiliary agencies are based on the same principles, which defined the League of Nations.

Despite this similarity in certain areas, the United Nations is a completely different and unique institute in other aspects— especially in the domain of ensuring international peace. Various member nations have agreed to contribute to military expertise and manpower and currently the UN peace-keeping force comprises of a distinct 100,000 peacekeepers.

Apart from learning from the shortfalls of the League of Nations, a multitude of factors defined the distinct nature of the United Nations. Post World War II decolonization; advent of Cold War tensions between the US and Russia; and the rapidly evolving nature of political, economic and social issues in the globalized world significantly shaped the decision-making mechanism and responsibilities of the United Nations.

The United Nations comprises of six core organs, namely— the General Assembly, the Security Council, the Trusteeship Council, the Economic and Social Council, the Secretariat, and the International Court of Justice. It should also be noted that five of the above-mentioned bodies are based in the United Nations headquarters in New York, while the International Court of Justice is based in The Hague, Netherlands.

Nearly all of the major agencies derive their power from the UN Charter, especially Article 2. The main statutes of Article 2 follow as:

- All sovereign members enjoy equality in status and importance
- Peaceful measures to settle disputes
- Member nations are prohibited to use any form of threat. Such actions would be counted as a breach of the UN's Charter
- Every member is bound by the nature of the membership and the Charter to assist United Nations with the enforcement of unanimous decisions
- Nation states that are non-members are also compelled to act in accordance with the guiding principles which are essential to maintaining international peace
- The last major statute prohibits United Nations to intervene in problems which are considered to be under the domestic jurisdiction of a sovereign state

Specialized Institutions

Apart from the six main bodies of the United Nations, there are several bodies and organizations associated with the UN. Some of the prominent agencies include:

- United Nations Educational, Scientific and Cultural Organization (UNESCO)
- Food and Agricultural Organization
- International Atomic Energy Agency
- International Labor Organization
- International Monetary Fund
- UNICEF
- World Health Organization (WHO)
- World Bank

Global Reach

The United Nations is a true international organization with a reach that extends to the far ends of the globe. Apart from the major contributions of conflict prevention, efforts directed towards peace through peacekeeping forces, and humanitarian assistance; there have been several aspects where the UN affects the lives of common citizens and individuals.

Other areas where the UN has excelled with significant strides include: promotion of democracy, sustainable development, disaster management, curbing proliferation of weapons, landmines, due attention towards international health issues, advancing gender equality and elevating the status of women.

However, there have been mixed reviews as to whether the UN has been successful in dealing with: conflict resolution in civil and regional wars, humanitarian assistances in times of crises, monumental refugee movements, sudden rise in international terrorism, unprecedented devastation from AIDs and other diseases, global financial meltdowns, and a staggering wealth disparity.

Nevertheless, all efforts by the United Nations and its specialized agencies are directed towards achieving a safer, secure, and sustainable world for the present and future generations.

The Mission of the United Nations

Founded in 1945 at the end of World War II, the United Nations is an organization that is made up of countries from around the globe who have united to maintain international peace and security, help to develop good relations between all nations, and to become a center for harmony among all nations.[165]

The United Nations is comprised of 193 member nations. It was founded to not only maintain peace and security, but to promote better standards of living, champion human rights, and promote social progress.[166] It was envisioned as a vehicle by which a New World Order could come about, a forum through which all nations could be heard and have a voice in the future. To a large degree, it has been successful in this respect. It has also been compromised by several nations who have an agenda who have blocked the UN from taking action in several parts of the world where they were needed.

United Nations Military Interventions

The United Nations has been a number of peacekeeping interventions over the years, with either observer groups or armed military forces.[167] In 1948, observer groups were sent to monitor the armistice between Israel and the Arab states of the region. They would return several more times over the next three decades. Other interventions have included the Belgian colony of the Congo when it achieved independence in 1960 to help the new government maintain order, monitoring the border between India and Pakistan, and creating a buffer zone on the island nation of Cyprus after a civil war broke out there.

Is the United Nations and United States Retreating?

Is the United Nations and United States retreating from the role they played as policeman for much of the 20th Century? It's no secret the American people are tired of war after long campaigns in both Iraq and Afghanistan. Since the end of World War II, the United States has been involved in countless direct interventions and threatened to intervene in many others.[168] Some of these campaigns were humanitarian in nature, some of them were to protect US energy resources and other interests. But there is no doubt the American people are tired of their government taking part in nation building, as results have been poor in Iraq and Afghanistan, and are tired of footing the bill for it.

One of the best indicators of the disgust of the American people can be seen in the Republican presidential primaries. Libertarian Ron Paul, a Texas Congressman who champions bringing troops home from foreign bases such as Korea, Germany, and other outposts and ending the wars in Iraq and Afghanistan has seen some substantial support. He was also a strong advocate of not deploying US military forces except when directly threatened.[169] While he was a long shot to win the Republican nomination, he no doubt had enough support to make his agenda heard at the national convention and more and more people seemed open to what once perceived as a radical position.

So it is clear that a new world order will take place in the next few years as either the United Nations or another entity stepping in to fill the void the United States will vacate as policeman of the world. But with a world-wide debt crisis there are very few countries that have the resources or the will to do the job. So it is clear that the job will fall into the lap of a reformed United

Nations; but the way it is currently set up, the question is can it get the job done?

United Nations Sanctions

The most effective tool the UN presently has and can apply in enforcing its deed is "political sanctions" against any member/country. Its enforcement of such policy was an effective tool against then apartheid South Africa

In 2003, UN sanctions on Liberia's profitable timber trade along with other sanctions, contributed to the demise of President Charles Taylor, who was charged with war crimes.

Libya is an example of success with such sanctions. Due to sanctions Muammar el-Qaddafi took responsibility for the 1988 Lockerbie bombings and vowed to end seeking weapons of mass destruction in order to normalize relations with the United States in 2006.

In the former Yugoslavia arms and economic sanctions subsequent to the war with Croatia weakened the regime of Slobodan Milosevic and aided in the succession by the Dayton Accords in 1995. It should be noted however, that sanctions did not alter the regime's behavior, which brought about sanctions again for treatment of ethnic Albanians in Kosovo in 1998.

Not all sanctions have been as successful. In the 1990's UN sanctions against Iraq set off brutal humanitarian issues spawning the oil-for-food program. Although the program helped feed Iraqis, corruption enabled Saddam's regime to take in an estimated $11 billion during the sanctions.[170]

UN arms embargoes against African states at war failed against Somalia and Rwanda in the 1990s, and the civil wars in Angola and Sierra Leone. UN sanctions against the Afghanistan

Taliban regime did not curb the Taliban leadership activities or stop al-Qaeda. The Security Council of the United Nations is the body of the organization that is charged with maintaining peace and security among all of the member countries. While other branches of the United Nations can only issue recommendations to member countries, the Security Council can make binding decisions.[171]

There are five permanent members of the council, the United States, China, France, Russia, and the United Kingdom. And there are ten members who are not permanent who serves two years terms. The current members are Colombia, India, Togo, South Africa, Portugal, Pakistan, Morocco, Guatemala, Germany, and Azerbaijan.

The problem in the past in getting things done, is that any of the permanent members can veto a resolution with only one vote. While the United Kingdom, France, and the United States tend to vote in a block, they have been stymied on numerous occasions by China and Russia. China and Russia have several times had their initiatives stopped by one of the three other permanent members. Hence the problem in getting the United Nations to act in several places where they may be required to help restore order and save human lives.

Initial Problems That Have Persisted to this Day

There has been some progress made in the years since the Cold War ended, and the United Nations has come to agreement to intervene several times over the last 20 years. But despite the gains that have been made during this time there is still one sticking point, and it involves Israel and the Middle East.

A large amount of time is spent by the United Nations in debating issues, resolutions, and other matters that are related to the Israeli-Arab conflict. This is a result of one of the first resolutions of the United Nations General Assembly that provided for the partitioning of Palestine in 1947.[172] While the plan to partition the land into Jewish and Arab states seemed like the right decision at the time, it has caused a great deal of grief in the years since. If the United Nations is going to be successful in maintaining peace in this region, some changes in the make-up of the Security Council may be necessary. Since this ongoing conflict takes up so much time, there is little left to work on protecting human rights in other parts of the world. A permanent solution to this problem needs to be reached, and the actions need to come from the United Nations, and not the United States or Israel. Part of the problem is that the United Nations lacks the necessary tools or military muscle it needs to get the job done in an effective manner.

Resolving Problems with the United Nations so They May Better Resolve Global Problems

Since the balance of power and wealth in the world has changed since World War II, it would seem obvious that the make-up of the United Nations Security Council should change as well. Germany, Japan, and the Czech Republic all have strong economies and influence and would be excellent additions to the UN Security Council. Japan and Germany would be logical choices since the Security Council attempts to balance power between the eastern and western parts of the world.

Other steps that could be taken could be to move some of the powers of the Security Council to the General Assembly. Military interventions and other action could be based on a majority vote by the General Assembly. Another step that could be taken is to remove the power of a nation on the Security Council to veto a military intervention with a single vote.

Once problems within the United Nations have been resolved, steps need to be taken to strengthen the military forces of the United Nations so they can be ready to respond to hot spots anywhere in the world within a matter of hours. Once these steps have been taken, the United Nations will have what it needs to help in human rights matters, take a bigger role in nation building and promotion of democracy, and take its place and fulfill what it was intended to do when it was founded, to lead a New World Order where war is not the answer to conflicts. And once there is a permanent solution to the Arab-Israeli conflict, there will be more time to focus on human rights issues.

To fail in this regard will result in more loss of life through wars, more starvation and human rights violations, and the possible risk of nuclear warfare between the countries that today have a bomb, and there are several scattered throughout the world that have them. For these reasons, it is imperative to address the problems now in the United Nations to make them a relevant entity capable of taking action and passing effective resolutions that will make a difference to the people who need them the most.

The Future of the United Nations

The future of the United Nations may not be as strong as anyone may think. At the beginning, the United Nations' goal was to "to promote international cooperation and to achieve peace and security."[173] In addition to this, they had a goal of promoting social progress, better living standards, and human rights. After World War II, this was really important, as the world had been fragmented by the war. Bringing the countries together was seen as a way to heal from the war and help to heal the animosities between the countries.

While most people know the term, United Nations, most people do not have any idea what its purpose is now in this day and age. Since we are not in time of a world war, they are supposed to be mainly concerned with the social issues of people in the world, as well as peacekeeping. However, many people are clamoring that they are not doing the job that they were created to do. With the high number of people who do not have safe drinking water or regular meals, frustration with the system can be understood. The United Nations has four main goals today:

- To keep peace throughout the world by serving as a peacekeeping agency
- To develop friendly relations among nations
- To help nations work together to improve the lives of poor people, to conquer hunger, disease and illiteracy, and to encourage respect for each other's rights and freedoms
- To be a center for harmonizing the actions of nations to achieve these goals[174]

The goal of helping nations work together to improve the lives of poor people is a hotly contested one. One of the biggest complaints is that "The UN has partnered with bodies who have never exhibited the slightest sensitivity to the world's poor—other than as a potential market for many dubious products necessity."[175] This is unfortunate that this has occurred, as they are supposed to increase the living standards of people all over the world, rather than just a select few—mainly corporations. Corporations are making money off of the misfortune of the people of other worlds, which is not why the United Nations was formed.

This corporatizing of the United Nations is what many people are crying foul about. They do not want this to be what the UN is about. "Corporatization of the UN effectively commenced at the Earth Summit in 1992 when the UN refused to circulate the recommendations of its Centre on Transnational Corporations concerning protection of weaker countries from predatory corporations through their appropriate regulation."[176] While this Centre was dissolved the next year, this was seen as the beginning of the end for the United Nations if changes are not made in several different areas.

"The way the United Nations regards international business has changed fundamentally. This shift towards a stance more favorable to business is being nurtured from the very top."[177] Being more favorable to business means that they are putting money into corporation's pockets, however, on the backs of people who are struggling to survive. They are creating products to help them, but these products are not given to the people, they are sold to the people. This is a direction that the UN definitely needs to change. Why are they moving to this direction? Because the UN itself is short on funds and are struggling to survive.

This shortage of funds is clearly seen in the fact that they threatened that they were unable to pay monthly salaries to civil servants. They have to find a way to add funds to their coffers if they have any chance of a future. This can be done in many different ways, from sponsorships to sales or rentals of services to corporate philanthropy to theme parks and more. The key is being open to these financial strategies to be sure that they have money to function in the way that they were created to. Finding that magic solution is said to be the most difficult part.

Mismanaging the funds that they do have is an issue as well. A report released in 2012 found that the UNHCR or United Nations High Commissioner for Refugees has misappropriated funds and has all around had sloppy bookkeeping. This mishandling of funds of the member countries may imperil future contributions, which could have an impact upon the people that they are trying to help. "This is a major risk for UNHCR," the auditors warned, "given the increasing pressures on donors to justify why they provide public funds to international aid organizations."[178] Although UNHCR says that they have made changes, time will tell the tale and this means that we will not really know if they have made the changes for years to come.

Another issue that is seen with the United Nations is the fact that they have seemed to turn a blind eye on some of the atrocities that have occurred in the world. Darfur, Sudan, Iran, and North Korea are just a few of the places where proliferation and genocide have occurred and many people wonder why the UN did not take a strong stance against these instances. This seemingly lack of attention is something that many people do not understand, as one of the main jobs of the UN is to keep the peace and they do not see this as happening. This is largely due to the way that the Security Council is set up with its five-member council voting on issues such as this.

Reforms must be made in the Security Council. Without these reforms, the United Nations will lose most of its power and legitimacy. The fact that five members are making decisions that affect the world is concerning. Having a consensus is almost impossible in any decision making and this causes difficulties in making an impact in the world in the way that they need to. They each have different political agendas as well, which is another issue that causes dissension within their group and makes issues impossible for them to come to any sound decisions.

A report after the 2010 conference came to these conclusions. "The efficiency of the UN development system and the need to reform it has been much discussed but with little progress and with gathering frustration and concern. The core problem is decision making; the historical design of the system and its fragmentation has resulted in the lack of any overall control which is not subject to the national interest of members."[179] The absence of a central government to make decisions is one of the biggest issues of the UN and could be causing irreparable damage that will be hard for them to bounce back from. This would take constitutional reform, which is almost impossible. They need to change with the times and so far they are not up for that as of yet.

Does the UN have a future? Only if genuine reforms are made and they are adhered to. Constitutional reforms, as well as Security Council reforms, will have to be made if the UN has a chance of being able to effectively do their job in the future. They must be able to respond to practical situations to be effective and this will take some changes that many believe will not be made. They also must be able to adapt to how the world is changing as well. Change is hard for any group, however, even when we are talking about change that could help the world to be a better place.

Universal cooperation is something that the UN greatly needs, but with the many different political agendas, as well as countries and cultures, this cooperation is difficult to find and this causes major issues when they are trying to make decisions for the good of the world, as well as separate countries. Most of the issues are attributed to the United States, which is something that most people do not realize. Other countries see this issue as "The US wants to use the UN to tell everyone else what they must do and is increasingly willing to use its power to bully and punish those who get in its way."[180] This is an issue that the United States needs to confront to be sure that we are working toward a cooperative system as much as possible to build a world that is committed to international justice. The U.S. is seen as the big bully in the UN, this harms the reputation of the US, and causes other countries to not back the U.S. agendas in some cases.

The question is "will they be prepared to accept the structures that are largely tailored as western liberal internationalism of the 20th century?"[181] Countries are changing and the UN needs to change with them to be able to meet the needs of the emerging world. Finding that middle ground is an important part of the UN being able to face the future strong and applicable to the world. With unity and reform, the United Nations could be restored to the peacekeeping and social problem solving function that was the reason for its creation in the first place.

Effective laws need to be in-place, well planned scenarios and action plans ahead of conflicts, rather than on-going arguments or discussions in the midst of crisis or conflicts!!! Rules of engagements need to be drafted and set in the books prior to conflicts.

Chapter IX. Green Environment and Technology for all

Providing a healthy, sustainable environment for generations to use is the prime responsibility of mankind. Excessive use of materials, or lack of attention to the environment that any individual or industry leaves behind for services or production they use can become disastrous on the long run. Responsible use of resources at all levels of society need to be controlled by an international body, through their respective societies or members. Rapid extraction of raw materials may affect the production level of different business enterprises, and hence certain prosperity levels at particular society. However, the process needs to be managed and controlled by an international body for the good of all nations to benefit. Same is valid with pollution level, industrial output effects, water and sanitary measures for mankind. In some cases, it may affect industrial development, or even business expansion and operating interests. Land use for resource allocation program across the globe can be regarded as a method to curb such a need—opium cultivation in Afghanistan, over fishing in North Seas, use of nuclear technology, etc.

Application of new technologies across the globe has similar impacts on development programs and business expansion, affecting all mankind. Intellectual property rights need to be reinforced to benefit the author(s); however with limited duration and reward to allow its application on a broad international basis for mankind. Medications, certain achievements in design, or products benefiting prosperity and well-being of people in different societies need to become available to all with an international protection mechanism for the author(s) in a meaningful, acceptable manner to benefit all. Therefore, this measure also needs to be governed by an international body, in cooperation with all nations concerned—a strong, workable UN.

Green Environment and Technology For all

The modern environmental movement was spawned in 1970 with the inception of Earth Day. At the time, Americans were driving V-8 muscle cars that used leaded gas, factories released pollutants into the air and into rivers and streams without consequences, and air pollution was accepted as the price that had to be paid for prosperity. With the inception of this event, people slowly began to take notice of their environment and the deadly effects of man's thumb on the balance of nature. Today, with green technology that has only recently become available, nations have the ability to produce the energy needed for the general public and for industries without pollution and depletion of vital natural resources that future generations will need.

Now there are many green measures being taken to reduce energy costs, preserve natural resources, and lessen the negative impact we have on the earth. These include many individual opportunities and choices such as installing solar panels, heat pumps, and energy efficient appliances and windows, recycling, and purchasing electric vehicles. Large scale measures for government and industry include reducing carbon emissions, utilizing wind power, geothermal energy, researching renewable energy sources, and examining current processes in order to increase efficiency and reduce pollution.

A Short History of the Environmental Movement and Legislation in the United States

In the year 1970, President Richard M. Nixon helped to create the Environmental Protection Agency (EPA). This agency was charged with the task of enforcing laws that are designed to protect the environment and the public health. The Clean Air Act was passed in 1977, and it was designed to regulate air emissions and gave the EPA the power to set air quality standards for all states. This law was later revised in 1977 and in 1990 to deal with the problems such as depletion of the ozone layer and acid rain.

Other groundbreaking legislation that took place during this decade include the Clean Water Act, which helps to protect the quality of surface water as well as manage polluted run-offs in an effect to protect the public and the wildlife of the nation. The Toxic Substances Control Act of 1976 gave the EPA power to track chemicals used in mostly manufacturing to determine if they pose a threat to humans or wildlife, and ban them if it is deemed that they do.

These and other initiatives passed in the years since have made a difference in the lives of Americans. Large urban areas that were once plagued with smog and pollution are now in much better shape and enjoy much healthier air than they did back in the 1970's.

Similar measures must be implemented and the funds devoted for research for country and industry specific and possibly new processes that reduce pollution in all countries.

Industrial Growth in Developing Countries Results in More Pollution

Industrial growth in countries such as India, China, Thailand, and other Far East countries have come at the expense of the environment in those countries and will eventually affect the world. A rapidly growing population and cheap labor have made these countries the choice for companies in the West and other parts of the world who are looking to outsource labor-intensive manufacturing in order to lower expenses and raise their profit margins.

Since the cost of living in these countries is low, the jobs have been welcomed with open arms and have helped many impoverished areas of these countries, but at what price? Today China and other countries from the region are facing an environmental crisis that is worse than what America faced in the 1970's. The water in many parts of China is no longer safe to drink.[186] Pollution is killing off aquatic life by cutting off their oxygen supply. China is also experiencing a dramatic increase in dust storms. These storms can also become deadly as they can pick up airborne toxins from the factories in the region. These storms are known to have spread as far as the United States, increasing tensions between the two countries. And these problems are only the tip of the iceberg of the mounting environmental problems in China and the Far East. Clearly, something must be done quickly or the future of coming generations will be compromised by polluted water and air, and the health care costs could put an end to the boom in this region.

Is Green Technology the Answer for China and the Far East?

Green technology is an evolving field that can help to provide methods, materials, and techniques for generating energy from non-toxic clean products, as well as providing sustainable design features—for products and services alike. The goals of green technology are to provide sustainability, to meet the needs of society without damaging or using up natural resources. It also helps to reduce waste and pollution by changing the manner factories are performing. The technology also strives to be viable, by creating technologies and products that benefit the environment, and people and provide careers for people in new industries.

There are several green energy applications available to mankind. By far the most important and pressing need is reduction in fossil fuels applications as the prime source of energy. It involves the development of alternatives to fossil fuels and new means of generating efficient energy. However, the initial design features play a great role in delivering the solutions. Green building technology is a wide application that involves everything from where a building is located to the choice of materials involved in constructing it. Green nanotechnology is the manipulation of materials on the nanometer scale that has the potential to change the method or manner the products are manufactured. It also encompasses the applications of green chemistry and green engineering principles that have the promise of revolutionizing everything in the manufacturing world. Governments can also get involved on the act with environmentally preferred purchasing. This is the search for products that have contents and methods of production that have the very smallest negative impact on the environment. While not all of these methods are viable at this time, the technology is evolving and improving on almost a daily basis, and the future will depend on engineers, scientists, and governments working together to make them a reality.

Green Technology That Can be utilized today and in the Future in the United States and Other Developing Nations

The time is coming when the demand for energy will outstrip the supply. Even in the United States, electric companies struggle in the summer months to supply their customers and rolling black outs have become more and more common every year. New technology must be utilized to meet this demand without further polluting the environment and using precious natural resources that are not infinite in supply. One green technology that can be utilized today is off-shore wind farms. Off-shore wind farms in Europe and other locations around the world have shown that they have the potential to be a viable alternative energy source that is cost-effective. New designs in wind turbines have made them much more able to withstand the elements and avoid costly maintenance that plagued the older type of turbine. The means are becoming available that would allow this energy to be outsourced to other countries, but until then the best way to utilize this technology is to build them in areas where the terrain is relatively flat and the wind is known to be blowing on a regular basis. With these stronger turbines, it should result in a quicker return on investment.

Another green energy technology that can be utilized as an energy source is energy from waste. There has been a great deal of debate over whether this is a viable source because of the potential health risks from fumes that are produced during the conversion process. It can also be said that it goes against everything that recycling stands for. But the simple fact of the matter is that waste is always going to be produced. And it is much more desirable to use it for energy production than just be buried somewhere in a landfill. And there is no scientific evidence at this point in time that shows fumes from production can lead to disease or other maladies.

Other green energy technology that looks promising, apart from variety of solar systems, is wave and tidal stream marine energy. It is one of the cleanest and most sustainable sources of energy available and a perfect solution for a country such as China that has an abundance of rivers, streams, and coastlines. The problem with this emerging energy source is the need to construct massive power plants on the coastlines, which is most always opposed by the residents of the area. Plus, the plant itself will require a considerable amount of capital to construct since it must be built ruggedly to withstand the destructive elements of the oceans, which can be powerful and destructive. This technology is probably a few years away from becoming viable, but it still commands attention because of the awesome power potential they hold.

Geothermal Energy

Another promising source of energy, which is being tapped in Europe since early 80's, is geothermal energy to lower the extreme demands of HVAC systems in buildings. Geothermal energy is heat from the ground found almost everywhere in the world. This energy source can be utilized in power stations or simple pumping systems, or even in residential dwellings. Geothermal energy is an inexpensive source being tapped now in many parts of the world. This is also a healthier energy that reduces global warming and dependency on fossil fuels.

Magma is the hot molten rock located below the earth's crust. The heat generated in the earth occurs naturally and is estimated to be 50,000 times more energy than all the oil and natural gas resources in the world. Enhanced Geothermal Systems (EGS) technology, enables the use of this heat for electricity production.

For every 100 meters you go below ground, the temperature of the ground increases about 3 degrees Celsius. Or for every 328 feet below ground, the temperature increases 5.4 degrees Fahrenheit. At 10,000 feet below ground, the temperature of the ground would be hot enough to boil water. Deep under the surface, water sometimes makes its way close to the hot rock and turns into boiling hot water or into steam. The hot water can reach temperatures of more than 300 degrees Fahrenheit (148 degrees Celsius). This is hotter than boiling water (212 degrees F / 100 degrees C). It doesn't turn into steam because it is under pressure.

Ground-source heat pumps tap geothermal energy and provide heat and cooling to buildings. Utilizing the 50°F constant year round temperature only a few feet below the ground's surface, they pump air or antifreeze liquid underground and then circulate in the structure. Liquid removes heat from the building into the ground in warm weather and supplies warmed air and water to the building in cold weather.

Geothermal energy heat pumps are the most energy-efficient and environmentally clean heating and cooling system available in some areas of extreme temperatures. According to the U.S.

Department of Energy heat pumps can save the average home enough money to pay for themselves hundreds of dollars in 8 to 12 years. Ground-source heat pumps furnish climate control in U.S. homes and buildings. Geothermal heat pumps are more costly to install, especially in existing structures as they require below ground excavations.

Geothermal plants currently produce 25 percent or more of electricity in the Philippines, Iceland, and El Salvador and in California more than 40 geothermal plants provide nearly 5 percent of the state's electricity. While the toxic gas hydrogen sulfide and traces of arsenic and minerals is released in the steam, there is a closed loop system with no emissions.

Iceland receives more than half of its energy from geothermal sources with most buildings in the country heated with hot spring water.

The Future of Geothermal Energy

Geothermal energy is an exciting source for electricity and climate control that has great potential. This is a renewable energy that can supply continuous efficient power with lower environmental impact. Electricity produced by geothermal facilities has been declining in cost. For geothermal energy to reach its' full potential, Enhanced Geothermal Systems (EGS) and production of geothermal electricity in oil and gas wells need further development.

Enhanced Geothermal Systems (EGS)

Enhanced Geothermal Systems pump water into dry areas where it does not circulate naturally. Plants pump water below the surface to break up rock and then through the broken hot rocks to create steam to generate electricity. The U.S. Department of Energy in collaboration with universities, corporations such as Google, the current industry on more research for the potential of this hot dry rock. Currently the countries such as Australia, France, Germany, and Japan are also funding research on EGS.

Co-production of Geothermal Electricity in Oil and Gas Wells.

Under, the American Recovery and Investment Act of 2009, $400 million of new funding was allocated to the DOE's Geothermal Technologies Program. One of recent methods of oil extraction from underground shale layers, using chemicals and high-pressure steam, known as "Fracking" are claimed to be endangering the environment. Admittedly, more investments would be needed to reduce the negative impact of current energy extraction technologies that have on the environment, and to ensure everyone will benefit from cleaner and more sustainable energy resources in the future.

It's clear that this will be a key century in the history of humans, and many other living species on this planet. With a population that is growing and putting more strain on present power grids and demanding more fossil fuel that is not infinite in supply, at some point something will have to be done. The planning needs to start now and the United States, China, and other top manufacturing countries need to join together and start a green technology initiative before it is too late, if it is not already too late. All of the future generations of humans and animals on this planet are depending on it.

The Origins of Extracting Natural Resources, Pollution and Environmentalism

As defined by Merriam Webster, *Pollution* is referred to as "the action of environmental degradation and contamination with man-made waste". Our world has rapidly changed in a few hundred years. Rapid economic growth, industrialization, urbanization, and exponential population growth have undermined the very existence of human race and the planet Earth.

Although such changes have contributed positively to technological advancements, leisure, one-click communications, global trade; the renaissance has also resulted in undermining our long-term sustainability and survival.

The negative consequences of growth and technological developments are simply immeasurable. Industrial wastage, chemical pesticides, sewage, and reckless burning of fossil fuels have put forth the monumental risks of Global Warming, Ozone depletion, and unpredictable climatic changes.

However the international scenario has experienced an increasing environmental awareness amongst thinkers, industrialists, activists and government officials. There is a heated debate raging between technological advancements and the associated effects of such change. Various environmental activists have successfully highlighted this issue and earned acceptance on the international front. A number of awards including the prestigious Nobel Peace Prize have been awarded to various non-profit organizations and individuals working towards building a sustainable future. Mr. Al Gore is just one of the successful individuals who helped increase awareness for ecological preservation and reducing carbon footprints.

Yet there has been much resistance to change and even discounting of the effects of environmental impacts such as global warming by industry and subsequently politicians. Meeting standards that reduce carbon emissions or other pollution controls for production and products themselves cost manufacturers money and affect their profit margins. Often this is no more than short sighted greed being exhibited by the people who will profit from polluting the environment.

In the U.S., opposition has come in the form of political campaign contributions and lobbyists that represent large corporations. Numerous U.S. based companies have moved production operations to other countries not just for cheaper labor but to take advantage of less stringent environmental controls.

History of Pollution

The menace of pollution has accompanied human kind from prehistoric ages. The lighting of the first *Fire* initiated the process of air pollution. Researchers have discovered the presence of carbon and soot in prehistoric caves associated with improper ventilation. As civilizations progressed, the need to develop improved weapons took over. Stone weapons were replaced with metal ones. The *forging of metal* is collectively designated as the key turning point in increasing air pollution. Scientists have collected samples from Greenland glaciers, and arrived at the discovery of carbon arising from metal production in Greek, Roman and Chinese civilizations.

The first major revolution which compelled human race to transform from hunting and gathering to agriculture and settling is the *Neolithic agricultural Revolution (8000-5000 BC)*. This change represented a wide-scale transition of human culture and paved the way for later developments in pollution. Societies developed a sedentary lifestyle and thus boosted sewerage and sanitation problems. Agricultural farming and cattle-farming lands were created after the removal of natural landscape and habitats fostering natural ecosystems. This practice not only forced animals to migrate but also resulted in water logging and soil erosion. This radical modification of natural environment resulted in specialized crop cultivation. Scarcity of food was not an issue anymore; surplus of food subsequently encouraged population growth. The sedentary lifestyle was marked by an exponential growth and spread of diseases, arising from domestication of animals and inadequate sanitary practices.

The world then experienced a brief period of no-growth or obscurity characterized as *Dark or Middle Ages*. This period succeeds after the fall of Rome and stretches from the 5th to the 13th century. Historians regard this age as a period of intellectual scarcity, no technological developments, depopulation, de-urbanization and increased barbaric activity. Much of the classical literature which was lost during the epitome of Middle Ages was gathered or retranslated. This revival of knowledge paved the way to enlightenment during the end of Middle Ages, historically known as *High Middle Ages.* The period stretching from 11th to the 13th century featured increasing population, certain technological developments, and increased militarization. Interaction with the Islamic world and the migration of intellectuals to Europe paved the way for the period we know as *Renaissance.*

The period from 14th to the 16th century, also known as Renaissance was the age of scientific revolution. Significant advancements were made in the fields of printing press, metallurgy and mining, iron forging and smelting, and weaponry. All these developments greatly benefitted the human race, but also initiated an unending cycle of environmental degradation. Knowledge was spread at the cost of cutting down trees and violating the ecological system. Iron and steel products created carbon emissions and negatively affected our atmosphere. Even though the Renaissance was more of an intellectual and cultural revival, it resulted in bringing more harm to the planet Earth.

But what really altered the world as we see it today is the *Industrial Revolution (1750-1850).* The technological changes arising from the industrial revolution influenced every aspect of everyday life—economic, social, political and cultural. The spark of intellectual revival originated in United Kingdom and eventually spread to the rest of the world. The profound effects resulted in an exponential growth in average per capita income and population growth worldwide. Statisticians noted that during the two centuries after 1800, the average per capita income increased by over ten times. This improvement in general living standards prompted population to increase by over six times as compared to 1800.

Mechanization

The 18th century brought great improvements in the field of machine-based manufacturing. The invention of iron and steel making on a commercial basis and the introduction of all-metal machine manufacturing facilitated the production of other machineries to be used in multiple industries. During the initial phase of the Industrial Revolution, steam engine was invented. This mechanical invention consumed coal as the primary source of energy. The steam engine brought drastic changes, affecting nearly all spheres of life. Transportation was radically improved where rail engines utilized steam power to cover long distances in a short span of time. The consumption of steam to fuel machineries also impacted industrial production. Textile manufacturing which initially was limited to a small scale was altered to manufacture final goods on a continuous and mass-production basis. Increased usage of coal and improper dumping of industrial wastage from a multitude of manufacturing companies adversely affected the environment.

The second phase of the Industrial Revolution experienced the discovery of oil and the invention of internal combustion engine and electrical power generation to produce energy for the respective industries. Even though the internal combustion engine was only moderately efficient in terms of carbon emissions, the process of exploiting Mother Nature by extracting fossil fuels continued. Initially only coal was utilized to generate steam power; however internal-combustion mechanism required burning of another non-renewable fossil fuel—*Oil*. Fossil fuels such as coal and oil, and other natural resources including water, trees and land were recklessly exploited for farming, clearing land for housing societies, creating electricity, driving locomotives and fueling industries.

Therefore it was the Industrial Revolution that eventually led to the development of the notion—*Environmental Pollution*, as we know it today.

The Impact of World Wars on the Environment

Even though many individuals and prominent thinkers attribute World Wars as a requirement for ending hostility and aggression and enforcing global peace; it is noteworthy to acknowledge that both the World Wars had devastating effects on our environment. The unending race between nations to prove their respective military superiority resulted in the discovery of an advance form of armaments and weapons.

The World War II witnessed the testing of *Nuclear Weapons* on two Japanese cities—Nagasaki and Hiroshima. Apart from immediate human deaths and total annihilation of two major cities around the world, the environment suffered from bombing, landmines and the radioactive proliferation arising from nuclear weapons.

Even after World War II ended, major superpowers continued to create, examine and test enhanced and more destructive versions of nuclear and many other weapons. Significant threats of World War III were quite imminent during the Cold War era. Development and sale of chemical and biological weapons of mass-destruction, initiated by the super-powers, and later delivered to tyrannical allies such as Saddam Hussein later became liabilities for the supplying countries! (Please expand on Iraq War, with not finding the WMD, however he used the chemicals received from the US and Germany against Kurds!).

Extraction of Natural Resources

The last few centuries have experienced an exponential increase in population, industrialization, and consumerism. All of these stated factors and other variables combine to result in a reckless approach towards extracting natural resources.

It is imperative to note that man has exploited and extracted Mother Nature in a method faster than the recovery rate. This has resulted to an extent where the intricate web of biodiversity and ecological balance has been disturbed.

Certain philosophers, including His Holiness the Dalai Lama has even said that, *"Without humans the world would be better off"*. It is a universal fact that the very existence of human race is dependent on the presence of natural resources. However environmental activists and conservationists that article do not suggest that mankind should despise knowledge and technology, revert to the Stone Age and completely abstain from extracting natural resource.

But driven by greediness, humans have exploited and over-extracted natural resources, attributed mechanisms which add to the pollution and ecological disaster and put in danger the very survival of our planet and the future generations.

The key word to be considered here is *'Survival'* and not *'Gluttony'*. Extraction and consumption of world's resources should be driven by moderation and bare necessity. However the vicious rules of our world are set by factors such as *Demand* and *Supply*. With wealth disparity touching new heights, free market apparatus has equally failed as the Command and Control of the infrastructure.

The process of commercially extracting natural resources developed in the 19th century. Since then the consumption of resources for basic consumption, energy needs, and commodities has exponentially increased during the 20th and the 21st centuries.

Presently there are three major forms of exploiting natural resources:

1. Meeting Energy Needs through Fossil Fuels

Scientists have estimated that roughly 80% of all energy needs are met by fossil fuels. Fossil fuels majorly comprise of oil, gas and coal and are non-renewable in nature. Non-renewable means that once consumed it is nearly impossible for Mother Nature to replace or reproduce the resource. This is the case because fossil fuels are formed over a period spread over millions of years. The problem lies in the fact that man is consuming these resources at such a faster rate that the depletion is way greater than the rate at which these resources are formed.

To worsen the situation, the burning of fossil fuels produce a staggering amount of *Carbon Dioxide*—approximately 21.3 billion tons of CO_2 per annum. It is estimated that natural processes (fauna and trees) can absorb only half of the CO_2 produced by man. This excess of 10.65 billion tons of CO_2 every year is disturbing the delicate balance of our atmosphere. It should also be noted that carbon dioxide is a *Greenhouse Gas* and the excess of this element in our environment contributes to trapping excessive sunrays in Earth's atmosphere. This phenomenon of rising temperature is termed as *Global Warming* and results in adverse atmospheric and climatic changes—melting of polar ice leads to rising sea levels, which in turn results in flooding of below sea level cities and islands. Skin diseases, extreme weather conditions, and extinction of natural species (fauna, plants, animals, birds, insects and reptiles) are only some of the devastating effects of global warming.

2.   Extracting Subsoil Minerals

Initially man utilized precious minerals for minimum usage, such as forging weapons, art and jewelry, and creating coins or currency. However as technology progressed, man started using these rare minerals for industrial and commodity purposes. Resources such as Aluminum and other metals were excessively utilized in heavy machineries as well as everyday necessities. Initially valued higher than gold and silver, aluminum was used exclusively as ornaments and exhibition items. The invention of Hall-Heroult process removed the difficulties in extracting aluminum from ores, thus leading to excessive extraction and a significant decline in prices. Today aluminum is extensively utilized for:

- Transportation (airplanes, automobiles, trucks, bicycles, etc.)
- Packaging (foils and cans)
- Construction material (aluminum windows and doors)
- Cooking appliances, utensils and crockery
- Consumer electronic products (computers and cameras)

Mankind has not only experienced but also culture based on consumerism and provision of extravagant commodities has fueled reckless extraction of precious minerals. It is also essential to understand that these minerals are naturally formed over a long duration and are practically non-renewable in nature.

3.   Agricultural Farming, Deforestation and Destruction of Natural Landscape

The population explosion which occurred in the last two hundred years has placed significant constraints on the resources of our planet. Increased population translated into an ever increasing need to fulfill the food and housing requirements. Various unsustainable methods of Intensive Farming were developed. This form of agriculture is starkly contrasted with Organic or Extensive Farming. Intensive farming involves increased mechanization and use of chemical fertilizers and pesticides to artificially boost agricultural growth.

Even though this modern-day intensive farming has greatly enhanced agricultural output; it has led to a dramatic increase in environmental pollution as well as disturbing the ecological balance. Synthetic agricultural commodities have adversely affected our environment by poisoning waterways (rivers, lakes and eventually oceans) and eroding soil.

Abundance of short-term crop solutions (pesticides and chemicals to protect crops against pests and insects) has not only increased health hazards for humans; it has also poisoned water channels and underground aquifers, thus destroying natural life present within rivers and lakes. Increased use of machines for farming requires burning of fossil fuels to generate the needed energy.

However before even initiating the food production cycle, humans often resort to clearing forests to attain arable land for farming. Deforestation is termed as clearing of trees from forestland for the following purposes:

- Agricultural Farming
- Cattle Farming
- Urban usage (Housing and settlement)
- Timber

Deforestation incurs devastating effects for the environment: Soil erosion, reduction in natural CO_2 absorbing mechanism, loss of habitat and biodiversity, extinction of a wide variety of living species, adverse climatic effects, and desertification.

Due to lack of knowledge, skills and expertise; deforestation is often achieved by burning down precious resources. Burning of trees add to the amount of CO_2 in the atmosphere. In developed countries, trees are recklessly cut down by advanced machineries for timber needs.

Industrial Pollution

Industrial Pollution is one of the leading contributors of pollution world-wide. Fossil fuels burned during the production process and improper disposal of industrial wastage in waterways are some of the major causes of industrial pollution.

Extensive research has been carried out to identify the specific industries which cause industrial pollution. Industries have been divided into six major categories on the basis of their nature of activities and contribution to industrial wastage:

1. **Toxic and Non-Toxic Chemicals**

   a. Fertilizers and Pesticides
   b. Cleaning Agents (Detergents)
   c. Paints
   d. Plastics and Resins
   e. Acids
   f. Explosive and Toxic Chemicals
   g. Rubber
   h. Cement

2. **Food and Pharmaceutical Products**

   a. Meat Production
   b. Poultry
   c. Fishing
   d. Agriculture
   e. Brewed and Carbonated Beverages

      f.   Canned products

      g.   Palm Oil

      h.   Pharmaceutical medicines and solutions

3. **Apparels and Textiles**

      a.   Leather goods

      b.   Textiles

      c.   Dry cleaning and Laundry processes

4. **Energy**

      a.   Coal

      b.   Petroleum

      c.   Bio-fuel

      d.   Oil and Gas Refineries

5. **Nuclear Generation and Radioactive materials**

6. **Other Miscellaneous Materials and Commodities**

   Pulp and Paper production

      a.   Steel

      b.   Metal

      c.   Iron

      d.   Timber

It is interesting to note that the presence of industrial pollution dates back to ancient times; however the industrial revolution significantly propelled this process. Nations and governments have yet to understand that they possess a collective responsibility for the entire planet, as the drastic effects of industrial pollution are not restricted by specific regional boundaries. Scientists are anxious to discover carbon particles and industrial pollutants in the barren tundra of Antarctica.

Awareness about Pollution

The need for environmental protection was recognized as early as 1272. A royal decree was passed by King Edward I to officially ban the burning of sea-coal in London. The *Great Stink on the Thames (1858)* and the worst air pollution incident in the history of Great Britain—*Great Smog (1952)* lead to public awareness, government regulations, and pollution acts.

Such events compelled activists and government officials in United Kingdom and subsequently in United States to enact environmental legislation, such as *The Clean Air Act (1956), Noise Control Act, Clean Water Act,* and *National Environmental Policy Act.*

Various organizations emerged and were created to safeguard and protect the environment. Some of the famous institutions include *United States Environmental Protection Agency* and *World watch Institute.*

International environment catastrophes such as the *Three Mile Island incident, Chernobyl nuclear disaster, Bhopal gas tragedy,* and numerous oil spills have resulted in creating and strengthening social and environmental protection movements across the globe.

Environmentalism is a growing philosophy to restore, preserve, conserve and improve the overall health of the environment by advocating a balanced relationship between humans and the encompassing biological environment of planet Earth.

Water Wastage, Sanitation and Land use Principles

I   Water Conservation and Treatment Principles

The water preservation notion is based on the principles of conservation, efficiency in usage and recycling. Such practices involve identifying and treating water leakages and introducing efficient irrigation methods—*Drip Irrigation System*. This water efficiency concept has also been introduced in commercial applications such as household appliances and sanitary plumbing. Reusing wastewater after proper treatment for toilet flushing and watering gardens is also an increasing custom.

II Land Ethics

The philosophy of *Land Ethics* extends the boundaries ethics to include nonhuman elements and organisms referred to as *"Biotic Community"*. This holistic and collective deliberation compels humans to consider the negative effects of any of his activities on animals, water, soil, and plants.

Various philosophers and thinkers have put forth multiple variants of Land Ethics. Some of the most prominent are:

- Ecologically based Land Ethics
- Egalitarian based Land Ethics
- Utilitarian focused Land Ethics
- Libertarian based Land Ethics
- Economic based Land Ethics

Recycling is not the only solution

It has long been advocated that *'Recycling'* is the only possible solution for conserving natural resources, preserving ecological balance and reducing pollution. It can be true in certain scenarios, but as often falsely misunderstood, recycling is not synonymous to being *'Green'*.

This is particularly true for scenarios where recycling only resort to reusing already used materials. Recycling does not address the dilemma of curbing the profound desire which lies at the heart of excessive needs and wants.

What is the Real Solution? Educating Environmental Respect

Instilling environmental respect through fundamental changes in the education system and curriculum is the need of time. It is futile to expect individuals to care for the environment if they lack basic understanding and practical experience pertaining to environment conservation and protection. The revised curriculum should comprise of a complete overhaul and inclusion of *'Environmentalism'* and educational trips and visits.

It is essential to include a quotation from Aldo Leopold,

"There are two dangers in not owning a farm. One is the danger of supposing that breakfast comes from the grocery, and the other, that heat comes from the furnace."

Barry Commoner's four laws of ecology would serve as a starting point for the reformed universal environmental education:

1. There is no such thing as a 'Free Lunch'.
2. Nature knows best.
3. Everything must go somewhere.
4. Everything is connected to everything else.

Individual Responsibility

Strong measures for environmental protection against industrial pollution in the United States has tipped the scales toward the significance of pollution contributed by individual activity.

A great deal of air pollution caused by individual activities that include yard equipment exhaust, driving, recreational equipment, burn piles, and wood burning fireplaces and stoves.

Educational programs that teach individual responsibility can increase awareness, empower people to change their activities and make personal contributions while curbing pollution.

Ocean Sustainability Now and For the Future

The oceans are the shared resources of many countries. The treatment of these waters by any one country can have a dramatic effect on the overall health of the water and resources within. The oceans require specific attention and regulation for protection and the benefit of all people.

The earth has supported humanity for millennia, and the oceans have provided a nearly limitless bounty. People have counted upon the oceans for food from the dawn of consciousness, and nature has responded by filling the waters with teeming life. Fish, whales, mollusks, and seals have all given food to hungry humans. For most of history, the balance between the supply of oceanic food and people was perfect—there was no way that fishermen could remove enough from the waters to cause a depletion of resources. Unfortunately, the balance has been upset and exploding human populations and too efficient fishing techniques now leave our oceans with the possibility of depletion. Now, one of the most abundant fish species on earth, the Atlantic Cod may actually go extinct within 20 years. Humankind simply cannot afford to be so careless, rapacious, and shortsighted if we continue to expect the oceans to feed our burgeoning populations.

Oceans at Risk

There are a number of reasons why our oceans are now at risk and overfishing is only one of them. As commercial fishing has developed the old methods of taking fish out on lines or in small, hand held nets is a thing of the past. Fishing fleets now use bottom trawlers that scoop up literally everything on the ocean floor. What is not needed is simply discarded, usually in a dead or dying condition. Also, the sheer number of commercial fishers is far too many for the capacity of our oceans—there are only so many fish in the sea. In many cases, so many adult fish are caught that there are not enough left to provide an adequate breeding population.

Pollution is another problem facing oceans, and this comes from a number of sources. Runoff from farms, factories, and sewage treatment all has a negative impact on the state of the water near shore. Many of these waters are actually the spawning grounds for many important fish species, and contaminated water can make it difficult or impossible for fish eggs and fry to live. Too many cities use the oceans as a dumping ground for garbage, and the unmentionable items that wash ashore on Long Island and Fire Island on the Atlantic Coast bear testimony to the harm that this practice is doing not only to ocean life, but to the ability of humans to enjoy the water.

As the following chart demonstrates, as of year 2009 . . . . we are using the earth's resources to manufacture disposable items, and then destroying what might be our greatest resource by carelessly disposing of these items! These account for eighty per cent of the debris items found in our oceans.

TOP TEN OCEAN DEBRIS ITEMS 2009			
Rank	Item	Approx # of Items	%
1	Cigarettes/Filters	2,182,252	21%
2	Plastic Bags	1,126,774	11%
3	Food Wrappers	942,233	9%
4	Caps/Lids	912,246	9%
5	Plastic Bottles	883,737	9%
6	Plastic Utensils	512,517	5%
7	Glass Bottles	459,531	4%
8	Beverage Cans	457,631	4%
9	Straws	412,940	4%
10	Paper Bags	331,476	3%
	Total Debris Items	**8,229,337**	**80%**

Too Little Concern

Unfortunately, it has always been an unfortunate aspect of human nature to view the oceans as infinitely able to provide food and be a bottomless repository of whatever we happen to dump into it. The oceans seem so vast and endless that people have a difficult time imagining that there could come a time when certain species, such as cod, are facing extinction or that marine life will be impacted by effluents from the shore. It has seemed for far too long that the oceans could 'take' whatever we did to them. However, the oceans are now showing definite signs of strain, and unless steps are taken to protect and help restore these mighty bodies of water, they could, literally, die.

World governments have been slow to try to apply brakes to overfishing and pollution, looking for short term political gains instead of putting politics aside and addressing the problems oceans are facing honestly. There have been some tentative steps taken to protect the oceans, but whether these will be sufficient to correct, or even slow the damage being done is uncertain. When the nets that should have been full of cod began to come in empty, action was taken to protect the remaining fish. There is still some controversy over the ban on commercial fishing will prevent the extinction of the species, but there is some indication that the cod may be starting to replenish their numbers. However, pressure is now on to partially lift the fishing ban. It is understandable that people want to be able to make a living by fishing, but unless the numbers of cod have grown enough (and many contend that they have not) another crash will undoubtedly occur.

The United Nations Convention on Law of the Sea takes the point of view that oceans, to be sustainable in the long run, must have certain protections and that individual nations will have greater control over the use of their territorial waters. As the economic zone of any country would extend out to 200 miles from the shoreline, this would help to assure that a high degree of protection would be afforded marine resources. Most fishing would be done by those who actually lived in the adjacent country, rather than by international fishing fleets. The United States has signed this convention, but it has yet to be ratified by Congress.

Marine Protected Areas

One way to prevent depletion of marine stocks is to create Marine Protected Areas. These have proven to be very effective in restoring populations in places that have suffered from overfishing. Because modern fishing techniques, including purse seines and bottom trawls are so catastrophically efficient, it is not unusual to find formerly productive areas basically stripped of life after a few seasons. Placing these areas, especially those that adjoin sovereign nations, under the MPA aegis has already proven to be a way to allow stocks to recover. Areas around Australia that had been basically denuded of ocean life have responded quickly to protection and in a few years had recovered enough to allow sport fishing. Marine Protected Areas not only protect ocean life, they also protect people who depend upon tourism or small scale fishing for survival. MPAs that come to be classified as multiple use areas are generally the most successful in the long run.

Although Marine Protected Areas have been an excellent way to restore ocean stocks, unfortunately there is no way to enforce these standards in international waters. Realistically, it would be difficult to convince many governments to adhere to rational standards, so at this point the best that can be hoped for is that territorial waters will be protected to one degree or another.

On the whole, there is a shortage of food available in the world, the shortages are in specific geographic areas and affect specific people. There are several major factors that present food shortages and cause mass hunger.

One cause of hunger and shortages is geography. There are areas on the earth that lack resources to adequately sustain human populations and the cost of supplying these areas is prohibitive.

Another contributing factor to food and resource shortages is how governing differences between countries have allowed some countries to flourish, while some countries have been ravaged or left without.

World hunger and resource shortages are affected by the overall population of the earth. Mankind has made little effort to curb growth of the world's population. There is a finite amount of resources available on the earth for a finite amount of humans. What those numbers are is not clear, however what is clear is how the human race has misused the earth's resources.

Changing how we use our resources is the first step to ensuring all people benefit and how we preserve more for future generations.

Improving Agricultural Productivity

While a primary goal of the U.S. Department of Agriculture (USDA) is to expand markets for U.S. agricultural products, they also work to support global economic development. The USDA and World Agricultural Outlook Board (WAOB) support this goal by developing monthly World Agricultural Supply and Demand Estimates (WASDE) for the U.S. and major foreign producing countries.

Because weather has a significant impact on crop progress, conditions, and production, WAOB prepares frequent agricultural weather assessments, in a GIS-based, Global Agricultural Decision Support Environment (GLADSE).

All agricultural producers and farmers around the world need to be educated about such information and how their particular environment; soil, sunlight, and water availability, affect their particular crops.

Biotechnology needs to be examined and governed to ensure developments and practices are intended to serve a greater purpose than mere financial yields.

Land for agricultural use needs to be evaluated. As populations have grown the need for commercial and residential land use has taken precedence over land devoted for agricultural use with little regard as to whether the land would serve a better long term purpose.

Water Conservation

In the U.S., the population has doubled in the last 50 years, and water use has tripled. More than half of U.S. states are expected to face water shortages in the near future.

The world's population has tripled in the 20th century and population is expected grow by as much as fifty per cent in the next fifty years. The demand for water could have catastrophic consequences on the environment. Currently one out of six, or over one billion people on earth do not have access to safe drinking water and more than 2.6 billion people lack access to sanitation. As of 2004 more than 3900 children die every day from water borne diseases and that number has only grown.

Water is also becoming scarce for agricultural use, industrial applications, and wastewater treatment. We have reached a critical point in time to make decisions about all the earth's waters if we want to make clean water available to all the earth's inhabitants now and in the future. How we use our water also affects the earth's ecosystems and all other species.

Why We Need Coral Reefs

Anyone who has had the opportunity to either visit a coral reef or even observe a reef aquarium will be fascinated by the life that abounds on and near reefs. To watch coral polyps sweeping the currents for food or to see a tiny crab reaching into crevices for tidbits can only arouse a sense of wonder and an appreciation for the diversity of living creatures. But, the value of coral reefs is not only an aesthetic one; coral reefs play an enormous role in the environment of not only the ocean, but nearby land as well.

Coral reefs are built up over the centuries by the skeletons of the polyps and are now considered to be among the oldest living entities on earth. However, although coral reefs seem to be strong and permanent living fixtures, they are actually quite delicate and are easily damaged by pollution, changing ocean temperatures, or physical damage.

Reefs offer protection to shorelines from storms blowing in from the ocean, helping to break up the larger and more destructive waves. Besides acting as a bulwark, coral reefs are also nurseries for numerous species of fish and other marine life such as clams, oysters, and scallops, which are all important commercially. Helping reefs to become healthier and grow will enable these 'bread baskets' to continue providing food for expanding human populations. Coral reefs are also important as they support tourism in a number of countries, providing income for a wide range of services.

Helping to Sustain the Ocean's Bounty

Laws and regulations that provide protected national zones are one way to make sure that breeding grounds are safe from overfishing. Thousands of no fishing or restricted fishing areas now exist worldwide, and these are one way to help allow species to reproduce without hindrance and rebuild stocks.

In some regions, cooperatives have been formed along with the restrictions placed on fishing. These cooperatives allow all the members to derive an income from the more limited fishing while still assuring that waters will not be depleted by large commercial concerns.

Fish farming (also known as aquaculture) is another way to restock diminished species and protect existing stock. Aquaculture has proven to be excellent at raising everything from mollusks to fish to shrimp. Not so many years ago, wild populations of the giant clam were being depleted by local people who use this for food. However, by starting to raise these clams in controlled conditions, it has been possible to not only provide enough food for those who need it locally, but also to supply clams for export, either for food or for the aquarium trade.

Many coral species are threatened today, not only because of outright degradation of their environment, but also because of the popularity of these animals for home aquariums. Now that a greater understanding of the physical needs of corals has been gained, a multimillion dollar business of raising corals in tanks specifically for aquariums has been founded. This will not only spare wild corals from being preyed upon, but also provide income for those raising the corals.

Sparing the oceans from overfishing, pollution, and other problems will certainly not be a simple project—there are so many nations with diverse objectives involved, as well as basically free-for-all international waters—but full and immediate attention need to be taken by individual countries to protect their own territorial waters, continental shelves, reefs, and estuaries, and even these measures will go a long way in helping to keep the oceans strong, alive, and productive.

Chapter X. Blue-Print for the Next Generation

World politics, everywhere, is in turmoil and major transition. Awakening of societies—with the effect of increased education and Internet—is adding to the swiftly changing political and economic landscape. Influence of certain interest groups in political affairs of societies is being questioned by masses. Influence of many financial organizations, strangling the societies are being challenged and curbed as advancements in educational level of societies are pursued. Major changes in the form of governance is on horizon, whether in the industrial West, or in awakened advancing nations, provided a coherent, organized and democratic movement are established for participation of all masses. Over population in certain areas causing gross inequality and consequent famine or poverty has become a major obstacle in economic development planning, challenging mankind. The whole world economic and political structures are in transition.

Inequality is derived from status quo and the lack of equal opportunities for all and has become the primary catalyst that has fueled frustration and resentment in people around the world. Over the years the world has seen the establishment of very specific lines that determine and define a person's place in society and in this world as a whole. This ascertains how much a person of a certain caliber can accomplish during his or her lifestyle.

Inequality starts off by separating class and caste, and then stems off into separating the state, church and ethnic backgrounds of people which is very pronounced in certain countries, while understated in other countries. However, it is present in every country even in modern times.

To some people, equality in terms of politics of the state, might sound like an ideology dangerously close to the communist agenda.

However, even though the root of the movement for equality might be based upon certain aspects of the communist ideology, the essential principles, practices, demands and strategies differ in every way possible.

The demand for equality is similar to Marx's demand of a proletariat revolution. The 'equality movement' asks for the end of a bourgeois driven capitalist regime to level the status quo for all individuals based on merit and accomplishment alone. However, the demand for equality does not mean equality in terms of the communist manifesto. The demand for equality today is inclined towards the equality of the availability of opportunities—equal opportunities for all, when it comes to education, jobs, careers, standards of living and human rights. These essential human rights include the basic right to equal opportunity for all, curtailing three cardinal factors which are the right for opportunities to live a life of equality, liberty and pursuit of happiness.

Unlike communism, equality does not mean granting everybody with equal amounts of income, living facilities, personal possessions and health-care. Equality does not mean the end of individuality to create a stagnation of state due to lack of motivation. The demand is only for the right of opportunity, so that individuals have the power to create such things for themselves based on their own credentials.

Opportunity is the operating word here, because of the general mindset nursed by the people of today. Many believe that it is perfectly fine for the government to play the role of Robin Hood, for a selective population, taking money from those who have money to spare to give to the economically challenged.

However, this is a gross misconception as many people who have managed to earn respectable sums of money through legitimate means do not deserve to have the fruit of their hard-work taken away and given to those people who are content on living on state sanctioned welfare.

It is also fundamental to consider that when contemplating equality, it is best not to confuse it with the liberal leftist interpretation of the term. Equality is desirable only if it presents you with the opportunity to be the best as a nation, or as an individual. It is not desirable if it is used to provide you with all the benefits earned through other people's accomplishments under a mask of homology as humans that share a planet.

The main reason developed countries like the United States are powerful, is because people desire to be a part of its functional economy. Because America is a free enterprise system, it is obliged to grant each and every resident with the opportunity to accomplish anything with the correct merits. People's participation in their own nation building is essential, otherwise they don't appreciate the efforts delivered to them by other nations or business enterprises.

Even if many claim that capitalism never really allows room for a balanced status quo where anybody can surpass the class that they were born into, if the constitution of a country includes the rights to grant equal opportunity for all, there is always room to implement the constitution as an applied practice.

Influential Budgeting Practices

The G8

The G8 is the most influential economic and political organization which is designed to discuss and affect revolution and change amongst the most powerful nations in the world. The 'G8' stands for 'Group of Eight'. These countries include the United States, Canada, Germany, Italy, France, Japan, Russia and the United Kingdom.

These countries are allies and constantly stay in touch to influence each other's integral decisions, but the most crucial decisions are made during the G8 summit. The G8 summit is the forum where all of these countries get together to decide and alter the world's political and economic situation.

The G8 has no permanent headquarters, budget or staff. However, wherever the summit takes place is where they decide the global budgeting practices, for their respective countries which in turn affect the world's economies.

The United States for example has a fixed budgeting practice which has been in effect since 1974. The president puts in a request for the budget at the starting of the New Year, which is then resolved by the United States House Committee and the United States Senate Committee on the budget. Then the funds vying for approval must be authorized through an enactment of legislature by an authorizing committee. After that it is appropriated by the Appropriations Committee of the House.

The decision of the United States budget has a significant impact on the economy of the entire world. This is how other nations appropriate their own budgets, especially if they are dependent on aid coming in from developed nations like the G8.

As long as this practice is continued, one can hardly hope for economic equality in the world, especially when different areas of the world have very different factors to consider when they are creating their budgets.

How Agenda-setting Global Institutions Influence World Economies and Politics

The world is classified into distinct geographical and economic segments, and these define not only geographically, but by their economic status which defines their classification into the infrastructure of the global power hierarchy. These divisions are done in terms of:

- The G8
- The European Bloc
- Emerging Economies
- Developing Countries

Since the G8 countries are the deciding authorities, their budgeting has an impact on the rest of the world. There is diversity in the type of economic and political structures among the European states. These states are divided by these sectors when it comes to economy and legislature:

- Scandinavian model
- Eastern bloc
- Western Europe

Economic analysts and political think tanks have long contested the notion that influential global institutions are nothing more than instruments used by elite nations to further their own political and economic agenda. Underdeveloped and developing countries have repeatedly voiced their concerns over how certain economic policies proposed by G8 nations have made their natural resources susceptible to exploitation by richer nations, having an adverse effect on their economies as a result.

It is an established fact that labor in developing countries is grossly underpaid when compared with what their counterparts receive in developed countries. African and Asian labor is among the most underpaid workforces today, even with their exceptional skill. This stark contrast in wage rates is the most obvious example of global economic inequality that stems from discriminatory and biased policies.

Developing nations consider International Monetary Fund and World Bank as two other global institutions that have repeatedly exploited the wealth and natural resources of poor nations and impeded their growth. For instance, much to the chagrin of the local populace, IMF-compliant governments of oil-rich nations like Nigeria, Guinea, Cameroon, Ghana and Chad have recently announced a sharp hike in oil prices as per the directive of the International Monetary Fund.

However, the widespread public protests and riots that ensued after the announcement were justified seeing how the citizens of oil-rich Nigeria have been forced to pay costs of fuel that are roughly equivalent to what the average American pays back at home. Such disparities are widespread in developing countries and are usually the brainchild of puppet regimes that are sycophantically compliant with the regional interests of hegemonic foreign institutions.

Needless to say, the enforcement of such biased and discriminatory economic policies in an underdeveloped economy will only stoke up economic and social inequality by segregating the poor class from the moderate-income households. This will inevitably hinder the nations' real progress towards economic growth and stability.

The World Bank has also played a significant role in advertently exploiting the natural resources of impoverished nations by introducing policies that have done more damage than good. Nigeria is the perfect example of the adverse effects of such structural adjustment policies, seeing how the living standards of the average Nigerian have been systematically reduced through time.

Using the carrot and stick approach, the global institution has enticed many an underdeveloped and developing nations into adopting stringent and, at times, suicidal economic policies such as devaluing their currency, lifting off trade tariffs, removing subsidies and introducing detrimental budget cuts in critical services such as health and education.

Borrowing countries that are strongly dependent on foreign-sanctioned loans and monetary assistance for driving unhindered economic development are persuaded to encourage production and export of domestic commodities and resources so that they are able to increase foreign exchange. However, as foreign exchange is highly prone to frequent value adjustments, the fundamental deficiency of a price control mechanism and an authentic currency rate lead to inflation and abject poverty, both of which are the precursors of anarchy and instability.

Without question, reason or thought, all the nations of the world seem to have partaken in the race for higher economic growth, showing utter disregard for other pressing social, national and global issues. This undeniable reality is the precursor that has caused increased global social inequality and this has led to the erosion of true democratic governance and public empowerment around the world.

An expanding body of evidence strongly suggests that aggressive expansionist policies aimed at garnering economic and political gains has been at the helm of growing global inequality. Economic growth, which is the universal religion, has disappointed many nations and created problems for many others. In many nations, the drive for higher economic growth has undermined critical educational and healthcare systems while in countless others, it has had an irreparable adverse effect on communities and the environment.

This universal economy-centric culture has played an integral role in breeding a ruthless agenda that encourages those occupying the highest echelons of power to exploit the natural resources and wealth of impoverished and developing nations.

This manufactured consumerism has dismally failed at meeting actual human needs such as creating significant job opportunities.

Introducing Economic and Political Reforms That Encourage Global Equality and Sustainable Growth

The world faces a grave challenge in building a new economic framework that fosters sustainable growth and development. Sustaining people, communities, and nature must henceforth be seen as the core goals of economic activity, not hoped-for by-products of market success, growth for its own sake, and modest regulation. The watchword of the sustaining economy is caring: caring for each other, for the natural world, and for the future.

When seeking an improved alternate to the current economic and political system governing the world, the ideal place to begin would be to think about the undeniable flaws that have caused the current system to fail so miserably. It is obvious that inherent weaknesses and flaws in the current economic system have rendered it highly susceptible to exploitation and manipulation at the hands of those who occupy the highest echelons of power and who have largely been responsible for unleashing its destructive potential.

A powerful and cohesive global initiative is an essential prerequisite in molding and regulating the socio-economic and political system in order to increase its effectiveness in terms of meeting environmental and social goals. Contrary to the commonly held belief that a strong economy should be the priority of a nation, a strong social and democratic system is a more pressing concern for a nation and a more important necessity if the objective is to encourage higher growth and sustainable development.

Today's economic apparatus offer little in this regard, reiterating yet again the need for a reinvented economic framework that encourages global equality and prosperity while simultaneously addressing pressing social and democratic issues plaguing most nations. In order to achieve these goals, many closely associated factors need to grow at a similar pace.

Among the most pressing issues that demand urgent attention is the need to create equal job opportunities for people of all nations as growth in good jobs will inevitably lead to better standard of living. Availability of healthcare is another issue that needs to be addressed along with the development of an efficient system to deliver it to the masses.

One of the primary reasons why mortality rate from curable ailments and diseases is low in developed countries is that they have an effective healthcare delivery system that makes it easily available to the general population. In order to advocate global equality, these basic necessities should be made widely accessible to the impoverished population of all the nations of the world.

Growth in education-based opportunities is yet another major factor that drives long-term sustainable growth in a nation through the development and training of skills. This increases the density of the educated workforce when compared with the labor workforce and this translates into higher earnings for the average citizen and better standards of living.

Many economies of the world have witnessed the devastating effects of unemployment and lack of job opportunities. The availability of equal job opportunities for all citizens, the well-being of people, and the health of communities should be stimulated through a determined federal initiative that encourages increased direct spending and investments along with the provision of incentives to create a greater number of jobs in democratically-determined high-priority areas.

All government policies should be molded in such a manner that they are conducive of long-term uniform socio-economic growth and development. The introduction of simple policies that encourage shorter work weeks and longer vacations, job security and benefits, greater labor protection and guarantees to part-time workers is a step in the right direction when encouraging equal opportunities and benefits for all. As long as the governments, and nations alike, realize that education, healthcare, communications are all infrastructures for the society, and should not be regarded as "profit centers", a humane and just community can flourish.

A reformation of the tax collection apparatus is a great way for governments to indicate their resolve towards introducing a positive change that fosters real economic and social development while also promoting equality and fairness. Fair tax reforms are the perfect tool for governments that seek to alleviate the scourge of poverty from their country. Governments must take a bold initiative and introduce genuine and fair taxation reforms that are effective in reducing to a minimum the tax incentives and benefits enjoyed by rich tax evaders. A greater tax collection from the rich upper class can then be directed towards poverty alleviation programs such as income support plans for the poor.

Apart from this, local production units should be offered attractive incentives so as to encourage them to promote equality, tolerance and secularism while also addressing pressing concerns like rapid environmental degradation, consumer health and protection among other social costs. The introduction of stringent ecologically-responsible global initiatives should also encourage nations to adopt quantitatively-restrictive measures that discourage resource-extraction beyond their regenerative capacity. Similar policies can be introduced to assure that the discharge of harmful chemicals into the human habitat does not exceed its assimilative capacities.

Moreover, all trade agreements should take into account actual social and environmental development rather than just emphasizing on growth in GDP and per capita income. Although it is evident that the combined effect of all these policies in a socio-economic system will significantly reduce GDP growth, genuinely progressive trade and taxation policies will inarguably stimulate greater economic and social equality and improve the standard of living of the population.

Devising a Result-Oriented Agenda

In an era where the nations' of the world obsess about higher GDP and greater economic growth, redirecting the strategic focus of economic systems to the development of social and environmental needs may be deemed by many economists as putting the cart before the horse. However, real sustainable economic growth cannot be achieved if more than two-thirds of the world's population continues to live below the poverty line and when social and economic inequality is on the rise. Therefore, the invention of a more socially and ecologically friendly political and economic system is an essential prerequisite in order to foster long-lasting social, economic and environmental development. Here are some initiatives that need to be implemented on a global scale:

Identifying Inherent flaws in the existing system

The first step is to identify inherent flaws that exist within the in the current system and that need to be urgently addressed and revised. A simple approach to achieving this objective is to identify the areas that demand positive transformative change such as:

- **Governance**—A *laissez-faire* system where there is an acute shortage of laws and rules to regulate the purchase and sale of goods and services

- Corporation—Shareholder hegemony and prime ownership
- Social conditions—Economic insecurity and vast inequities
- Economic growth—GDP-obsessed economic systems that promote consumerism
- Consumerism—Conspicuous unregulated consumption of goods and services
- Communities—Fragmented and polarized communities
- Politics—Weak democratic framework that is easily susceptible to manipulation and exploitation
- Foreign policy and military—Interest-driven foreign policies that encourage pre-emptive strikes, muscle-flexing and display of military might

Envisaging a new system—after the inherent flaws in the existing system have been successfully identified, the next step is to envision an alternate system that should ideally address the following:

- The core values that the proposed initiative seeks to prioritize and harmonize
- The transformations required in order to achieve defined core values
- The measures that need to be implemented in order to undergo planned transformations

Building the system that delivers change—In order to bring about the proposed positive changes, it is imperative to:

- Implement a commonly acknowledged and accepted progressive agenda
- Unite allies with the help of shared values rather than caste, creed or ethnicity
- Building a strong global movement that drives progressive transformative change
- Introducing a more balanced economic model

- Engaging local governments, youth, religions, colleges and universities
- Preparing against imminent threats or crises

Democratic and advanced Capitalism can steer the societies to economic prosperity, peace and stability only through education, adopting vigorous implementation plans. Educated and democratic societies—if influential elements from business ventures and interest groups or clans are barred from promoting their views and agenda through mass advertising, lobbying or otherwise—can produce stable and loyal partners in promoting peace across the globe and resist any acts of terrorism. On the other hand, lack of education, and strangulation of business enterprises and certain interest groups on societies will lead to frustration, revolt, upheaval, and even explosive revolutions or wars, which would be catastrophic and against the safeguard of humanity. We have experienced such environment during Saddam Hussein era of Iraq, in Libya or Syria of early 21st century, or Russia of early 20th century, with all that mighty military power collapsing under people's pressure in late 20th century. It would be up to the political statesmen to steer their country through this turmoil with a long-term vision for the progress of humanity.

Although major changes in many advancing societies are taking a revolutionary path in this transition, however, it should be emphasized that such revolutions do not need to be bloody or violent, if managed with visionary leaders at the helms—like Gorbachev's in Russia of late 20th century. More involvement of educated masses in their own affairs will guarantee a swift implementation of democratic values in their society. Educated, and disciplines societies, using their democratic means in managing their own societies never entertain extremism or radical movements, which endangers their political stabilities—they can become good, reliable partners in building a network to preserve peace across the globe.

The Future of the World

In order for countries not to fall to the same pit-falls as the advanced nations (on financial/banking runs), they need to formulate a democratic sphere/manner to benefit from capitalism without the influence of financial and big brothers (Corporations) right at the very beginning.

The role of the press and the internet should remain sacred and independent of governing bodies, similar to a supreme court so that the governments cannot close them down, or restrict them in passing the truth to the societies. A national board under the legislative branch can oversee such an arrangement, and even put that in their constitutions.

Balancing the national budgets of countries cannot be exploited by big brothers (World Bank, etc.). Each country must be fiscally responsible and live within their means. They cannot leave financial burden and debts for generations to come!

Each country must concentrate on their national productivity to safeguard job opportunities, and economic growth for better prosperity, coupled with internal research and innovations.

There is a great NEED for a national development planning for sustainable economic growth, considering the role of technology, education and democracy to yield the best results.

Each country must have a flexible, dynamic constitution to adopt policies with respect to time and not follow a specific dogma!

Societies need to be managed with devoted statesmen, rather than opportunist politicians under the influence of interest groups and advertising media!

Corruption must be curbed at any level; since the spread of this disease will undermine democracy, and eventually the political structure of the country.

Each country must practice total separation of religions and state affairs, to protect the faith of a nation in any religion, and human rights.

Taking the future of the world to heart in consideration with the needs of all people on our planet is essential to sustaining life and advancing our race. The future of our world is in the balance and in your hands. You can help tip the scales toward a better and brighter future for all people!

Index

U

V

W

Reference Notes

[1]   The Complete Idiot's Guide to Economics Tom Gorman

[2]   The Complete Idiot's Guide to Economics Tom Gorman

[3]   http://www.npc.umich.edu/poverty/#2

[4]   http://www.dailykos.com/story/2011/11/27/1040237/-Elites-Are-Attempting-a-Controlled-Demolition-of-the-Old-Social-and-Economic-Order

[5]   http://theroyaluniverse.com/current-monarchies/europe/britain/

[6]   The Smithsonian Museum of American History. Brown v The Board of Education, 2008. Web. 1/27/12

[7]   Roberts, Russell (October 10, 2003) "How Government Stoked the Mania." *The Wall Street Journal.*

[8]   Christie, Les (April 30, 2007) "Homes: Bid Drop in Speculation." *CNN.*

[9]   "The End of the Affair." (November 20, 2008) *The Economist.*

[10] Swaminathan, Mahesh (May 2010) "Agency MBS Trends." *Credit Suisse.*

[11] Zandi, Mark (2009) *Financial Shock.* FT Press. Cited on *Wikipedia*, "Subprime Mortgage Crisis."

[12] Geithner, Timothy (June 9, 2008) "Reducing Systemic Risk in a Dynamic Financial System." Speech to the Economic Club of New York.

[13]   Louis, Brian (May 10, 2010) "U.S. Mortgage Holders Owing More Than Homes are Worth Rise to 23% of Total." *Bloomberg.*

[14]   Labaton, Stephen (September 11, 2003) "New Agency Proposed to Oversee Freddie Mac and Fannie Mae." *New York Times.*

[15]   Declaration of G20 (November 15, 2008) Whitehouse.gov. Retrieved February 15, 2012.

[16]   Pelley, Scott (April 3, 2011) "The next housing shock." *CBS News, 60 Minutes.*

[17]   ADB. The Rise of the Middle Class in the People's Republic of China, February, 2011. Web. 2/10/12

[18]   Knowledge@ Wharton. The New Global Middle Class, 2008. Web. 2/10/12

[19]   Knowledge@ Wharton. The New Global Middle Class, 2008. Web. 2/10/12

[20]   China Knowledge. Ulrich Theobald, 2000. Web. 2/10/12

[21]   http://maps.unomaha.edu/peterson/funda/sidebar/oilconsumption.html

[22]   http://2010.census.gov/2010census/data/index.php

[23]   Data taken from the USDOT Federal Highway Administration and U.S. Census Bureau

[24]   Edward Harris and Frank Sammartino, Trends in the Distribution of Household Income between 1979 and 2007, Congressional Budget Office, October 2011, 3

25 Arthur F. Jones Jr. and Daniel H. Weinberg, The Changing Shape of the Nation's Income Distribution, United States Census Bureau, June 2000, 8

26 Emmanuel Saez, Striking it Richer: The Evolution of Top Incomes in the United States (Update with 2007 estimates), University of California, Berkeley, August 2009, 3

27 Ibid, 7

28 Tax Foundation, "Federal Individual Income Tax Rates History Nominal Dollars Income Years 1913-2011," February 2012

29 Data compiled from the Tax Foundation, www.taxfoundation.org, Accessed February 2012

30 Matthew Sherman, a Short History of Financial Deregulation in the United States, Center for Policy and Economic Research, July 2009, 7

31 "A Series of Issue Summaries from the Congressional Budget Office," Economic and Budget Issue Brief, Congressional Budget Office, February 2004, www.cbo.gov, accessed February 2012

32 Nicole Stoops, "Educational Attainment in the United States: 2003," Population Characteristics, June 2004, 7

33 "20 Facts about U.S. Inequality that Everyone Should Know," http://stanford.edu/group/scspi/cgi-bin/facts.php, Accessed February 2012

34 "Union Members in 2007," Bureau of Labor Statistics, January 2008, Accessed February 2012

35 Frank Levy and Peter Temin, Inequality and Institutions in 20th Century America, June 2007, 34

[36] DeParle, "Harder for Americans to Rise from Lower Rungs", New York Times, January 2012

[37] Joseph E. Stiglitz, "Of the 1%, by the 1%, for the 1%," Vanity Fair, May 2011, Accessed February 2012

[38] http://en.wikipedia.org/wiki/Czechoslovak_coup_d'%C3%A9tat_of_1948

[39] Velinger, Jan (28 February 2006). "World Bank. Radio Prague

[40] http://archiv.radio.cz/history/history15.html

[41] http://www.internetworldstats.com/eu/cz.htm

[42] "Promotion Strategy of the Czech Republic. Czech Tourism. Archived from the original on 28 March 2007. Retrieved 19 December 2006

[43] http://gulfnews.com/business/economy/uae-oil-reserves-enough-to-support-growth-for-30-years-1.580786

[44] http://www.dubaitourism.ae/

[45] http://www.thedubaimall.com/en

[46] http://www.dubaiworldcup.com/

[47] www.**emirates**.com/us

[48] http://geography.about.com/od/populationgeography/a/chinapopulation.htm

[49] http://edition.cnn.com/2001/WORLD/asiapcf/central/11/10/china.WTO/index.html

50 http://www.importexporthelp.com/china-sourcing.htm

51 http://www.jimpinto.com/writings/chinachallenge.html

52 http://matadornetwork.com/change/10-environmental-atrocities-in-china-that-you-didnt-know-about/

53 http://dpc.senate.gov/healthreformbill/healthbill04.pdf

54 http://www.nationalreview.com/articles/283458/obamacare-court-andrew-c-mccarthy

55 http://www.civilization.ca/cmc/exhibitions/hist/medicare/medic-5h23e.shtml

56 http://www.parl.gc.ca/Content/LOP/ResearchPublications/944-e.htm

57 http://www.nejm.org/doi/full/10.1056/NEJMp068064

58 http://www.cbc.ca/news/health/story/2011/06/24/doctor-survey.html

59 http://pm.gc.ca/eng/media.asp?category=1&id=1611

60 http://www.forbes.com/2008/04/07/health-world-countries-forbeslife-cx_avd_0408health_slide_9.html?thisSpeed=undefined

61 http://gbcnet.com/ushighways/history.html

62 http://www.eyewitnesstohistory.com/ford.htm

63 http://nationalatlas.gov/articles/transportation/a_highway.html

[64] http://www.emich.edu/studentorgs/place/Officers/andrew/
Econ%20375%20-%20The%20Construction%20of%20the%20
IHS-B.pdf

[65] http://www.randomhistory.com/2008/07/14_truck.html

[66] http://www.publicpurpose.com/freeway1.htm#def

[67] http://www.historynet.com/railroads-critical-role-in-the-civil-
war.htm

[68] http://www.ameinfo.com/sheikh_zayed_bin_sultan_al_nahyan/

[69] http://daniel-workman.suite101.com/
top-uae-exports-imports-a58360

[70] http://www.uaeinteract.com/travel/

[71] http://www.dubaidutyfreetennischampionships.com/

[72] http://www.wto.org/english/thewto_e/countries_e/
united_arab_emirates_e.htm

[73] http://www.tradingeconomics.com/united-arab-emirates/
unemployment-rate

[74] http://mises.org/econsense/ch51.asp

[75] http://en.wikipedia.org/wiki/
Public%E2%80%93private_partnership

[76] http://en.wikipedia.org/wiki/History_of_economic_thought

[77] http://www.iie.com/publications/papers/schott0608.pdf

[78] http://en.wikipedia.org/wiki/Globalization

[79] http://www.wto.org/english/thewto_e/thewto_e.htm

[80] http://en.wikipedia.org/wiki/Capitalism

[81] http://en.wikipedia.org/wiki/Structural_adjustment

[82] http://en.wikipedia.org/wiki/Brain_drain

[83] http://en.wikipedia.org/wiki/Protectionism

[84] http://www.fao.org/docrep/u8480e/U8480E0x.htm

[85] http://www.rswr.org/resources/plan-a-workshop/walking-a-while-in-their-skin/

[86] http://www.oecd.org/dataoecd/29/6/42613423.pdf

[87] http://www.oecd.org/dataoecd/29/6/42613423.pdf

[88] http://en.wikipedia.org/wiki/International_trade

[89] http://www.smetimes.in/smetimes/in-depth/2011/Mar/07/familiarising-with-import-export-business52320.html

[90] http://en.wikipedia.org/wiki/List_of_countries_by_exports

[91] http://en.wikipedia.org/wiki/List_of_countries_by_imports The above lists have been prepared using latest data from WTO, World Fact Book of CIA and Wikipedia

[92] http://www.oecd.org/dataoecd/29/6/42613423.pdf

[93] http://www.udc.edu/cere/docs/Solar%20Power%20and%20Sustainability%20in%20Developing%20Countries.pdf

94 http://articles.cnn.com/2008-08-31/world/eco.
affordablesolar_1_solar-power-solar-panels-solar-
product?_s=PM:WORLD

95 http://www.un.org/en/africarenewal/vol20no3/203-solar-power.
html

96 http://green.blogs.nytimes.com/2009/10/28/developing-countries-
will-be-a-booming-solar-market-industry-panelists-say/

97 http://www.observer.com/2011/09/
the-wall-street-protesters-what-the-hell-do-they-want/

98 http://www.newyorker.com/
reporting/2011/11/28/111128fa_fact_schwartz

99 http://www.observer.com/2011/10/
occupy-your-playlist-original-songs-from-zuccotti-park/

100 http://www.observer.com/2011/10/operation-occupy-wall-street-
cleanup-hits-the-new-york-stock-exchange/

101 http://www.nerditorial.com/newsandopinion/what-does-the-
occupy-movement-want.html

102 http://www.mapsofindia.com/outsourcing-to-India/

103 http://ideas.repec.org/h/eee/devchp/5-56.html

104 http://www.ajcn.org/content/68/4/873.short

105 http://www.greatschools.org/improvement/quality-teaching/61-no-
child-left-behind.gs

106 http://www.followingtheleaders.org/benefits-of-the-no-child-left-
behind-act.htm

[107] http://usliberals.about.com/od/education/i/NCLBProsCons.htm

[108] http://www.nytimes.com/2008/01/08/education/08child.html

[109] http://learning.blogs.nytimes.com/2010/02/05/
teacher-q-how-would-you-reform-nclb/

[110] http://sitemaker.umich.edu/klein.356/tracking

[111] http://news.bbc.co.uk/2/hi/europe/4736910.stm

[112] http://www.spiegel.de/international/0,1518,416429,00.html

[113] http://4brevard.com/choice/international-test-scores.htm

[114] http://www.huffingtonpost.com/2011/11/11/teachers-facing-low-
salar_n_1088367.html

[115] http://www.pep-net.org/fileadmin/medias/pdf/
files_events/4th_colombo/Madjan-pa.pdf

[116] http://www.good.is/post/laptops-of-the-world/

[117] http://storify.com/sunnyindc/
education-how-can-we-improve-education-in-thirdwor

[118] http://keylingo.com/hostetler-blog/2012/03/03/
technology-impact-on-professional-translation-services/

[119] http://datacenteroutsourcing.org/

[120] http://education-portal.com
articles/10_Sources_for_Free_Computer_
Programming_Courses_Online.html

[121] http://seotopblogs.blogspot.com/2011/08/top-online-outsourcing-jobs-sites.html

[122] http://www.huffingtonpost.com/2010/08/26/7-industries-in-need-of-w_n_693173.html#s130697&title=Skilled_Trade

[123] http://www.economist.com/node/16380980

[124] http://www.huffingtonpost.com/2012/04/22/job-market-college-graduates_n_1443738.html

[125] http://www.napcse.org/specialeducationlaw/perkinsvocational.php

[126] http://www.edweek.org/ew/articles/2006/03/15/27voced.h25.html

[127] http://www.vbisd.org/Page/286

[128] http://www.briarcliffe.edu/

[129] http://www.socialistworker.co.uk/art.php?id=18041

[130] http://www.economywatch.com/world_economy/china/?page=full

[131] http://www1.aucegypt.edu/src/skillsdevelopment/pdfs/EAST%20ASIA%20good.pdf

[132] http://www.reuters.com/article/2012/02/13/Us-use-budget-education- idUSTRE81C1Z620120213

[133] https://www.itmatchonline.com/itoutsourcing_trends.php

[134] http://www.sourcingmag.com/content/what_is_outsourcing.asp

[135] http://www.atlantic-it.net/

[136] http://jcwarner.com/writing/2-11-outsourcing.html

[137] http://www.lsu.edu/faculty/jwither/Essays/Immigration_Trade/Dyer_Essay.html

[138] http://www.leavcom.com/ieee_dec07.htm

[139] http://www.reuters.com/article/2011/11/11/us-china-pollution-idUSTRE7AA30420111111

[140] http://www.entrepreneur.com/article/204652

[141] http://outsourcingdefined.com/

[142] http://www.businessweek.com/magazine/content/06_05/b3969401.htm

[143] http://www.nytimes.com/2011/12/07/world/asia/beijing-journal-anger-grows-over-air-pollution-in-china.html

[144] Richard Wolff University of Massachusetts

[145] http://www.wfp.org/

[146] http://www.huffingtonpost.com/2010/08/03/the-10-poorest-countries_n_668537.html#s122149&title=1_Niger

[147] http://www.census.gov/hhes/www/poverty/about/datasources/description.html

[148] Willoughby, P. R. (2007) the Evolution of Modern Humans in Africa: a Comprehensive Guide. AltaMira Press, Lanham, MD.

[149] Brehm, S. S. and Kassin, S. M. (2006) Social Psychology. (Third Edition.)

[150] Lewis, O. (1966) "The Culture of Poverty" *Scientific American.*

[151] Horton, P. and Hunt, C. (1982) *Sociology,* McGraw-Hill.

[152] Belsky, J. (1993) "Etiology of Child Maltreatment: A Developmental-Ecological Analysis," *Psychological Bulletin, 114.*

[153] (Recorder Report) (2009) "Pakistani Children's Condition the Worst in South Asia," *Business Recorder,* Nov. 21, 2009. Retrieved from *General OneFile,* March 8, 2012

[154] (Reporter Report) (2006) "Children's Plight Documented," *National Catholic Reporter,* Feb. 3, 2006. Retrieved, *Academic OneFile,* March 8, 2012.

[155] Malinosky-Rummell, R. and Hansen, D. (1993) "Long-Term Consequences of Childhood Physical Abuse," *Psychological Bulletin, 114.*

[156] Zigler, M. and Hammer, A (1988) "Do Abused Children Become Abusive Parents?" *Parents.*

[157] Feminist Theory Website: http://www.cddc.vt.edu/feminism/enin.html

[158] People, J. and Bailey, G. (2006) *Humanity: An Introduction to Cultural Anthropology.* Thomson Wadsworth.

[159] Whitehead, A (2003) Failing Women, Sustaining Poverty: Gender in Poverty Reduction Strategy Papers.

[160] Clinard, M. (1984) *Sociology of Deviant Behavior.* Holt, Rinehart and Winston.

[161] Shiraev, E. and Levy, D (2004) *Cross-Cultural Psychology: Critical Thinking and Contemporary Applications.* Pearson

162 http://www.washingtonpost.com/opinions/us-food-aid-to-n-korea-sends-the-wrong-messages/2012/03/07/gIQA6MM1zR_story.html

163 http://www.who.int/gho/publications/en/

164 http://www.theghanaianjournal.com/2012/03/09/kwame-nkrumah-versus-african-leaders/

165 http://www.un.org/en/documents/charter/chapter1.shtml

166 http://www.un.org/en/aboutun/index.shtml

167 http://www.nobelprize.org/nobel_prizes/peace/laureates/1988/un-history.html

168 http://academic.evergreen.edu/g/grossmaz/interventions.html

169 http://www.ronpaul.com/

170 http://www.cfr.org/

171 http://news.bbc.co.uk/2/hi/europe/country_profiles/2293441.stm

172 http://www.mfa.gov.il/MFA/Facts+About+Israel/Israel+in+Maps/1947+UN+Partition+Plan.htm

173 http://www.un.org/en/aboutun/history/

174 http://www.un.org/en/aboutun/index.shtml

175 http://www.laetusinpraesens.org/docs/globcomp/globcom6.php

176 http://www.laetusinpraesens.org/docs/globcomp/globcom6.php

177 *International Herald Tribune*, 6 February 1998.

[178] http://www.foxnews.com/world/2012/03/14/united-nations-high-commissioner-for-refugees-blasted-for-poor-financial/

[179] http://futureun.org/

[180] http://news.bbc.co.uk/2/hi/programmes/2969184.stm

[181] http://www.irishtimes.com/newspaper/ireland/2011/1102/1224306912018.html

[182] http://www.earthday.org/earth-day-history-movement

[183] http://www.epa.gov/

[184] http://www.epa.gov/owow/watershed/wacademy/acad2000/cwa/

[185] http://www.epa.gov/compliance/civil/tsca/tscaenfstatreq.html

[186] http://matadornetwork.com/change/10-environmental-atrocities-in-china-that-you-didnt-know-about/

[187] http://www.green-technology.org/what.htm

[188] http://www.dallasnews.com/news/local-news/20110804-ercot-warns-of-high-probability-of-rolling-blackouts-as-heat-wave-strains-power-grid.ece

[189] http://www.environmentalgraffiti.com/sciencetech/green-technologies-change-world/7797

[190] http://www.ucsusa.org/clean_energy/our-energy-choices/renewable-energy/how-geothermal-energy-works.html

[191] http://www.energyquest.ca.gov/story/chapter11.html

[192] http://www.ucsusa.org/clean_energy/our-energy-choices/
renewable-energy/how-geothermal-energy-works.html

[193] http://www.ucsusa.org/clean_energy/our-energy-choices/
renewable-energy/how-geothermal-energy-works.html

[194] http://www.ucsusa.org/clean_energy/our-energy-choices/
renewable-energy/how-geothermal-energy-works.html

[195] http://www.epa.gov/oaintrnt/water/

[196] http://www.worldwatercouncil.org/index.php?id=25

[197] WHO/UNICEF JMP, 2004

[198] WHO Marks Czech Republic's Graduation to 'Developed' Status" in
2004-2010"

About the Author

B. Bahramian graduated from the University of Birmingham, England with a B.S. & Ph.D. in Civil Engineering, and later from the University of Dayton, Ohio with M.A. in Political Economics (major in Business Administration). As an associate professor of Engineering, he served the academic circles of University of Dayton, and University of Cincinnati in Ohio for many years.

Early in the 1970's, B. Bahramian served as Director of an academic development program at the University of Dayton, Ohio and as a designated Vice Chancellor for Tehran Polytechnic Institute in Iran, to implement an affiliation program between the two institutes, with cooperation and funding of the United Nations. Between 1973 to 1978, he structured and established Building & Housing Research Center, and National Science & Research Center for Iran. Between 1972 and 1979, he also served as a negotiator between late Shah of Iran and his major political opposition group to design a path for a peaceful transition of power to a more democratic form of governance, prior to 1979 revolution.

After the revolution, Mr. Bahramian served under the new Prime Minister, in charge of development & industrial planning for the country in the transition government of Mr. Bazargan. During the hostage crisis of 1979, he served as a negotiator with the U.S. Government in an attempt to resolve the crisis.

Since early 1980, Mr. Bahramian has resided in the United States, engaged in his profession as systems designer and program manager in different industries. Since 2005, he has served as a Director & Professor at the University of Maryland, where he is teaching Technology Management and International Affairs courses at the graduate schools. He has also been involved in the planning and implementation of business and economic development programs in Russia and China since early 1990s, with great interest in implementing technology and education as the backbone of industrial developments for advancing societies to prosper under democratic form of governance.

On the professional side, as the founder and Chairman of Center for Technology Management, Inc., Mr. Bahramian has been engaged in the design and development of a few high-tech and Energy Saving products in the U.S., and received U.S. Patents on a few products.

Printed in the United States
By Bookmasters